STUDIO JACKSON

CREATIVE CULTURE IN THE MISSISSIPPI CAPITAL

NELL LINTON KNOX | *Photography by* ELLEN RODGERS JOHNSON

THE History PRESS

Published by The History Press
Charleston, SC 29403
www.historypress.net

All images by Ellen Rodgers Johnson unless otherwise noted.

First published 2014

Manufactured in the United States

ISBN 978.1.62619.718.3

Library of Congress CIP data applied for.

Notice: The information in this book is true and complete to the best of our knowledge. It is offered without guarantee on the part of the author or The History Press. The author and The History Press disclaim all liability in connection with the use of this book.

This book is dedicated to the creative visionaries in Jackson, Mississippi.
Thank you for inspiring us.

CONTENTS

FOREWORD

I recently learned of an ornithological study in which crows were discovered to share their nests with cuckoos in an attempt to increase the survival rate of the young crows. As it turns out, cuckoos possess a unique methodology of warding off predators to protect their young, and when the baby crows shared the nest with cuckoos, it increased the crows' chances of reaching maturity as well.

Like the crows and cuckoos, artists and creative types traditionally fare better when they cluster together, sharing spaces and proximity with one another. This has certainly been my observation throughout my career as a patron, a producer and a director of the Mississippi Arts Commission in Jackson, Mississippi. When creative economies and creative clusters form, either out of necessity, out of coincidence or by design, success rates for all the artists therein increase, and the concept of collective, shared and cooperative strength is artfully demonstrated.

In *Studio Jackson: Creative Culture in the Mississippi Capital*, Nell and Ellen set forth the foundation of our community's creative spirit, exploring the offbeat, intimate and sacred spaces where their friends and fellow artists work. In their studios, these artists explore, seek their voices and chart their passageways toward creative expression and, ultimately, sheer vulnerability. Our creative spirit is historically and aptly sustained in this volume through words and brilliant, artful images. Our creators, our crafters, our makers of art and ingenuity are paraded before us in this imaginative, funky fanfare.

The third and final capital city in our two-hundred-year history of statehood, the city of

Jackson is our state's only truly urban setting. Through our storied history of tremendous struggle and through the ingenuity born of necessity, Mississippi has created great art, artists and storytellers. Within Jackson, the neighborhoods of downtown, Midtown and funky Fondren not only permit but also encourage creativity and innovation as an extension of our diverse and complex character. In this fertile environment, the creative economy grows wildly like kudzu. The unique compositions of the three counties and nearly dozen communities that fall within the metro Jackson umbrella comprise an extensive pallette of personality and culture unlike any other in the state. This eclectic collective encourages unorthodox expressions of creative spirit. It establishes centers of culture like Lemuria bookstore, the Mississippi Museum of Art, Koinonia, Sneaky Beans and Cups Coffee shop. It inspires other artists, such as Eudora Welty, Beth Henley, Richard Ford and Cassandra Wilson. Inventors, such as NunoErin and CSpire, find freedom of enterprise, entrepreneurial opportunities and innovative business latitude. Jackson is the city that social and artistic revolutionaries—such as Medgar Evers, Governor William Winter, Karl and Mildred Wolfe, Keith Tonkel, Richard Wright, James Meredith, Chokwe Lumumba and Dr. Blair E. Batson—call home. Perhaps most significantly, artisans and craftsmen within our community are encouraged just as businessmen, lawyers, politicians, journalists, teachers and doctors are encouraged; all are welcome, all are equal and all are necessary. Our Jackson art community is vividly diverse and its members deeply dependent on one another. We either succeed as a union of like-minded souls—just like the cuckoos and crows—or risk the certain failure that comes from self-reliance for the sake of standing apart. Here, art is not "I"; art is "we."

MALCOLM WHITE
Tourism Division Director
Mississippi Development Authority

INTRODUCTION

This past January, Mississippi governor Phil Bryant named 2014 the "Year of the Creative Economy." In his speech, Governor Bryant lauded various sectors of the creative culture in Mississippi. He mentioned creative people, creative enterprises and creative community, which together form a creative collective that makes a positive contribution to Mississippi's economy each year. This is the year, he said, to celebrate that creativity.

Growing up in Mississippi's capital city of Jackson, I was a consumer of the creative economy before the phrase "creative economy" was even coined. My mother took me to Kay Holloway's studio in Midtown to have my photograph taken when I was five years old. I grew up on Redwing Avenue in Fondren, where every year our neighbors built a giant float for the St. Patrick's Day parade. Wolfe birds and Richard Kelso paintings were household treasures. My uncle Carl hung Pearl River Glass ornaments on the Christmas tree, and I was surrounded by Fletcher Cox's woodwork at the home of my friends, the Mabus family. I watched the Wildlife and Fisheries building transform into the Fondren Corner Building in the early 2000s and have enjoyed the art haven that blooms inside that iconic structure.

Many of you, like me, have been contributing—consciously or unconsciously—to the creative economy for years as consumers. We have chosen to "shop local" at Chimneyville Crafts Festival and local art galleries; we have gone to celebrations at the Mississippi Museum of Art (MMA); and we have eaten at Walker's Drive-In, the Mayflower and Crechale's for decades. The Jackson creative culture continues to win us over. In fact, in November 2013, the *Atlantic* published an article titled "The Best City for the Next Generation of Artists Just Might Be Jackson." The article touted factors such as affordable rent and—most notably—an encouraging community of other artists.

But perhaps you, like me, have stopped to wonder: Why are all these creative people choosing to form a community in Jackson? How have they survived all these years in a city that is not infrequently rife with turmoil? As I roll over yet another pothole on North State Street, sometimes I wonder, "Why do I live here again?" Yet artists and craftsmen continue to live and work in Jackson, and new creative people start businesses here every day.

Over the last year, I interviewed visual artists and craftsmen who currently live and work in Jackson. My goal was to gain an understanding of the history and future of our creative culture through the perspective of those who are living it each day. The artists and craftsmen featured in this book are a selection of the many who have chosen to live and work in and around Jackson's downtown, Midtown and Fondren communities, earning their income primarily as artists, craftsmen and creatives. The artists in this book personify a microcosm of the larger creative economy that Mississippi celebrates this year, and I have endeavored to explore the many facets of these artists' individual points of view, as well as the history of their studios and work in Jackson. Along with Ellen Rodgers Johnson, I have visited their studios—their personal sanctuaries—documenting their work, exploring their histories and hearing the stories of their survival and success as visual artists, craftsmen, creative producers and small-business owners in Jackson today. Throughout this process, it was my observation that the artists and craftsmen I spoke with view one another's successes as collective wins for the entire art community. It is my hope that this book serves as another collective win.

NELL LINTON KNOX

1

FLETCHER COX

When potential clients approach Fletcher Cox with a project, he prefers to begin with the basics. Say, for example, they want a new desk. To get the client to visualize the end result, Fletcher asks them, "What color is it?"

"Most people know," he explains. "Very rarely does a commission come along that's open ended."

Once a client shares enough details, the first real decision Fletcher makes is determining what species of wood is suitable for the project.

"The woods feel different to me," he relates. "Cherry feels feminine; maple feels masculine. Each species carries a sense of proportion. Maple is strong, so legs can be half the size than those of walnut."

Then, Fletcher likes to visit the place where the commissioned piece is going to live to get a

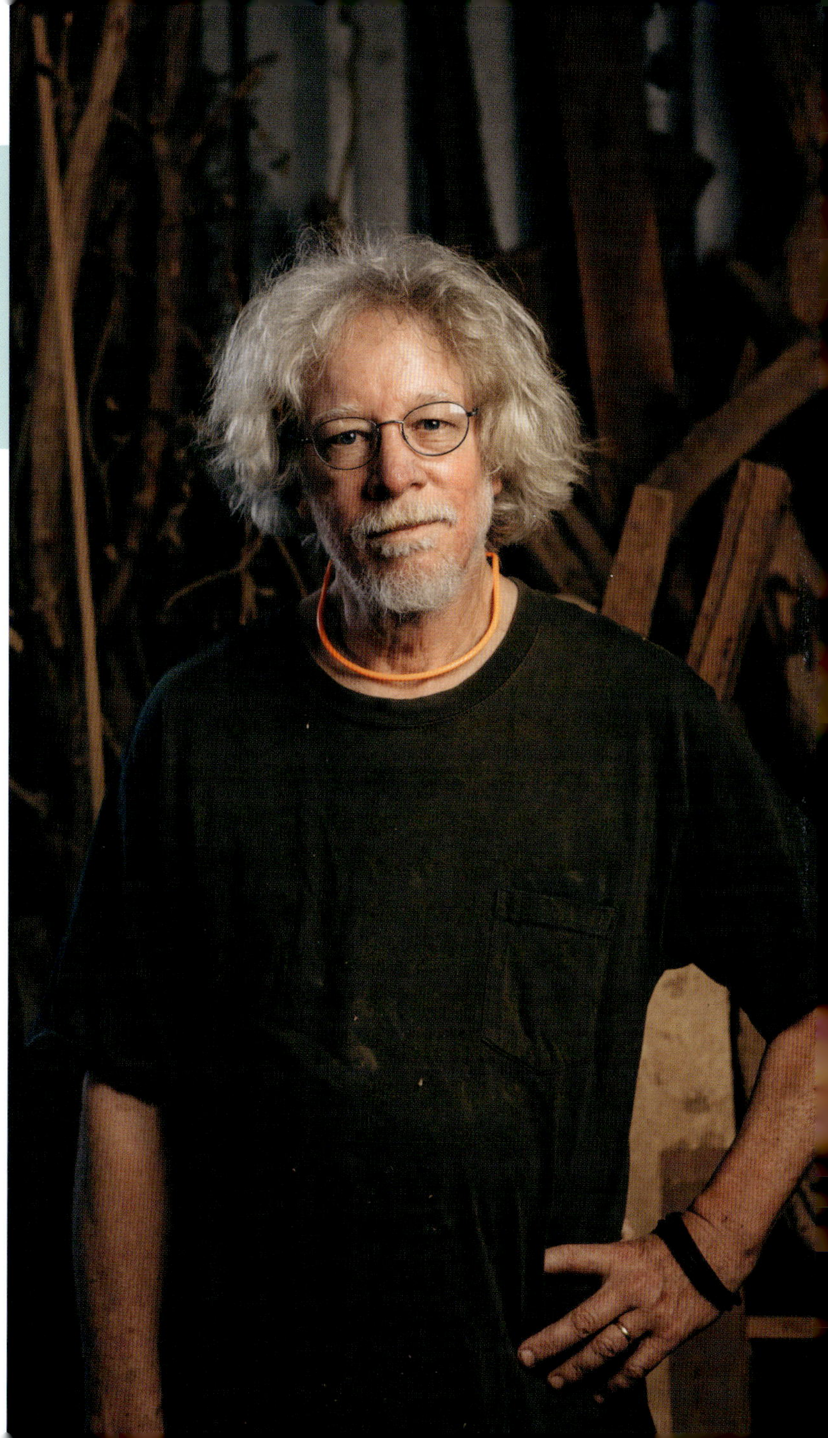

Fletcher Cox is pictured here in his downtown Jackson studio.

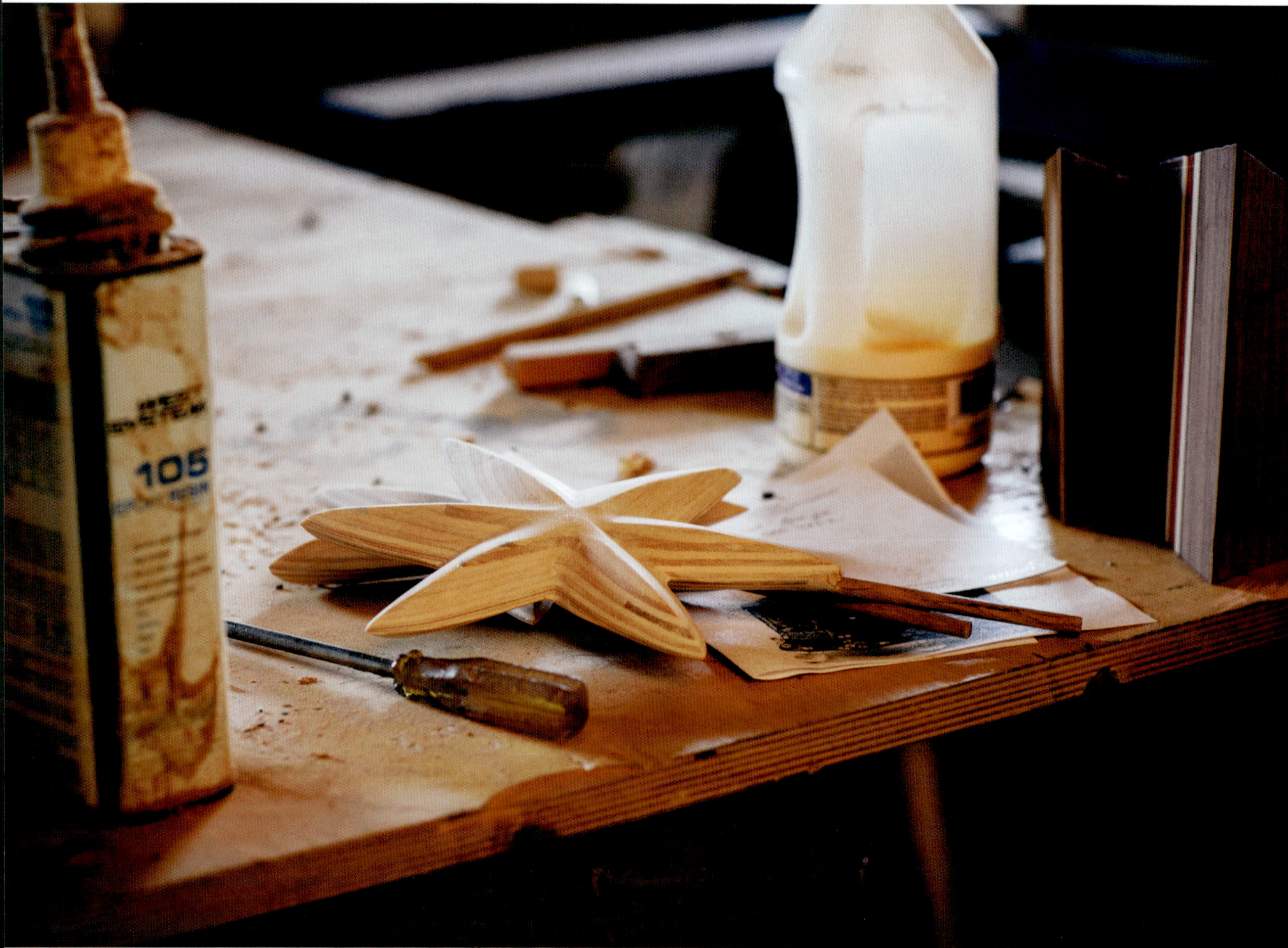

Fletcher moved his studio to downtown Jackson from Midtown so he could have a larger workspace.

feel for the client's particular aesthetics. Some people, he finds, are very somber and refined in their taste; some are over the top. Both types of people come to Fletcher, whose innovative style of craftsmanship has been featured in a variety of national publications, including *House Beautiful*, *The Robb Report*, *House and Garden* and the *New York Times*. His historic renovations and original craftsmanship are features of many iconic Mississippi buildings, including the Mississippi Museum of Art, the U.S. District Courthouse in Jackson, the Governor's Mansion and the Eudora Welty library, and his work is treasured by both private collectors and countless business organizations across the United States. His heart and home base, however, remain in Jackson, Mississippi, where he works in a studio downtown off Gallatin Street.

Background

Originally from Virginia, Fletcher attended Columbia University in New York after hearing a pitch from a Columbia graduate who was asked to speak to Fletcher's high school class. At Columbia, Fletcher took art history classes, majoring in English and enrolling in graduate-level courses when he was only a junior. He met his wife, Carol, at the English graduate school, where she worked as a receptionist.

During the spring of 1968, riots broke out at Columbia, and Fletcher, who was active in the student occupation of the school, participated in tearing down the construction fence where the school was allegedly building a segregated gymnasium. Together with his classmates, Fletcher occupied the main administration building until black students caucused, telling the white students, "This is our fight." Later, Fletcher was among the undergraduates who were dragged out of the building by the police. As part of his nonviolent protest, Fletcher remembers how he and other students all went limp, but that did not stop police from beating the students with flashlights.

Later, Fletcher was drafted to go to Vietnam. He declared himself a conscientious objector on religious grounds: to this day he remains a practicing Buddhist. Conscientious objectors were still given civic duties, so Carol and Fletcher were forced to move to Wyoming, where Fletcher was assigned to teach science classes at a state reform school. His science background was limited to what he had learned in high school classes, and he and Carol found the rest of the faculty members very different from the friends they had made at Columbia.

"Faculty parties were like the 1950s all over again," he recalls. "Women in one room, men in another."

As the temperatures dropped in Wyoming, Fletcher and Carol went to spend Christmas in the milder climate of Jackson, Mississippi, where Carol's parents worked at Millsaps College. After the holidays, the young couple returned to Wyoming in the midst of a blizzard, during which temperatures eventually dropped to thirty-three degrees below zero. Fletcher was miserable in the cold, and as soon as he had served his designated time, he relates, "We came back to Jackson to warm up."

In 1973, Carol took a job as a secretary at Tougaloo College, a historically black college located in northwest Jackson. They moved into the Tougaloo neighborhood, living in a converted double shotgun home. Later that year, they visited Fletcher's parents, who had since moved to D.C. Carol and Fletcher went to tour the Renwick Gallery, where there was a woodworking display of five craftsmen showing their work.

"The more we looked at it, the more entranced we became," Fletcher recalls.

Weary with the world of academics, Fletcher and Carol decided to pursue woodworking, saying, "We wanted something tangible in our lives."

Back in Jackson, Fletcher began attending a night class in Enochs Junior High School's woodworking shop. He became apprenticed to a furniture repairman named T.E. Mooney and "read every book [on woodworking] I could find at the Jackson public library, which was about six books." He remembers reading the entire *Encyclopedia of Furniture Design.*

Fletcher set up shop in their home and started out making small things, such as boxes and spoons. Until he purchased his first lathe at an estate sale, he was doing all his work by hand during the week and finishing the heavy woodworking on the weekends at the Enochs Junior High woodshop. Carol also did woodworking on the weekends.

Fletcher recalls the early years of his craft, noting, "We tried a lot that didn't work to figure out what we wanted to do."

A friend arranged for Fletcher to meet with a man named David Prewitt, who was working in Natchez, Mississippi, doing antique reproductions. Fletcher decided that he was more interested in modern design, and he and Carol took a road trip to Wisconsin to meet woodworkers there who were designing and making modern furniture.

Although his skills and knowledge were growing, Fletcher was not making much money. He was only able to buy a few tools, and his work was time consuming; Carol helped him with all the carving, shaping and sanding.

In 1975, Fletcher joined the Craftman's Guild of Mississippi, which had formed in 1973 with thirty original members. Fletcher was part of the second group of members to be juried into the guild.

"Any member of the Craftsman's Guild could set up shop in the log cabin on the Natchez Trace,"

Fletcher explains. Sales were steady, but Fletcher recalls, "We were really poor."

In 1975, Fletcher received a scholarship from the guild. He used the scholarship to go to a workshop at the Arrowmont School of Arts and Crafts in Tennessee. Then, Fletcher finally got his big break. Vatican II changed the liturgy of the Catholic Church, meaning that many churches had to change their furnishings, updating their altar tables, pulpits and credence tables, and Fletcher was hired by the Immaculate Heart of Mary Church in Greenwood, Mississippi. He remembers the commission well, describing it as "extremely difficult and challenging, a baptism by fire." He assembled and sanded some of the pieces in his truck, finished the job in time for the Christmas deadline and then went home to sleep for a week. He was subsequently hired to work on almost a dozen Catholic churches in Mississippi.

"Every parish priest I have met has been an outstanding person," Fletcher relates. "An institution that is a force for evil worldwide is a force for good locally."

Fletcher began to work on a larger scale, doing dining room tables and seating systems. He also began taking on more commission work. Fletcher was influenced by the ideals of the American Craft Revival, which promoted, among other things, self-sufficiency and organic gardening. When the American Craft Council caught on in the Southeast, nearly all the members, he recalls, were academics. He began entering craft competitions as a way of getting his name and work in the national eye, winning awards for his woodwork in 1978, 1981 and 1983.

"The aesthetic in Mississippi is very traditional, even backward, looking back to the eighteenth century. I had to expand my sphere of influence to do what I wanted to do," Fletcher explains. "Plus, it's an ego boost to win a prize," he laughs.

In 1989, Fletcher served as an adjunct professor for the Mississippi State University School of Architecture, which he continued to do until 2002. He has also taught at the Memphis Center for Architecture and the Tulane University School for Architecture.

As Fletcher's craft continued to evolve, he began improving the business end of his work. He quit giving ballpark prices on commissions and began calculating exactly how much time and effort went into each piece. Around the same time, he says, he realized that nothing that he could make out of wood would be as beautiful as a tree.

"I wanted to make wood look improvisational," he explains, comparing the history of woodworking with pottery. Fletcher believes that pottery has experienced a much richer aesthetic tradition due to the organic developmental process—most potters shape their work as they go, becoming one with the clay and letting the natural inclinations of the clay guide the final outcome of their craft, whereas Fletcher saw furniture as only creative in the design stage with little room for organic developments once the construction phase is begun. According to Fletcher, the Industrial Revolution, with its fascination with rectilinear boards, "killed woodworking."

Inspired by the Japanese tradition of woodworking, particularly the works of George Nakashima, and by African improvisational furniture, Fletcher's creations returned to the "raw" phase of wood, avoiding the "cooked" world of industrial design. Fletcher began sourcing and harvesting wood from sources other than the lumberyard, using entire downed trees, including their bark edges. He mentions being driven by a sort of "philosophical imperative" to work the way he does. Recently, for example, he was commissioned to build a desk for a new building at the University of Arkansas. Fletcher built the desk but used only the wood from trees that were cut down to make room for the new building, which were mostly red oaks, with boards weighing 250 pounds.

"You can actually watch the tree grow as you walk from one end of a table to the other," he explains.

The Mabus House

One of Fletcher's most comprehensive projects is the work he has done for former Mississippi governor Ray Mabus. Mabus served as governor of Mississippi from 1988 to 1992, during which time Fletcher was contracted to restore moldings and furniture in the Governor's Mansion. Fletcher was subsequently hired by Mabus to create additional, custom furniture for the governor's private living quarters. One of the custom pieces included a four-poster bed featuring a traditional Chinese pattern known as "ice ray," which Mabus favors.

After leaving office, Mabus built a stately home in Ridgeland, where Fletcher's detailed craftsmanship and organic approach to woodworking converge in many aspects. In 2003, Fletcher began his work at the Mabus house by fabricating the kitchen using bird's-eye maple. The project took a full year. Fletcher then crafted a dining room table made from an African wood called wenge and inlaid with the ice ray pattern that Mabus admires. Fletcher constructed a table for the breakfast nook out of an old tabletop that once belonged to Mabus's father; Fletcher added walnut inlay and curved legs to create a new design. For Mabus's extensive collection of textiles, Fletcher created custom stands that mimic the gentle curves of the limbs of a tree; a console for the projector in Mabus's media room

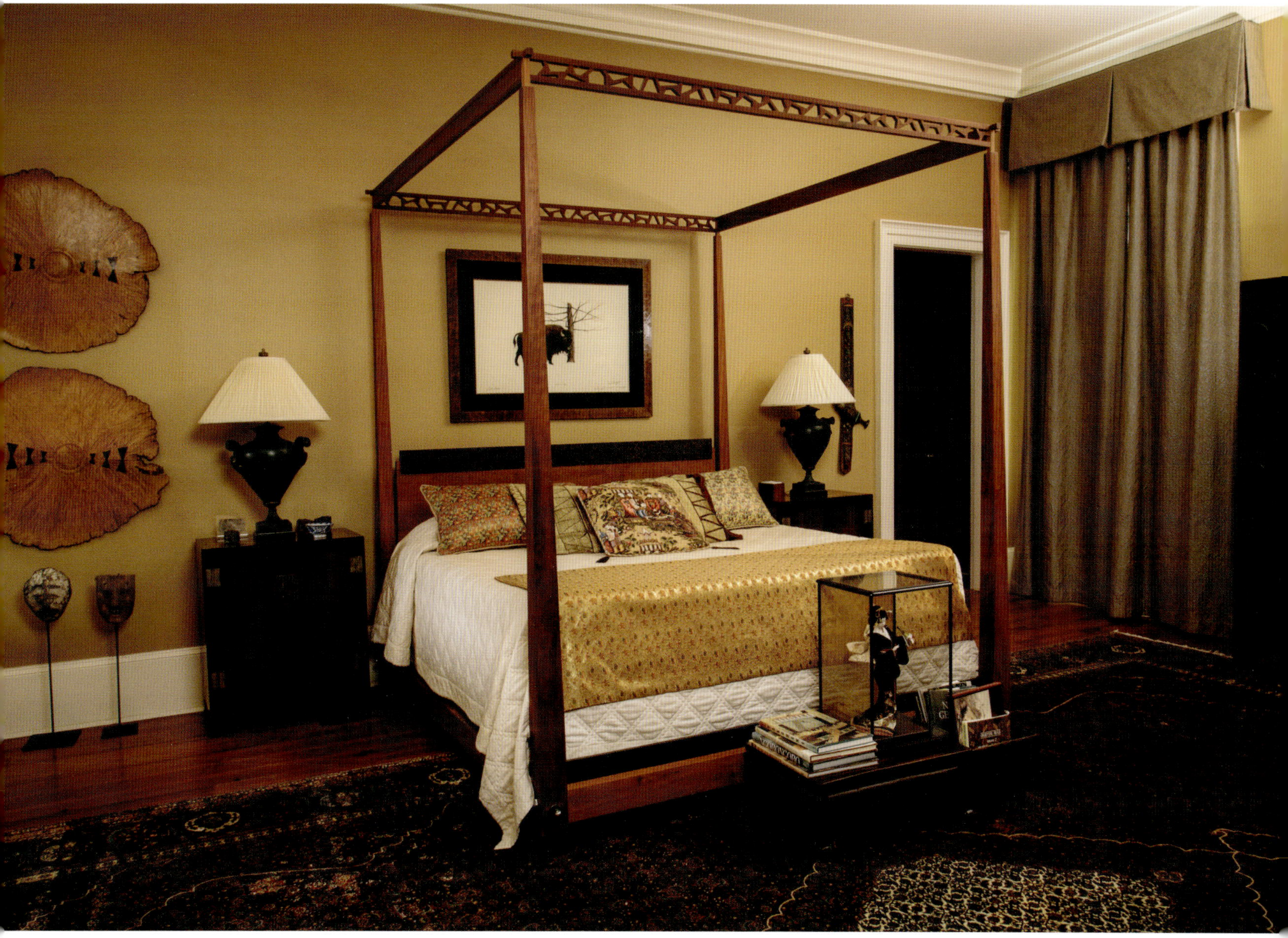

Fletcher is the only person permitted to disassemble and move this bed, which he built as a private commission for Mabus during Mabus's time as governor.

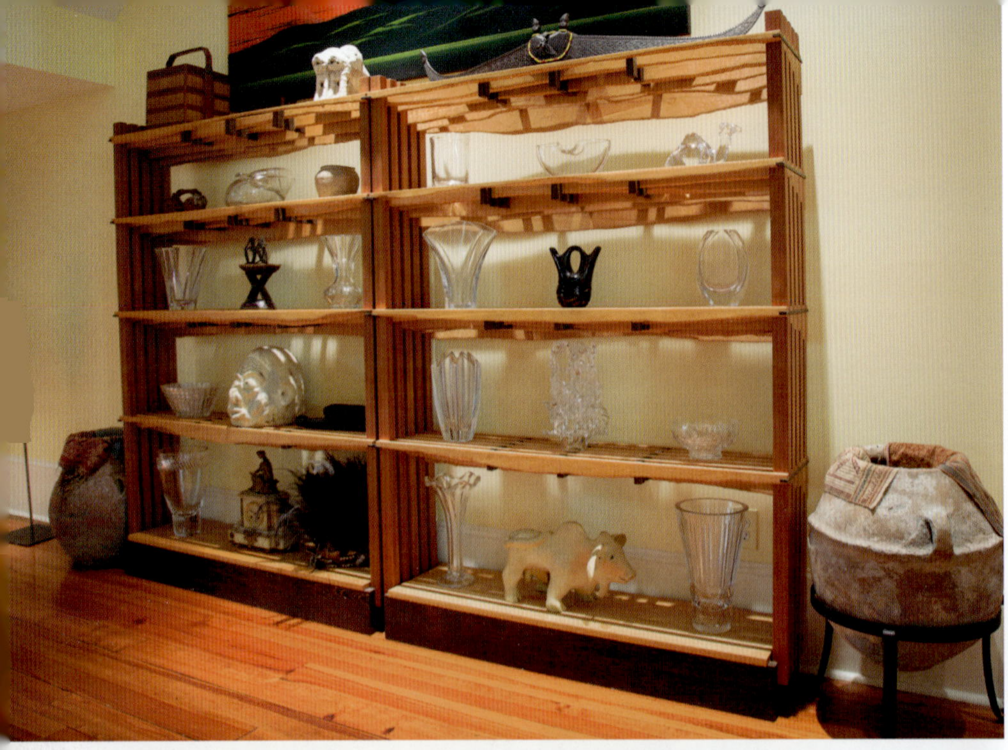

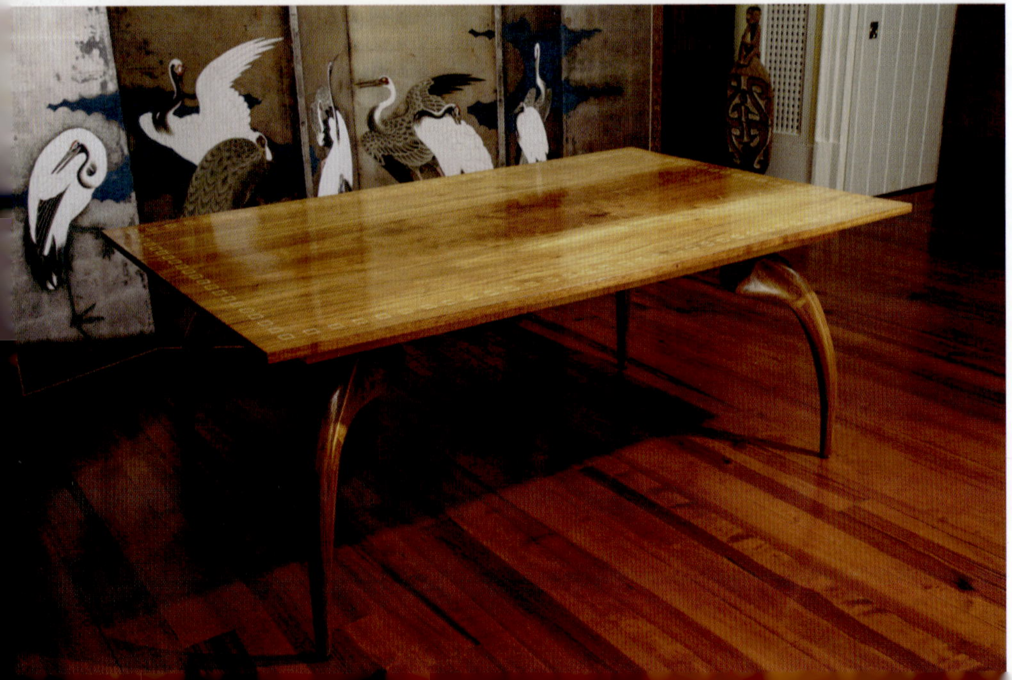

Left, top: This shelving unit was built by Fletcher Cox and commissioned by Ray Mabus during Mabus's time as governor of Mississippi.

Left, bottom: The walnut desktop belonged to Ray Mabus's father. Fletcher refinished the top, adding the maple inlay and unique curved legs.

Opposite: The Mabus kitchen is fabricated from bird's-eye maple. The project took a year to complete.

becomes a work of art in Fletcher's hands. Fletcher also designed and built Mabus's mantel and many other features of Mabus's home. The keen detail of Fletcher's craftsmanship complements Mabus's taste and overall aesthetic, which Fletcher describes as "postmodern."

In the Studio

After working from his home for many years, Fletcher bought a studio in Jackson's Midtown neighborhood. Fletcher expanded

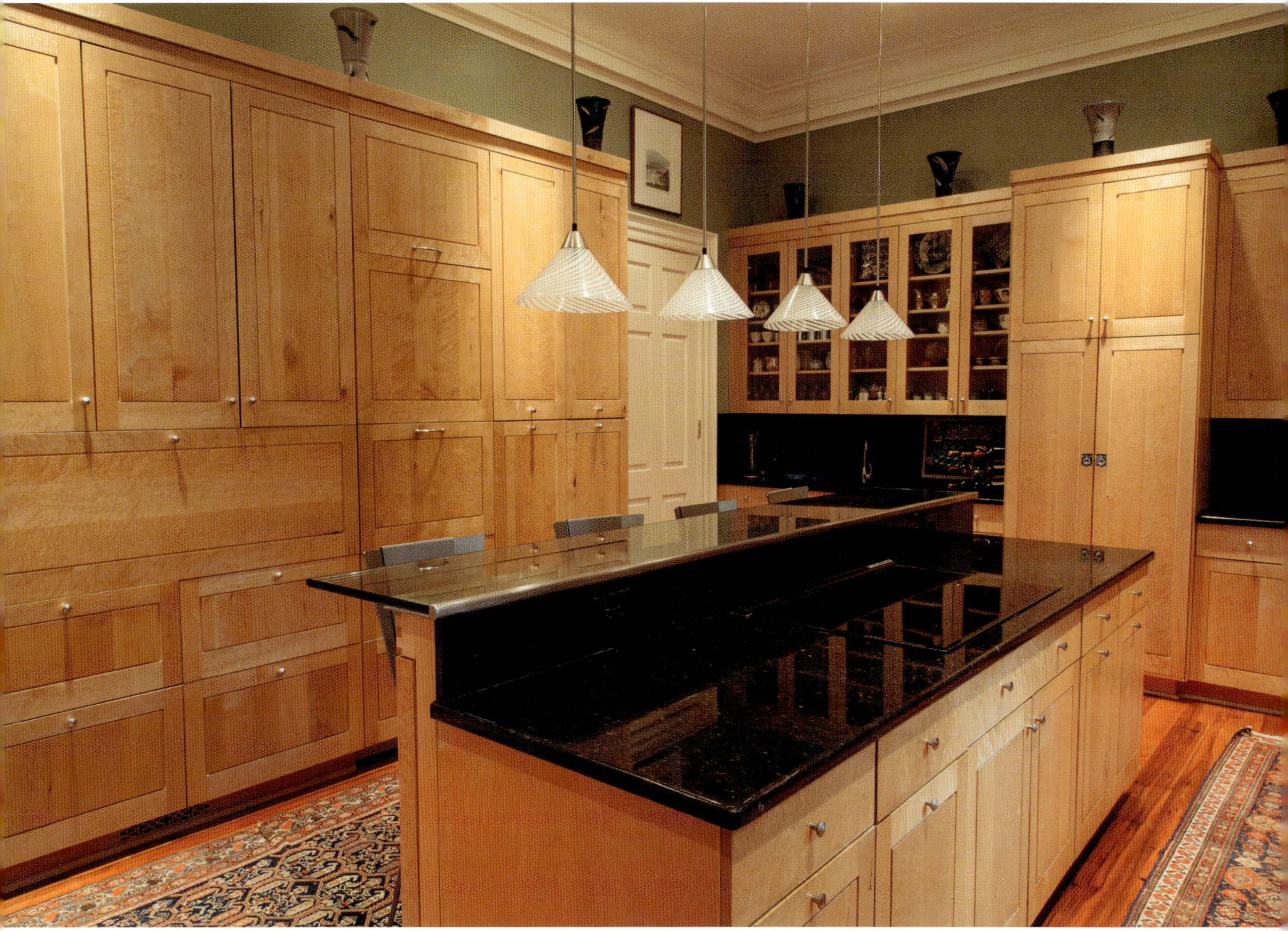

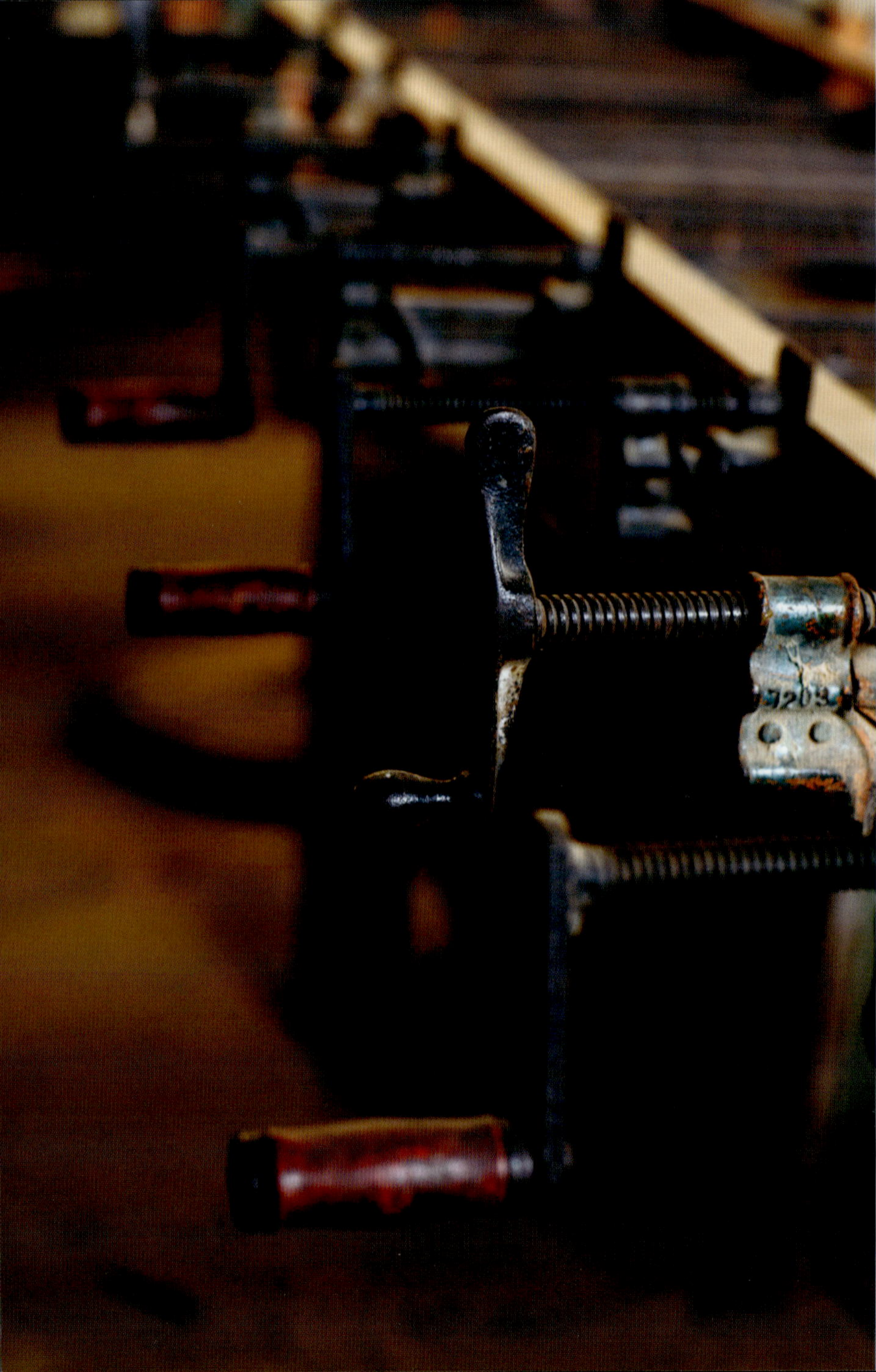

his studio into his current downtown Jackson location to have more space, which he uses to store his many woodworking tools and salvaged wood. It would be considerably more expensive for Fletcher to have such a large studio in any other city. Fletcher shares a large warehouse with like-minded woodworkers, and throughout his vast studio are various projects laid out in many states of completion. Fletcher is quick to acknowledge the massive buildups of sawdust and wood chips and the lack of heat and air conditioning, which he says are par for the course. Woodworking creates a mess and generates a lot of scrap material, but Fletcher saves wood scraps for smaller projects; with his leanings toward wood harvesting and conservation, he is not one to waste.

Space is important to a woodworker, and Fletcher has chosen his studio accordingly. For a project completed in 2012, for example, Fletcher was asked to create a sculpture using a bur oak tree that had fallen in a client's yard. Fletcher disassembled and shipped the tree from Illinois to Mississippi, where he turned

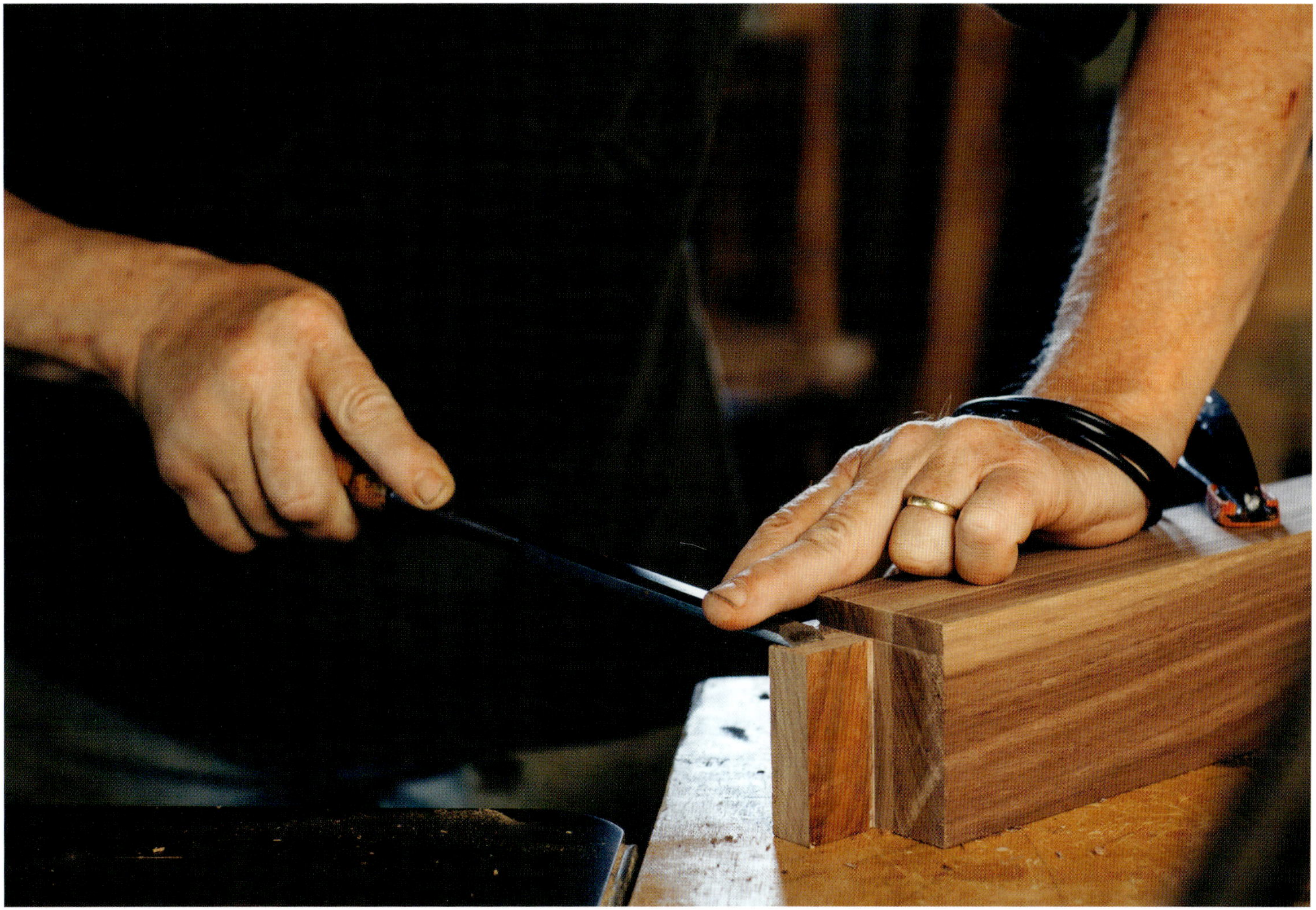

Fletcher is the recipient of numerous awards and prestigious grants, including the Governor's Award for Artistic Excellence.

Opposite: Fletcher's first studio was in his house, where he built smaller objects, such as boxes. A larger space allows for bigger projects and more work.

the tree into a sculpture reminiscent of the tree itself. The final product was enormous when reassembled, but Fletcher had the space to put it together before breaking it down to ship.

Fletcher plans to continue working in his current studio space, and he is pleased with the opportunities that living in Jackson for so many years has provided him.

"Lately, it's been one deadline after another," he relates. He maintains that his future goal is simple: "Make as much really cool stuff as I can."

2

JERROD PARTRIDGE

Jerrod Partridge grew up in Mobile, Alabama. In the tenth grade, his family moved to Forest, Mississippi, where he attended the local high school. In high school, although Jerrod loved to draw, he received no artistic training; Forest High School did not offer art classes.

"I think a Degas exhibit came to Jackson while I was in high school," he remembers, "but I never saw it. I wouldn't have known who Degas was."

Jerrod started dating his wife, Jesse, his senior year of high school, and they both went from Forest to Clinton, where they attended Mississippi College.

Jerrod recalls an uncertainty as to what he wanted to study in college. A family friend had shown Jerrod drawings in a medical journal,

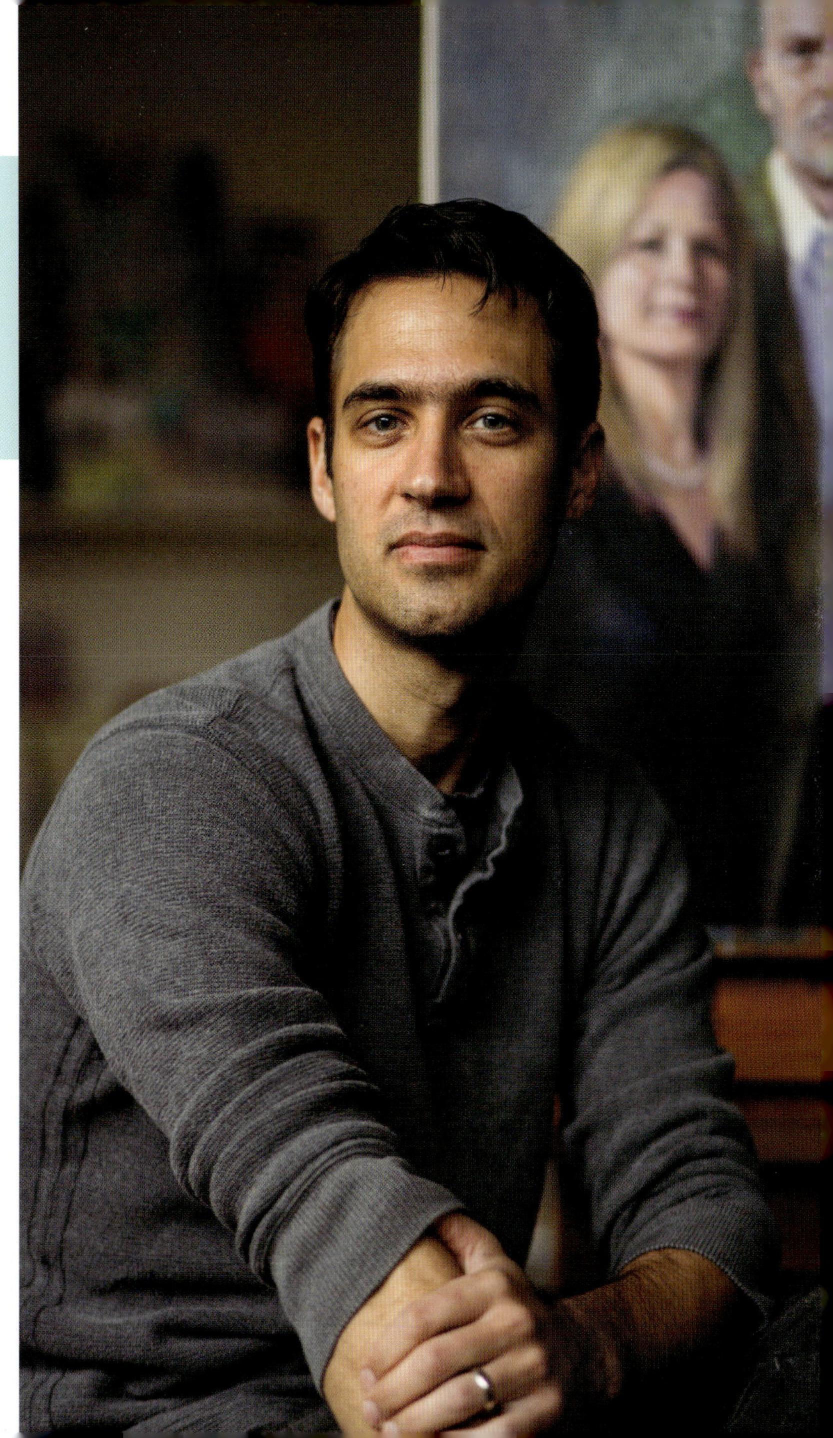

Jerrod Partridge in his Fondren studio.

and Jerrod liked the idea of illustrating medical textbooks. Freshman year, he registered for mostly biology classes, throwing an art class into the mix.

"I took that first art class, and a whole new world opened up for me," he says, smiling broadly.

Jerrod majored in art with a focus in graphic design, touring Italy and studying art history in London. After college, he eventually went to work full time for the marketing department at JBHM Architects in Jackson, Mississippi. He left JBHM in 2002 to attend the New York Academy of Art, where he received his MFA in painting in 2004, only to return to his job at JBHM.

"I enjoyed painting so much that I worried if it became a job I might not enjoy," Jerrod explains of his reluctance to do his art full time. "But the other consideration was that I might never reach my full potential without going into art full time."

In 2007, with the support of his wife, Jesse, Jerrod took the plunge into becoming a full-time artist. With a studio set up in the back room of their Fondren home, he took a job for a year at Pearl River Glass in Midtown.

"Pearl River Glass is an incredible foundry for artists," Jerrod says. "You go there and get inspired and learn about art as a business."

Since 2008, Jerrod has worked as self-employed full-time artist, showing his work at Southside Gallery in Oxford, the Attic Gallery in Vicksburg and Søren Christianson Gallery in New Orleans. He also teaches art lessons and figure-drawing classes at the Mississippi Museum of Art. To him, teaching is a way to practice his own craft.

"At any level, you need to practice to get better," he explains. "I always see what I wish I could have painted, so it's exciting when I see other people get excited."

As a professional artist, Jerrod understands the delicate balance between working on commissions, doing art for galleries and teaching.

"I juggle those three things, and if one slacks off, I try to build another one up. It's worked so far," he laughs. "My passion grows every year as I learn more, see more, see other people's work and struggle with my own work. There's never a finished point with art," he says. "You keep growing. That's the exciting thing about art—you never stop learning."

Jerrod has done commissions for notable clients, including Hinds Community College, Galloway Memorial United Methodist Church and Millsaps College. Last summer, Jerrod took a group of painters to Italy for a week so that they could stay in a villa in Tuscany and paint. The trip resulted in a series of commissions for Italy paintings, but Jerrod finds that he is frequently commissioned to paint portraits. One of his first notable portrait commissions came from Millsaps College, which asked him to paint former

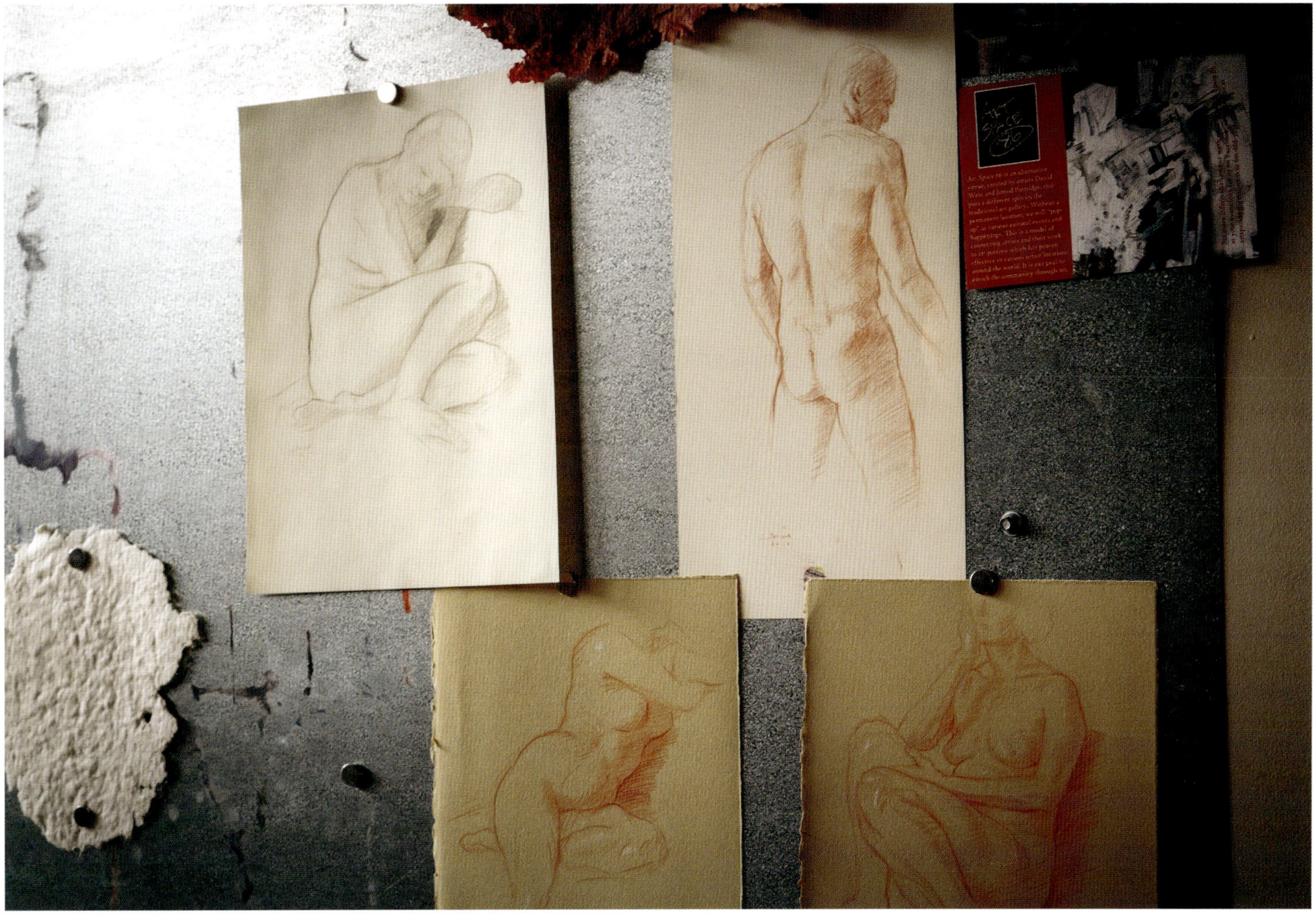

Figure sketches hang from a magnet board, which Jerrod finds is a useful way to keep ideas on display.

president Dr. Frances Lucas. Dr. Lucas came to Jerrod's Fondren home to sit for portrait sessions in the back room where Jerrod painted.

"I thought, 'Man, I wish I had a better setting for the president of a college to come and sit,'" he recalls. He decided it was time to build a studio.

A Backyard Studio

"I wanted to create a professional and appealing environment for people to come and sit for portraits or take classes," he says of his studio concept. Today, Jerrod's studio is an inviting space nestled in his own backyard, surrounded by plants and found objects. Propped up against the fence in his garden is an old porcelain sink filled with organic growth; a flock of chickens roosts nearby.

"The chickens were Jesse's birthday present," he clarifies, picking up a particular red hen and cradling it against him. "They're quite docile."

Venturing into Jerrod's studio, it is apparent that the space is designed to employ a high level of natural light, with a slanted roof and windows installed along the highest wall. The main room of the studio is a multifunctional space, with sawhorse tables that are easy to move and set back up in different positions. Since Jerrod does a large amount of work on paper, he has installed magnet boards on the studio walls so that he can easily hang up his work or arrange a series of paintings together. One group of paintings is a series of faces lit up with a blue glow; Jerrod explains that this is a study of how the face is touched by the light from computer screens. His bookshelves house the artists who inspire him, including Walter Anderson, John Singer Sargent, Degas, Benny Andrews and Henri Cartier-Bresson. He also admires street photography, such as the work of Gordon Parks.

"I'm not trying to make photographic images, but when someone can really capture life, that's powerful to me," he explains.

One of Jerrod's magnet boards is covered with his children's own artwork; their childhood interests influence their father's art.

"I'm working on a series of paintings of children with weapons," he says. "I've been observing my own kids and their fascination with weapons from such a young age."

In a southern state where children are taught to hunt for sport, Jerrod is somewhat surprised that

Opposite, left: In the top paintings, Jerrod has studied the light of a computer screen on the human face.

Opposite, right: Jerrod keeps inspiring books about his favorite artists at hand.

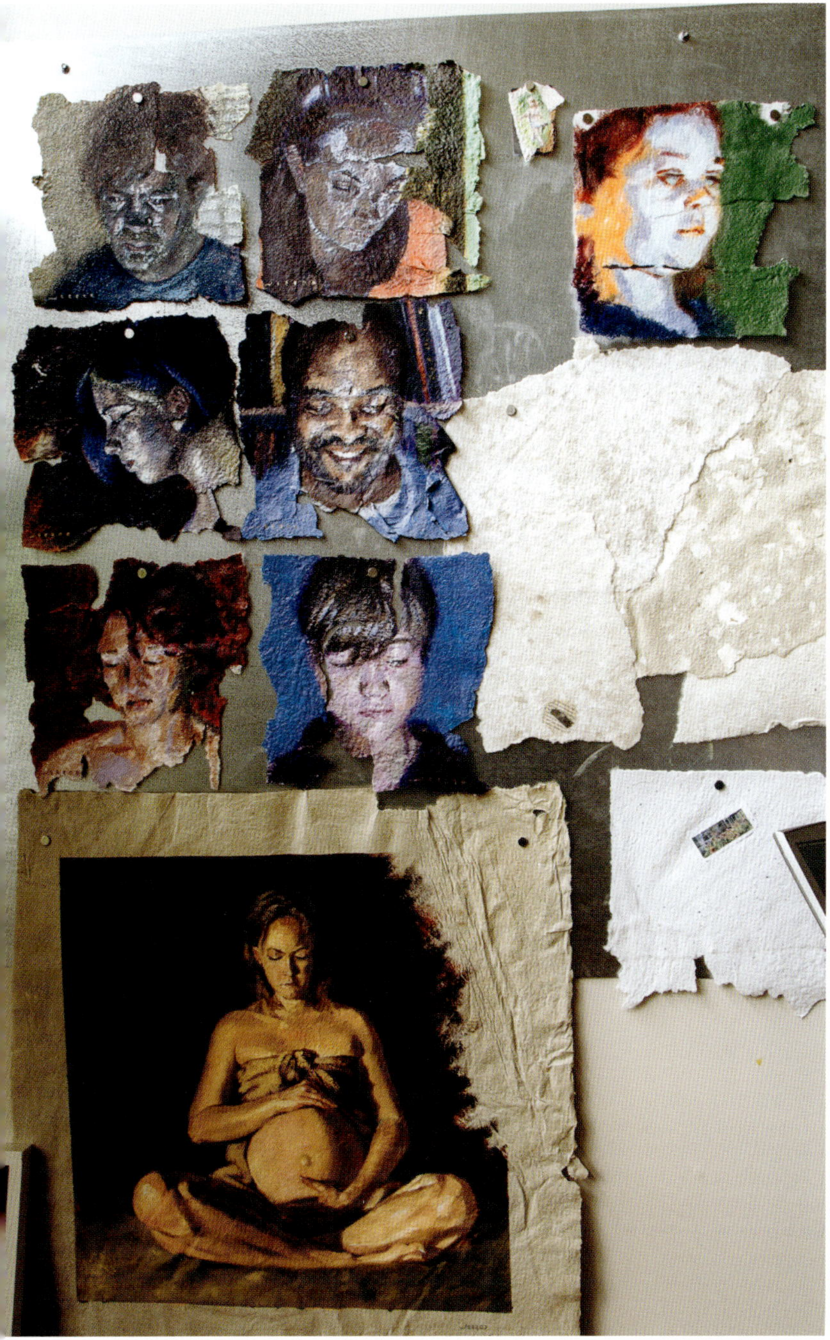

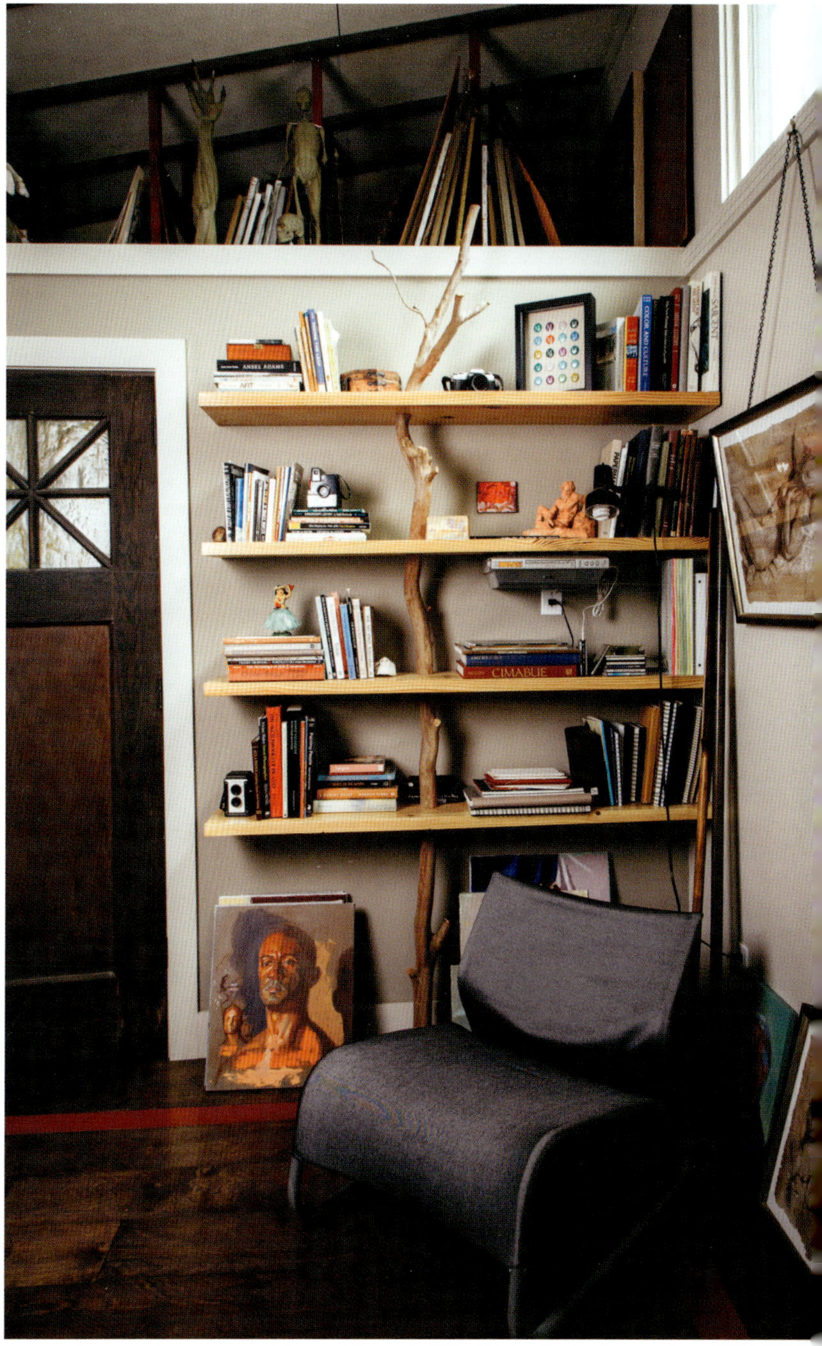
ANSEL ADAMS
CIMABUE

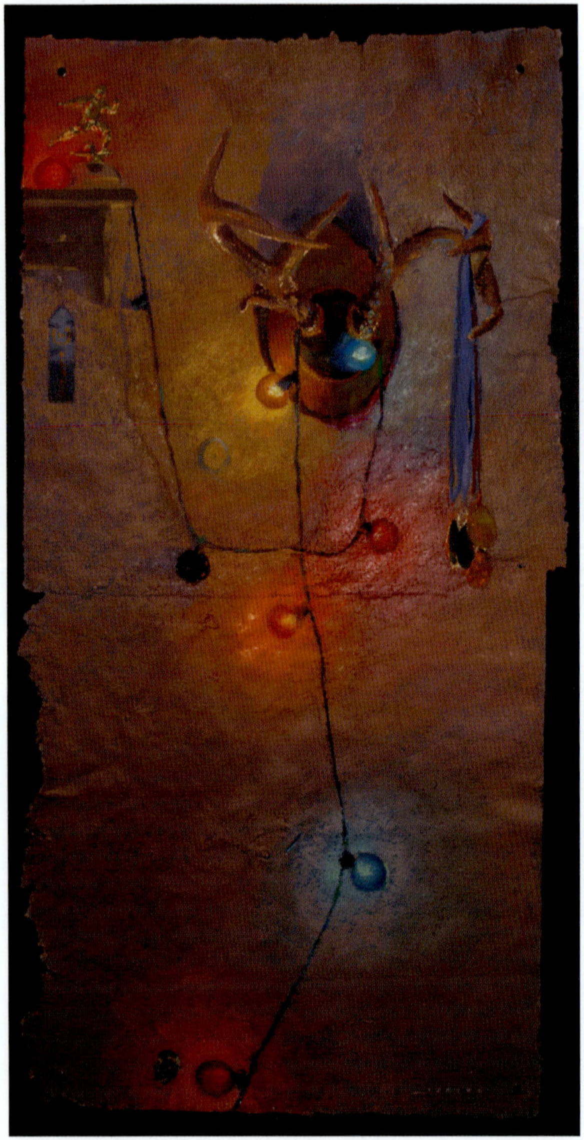

Great American Dream IV (Trophies) by Jerrod Partridge.

the paintings of children wielding weapons have been met with adverse response. He remains unfazed by criticism leveraged against some of his more controversial subject matter, revealing that he deliberately paints things that are uncomfortable or bothersome to him, frequently including skulls and antlers in his art.

"You want paintings to speak to people in a different ways," he explains.

Jerrod also uses his studio space to make his own paper using newspapers, scrap paper and cotton fiber. He occasionally incorporates images on the paper into his art, allowing the elements of the paper to merge with the elements of the painting.

"With handmade paper, there's another level of appreciation for the viewer," Jerrod says. "A good painting has elements you might not find right away, and if you live with it, you keep discovering."

Working in Jackson

Jerrod resides in the Fondren community and is a Fondren Renaissance Foundation board member, but overall, he has found a supportive artistic community throughout the city.

"I'm friends with basically all the artists in town," he says. "Because this is such a small town, you'd think there would be competition between artists. But there's not."

Jerrod cites special friendships with fellow artists, including Bob Pennebaker, Richard Kelso and David West, the latter of whom he worked with to co-found Art Space 86, a pop-up gallery.

Jerrod relies heavily on social media to promote art events in Jackson, stressing that social media is a way to improve the art community, not just a way to showcase his own work. For a while, he ran a blog highlighting community art events because he felt that it was important for people to have a social and artistic investment in their neighborhood. Jerrod has considered the idea of moving to a bigger city with a larger art scene, but ultimately, community and family have strengthened his resolve to stay in Jackson.

"When we lived in New York, I absolutely loved it," he admits. "New York City is one of the most magical places on earth. I would be happy to raise a family there, but our families are here. Jackson is such a rich and interesting place. Family and personal connections are a foundation to our lives. The narrative and storytelling traditions here are so deep, and there is enough support and interest here to keep me going."

Jerrod has received support in the form of grants from the Mississippi Arts Commission and the Mississippi Council for the Arts. He is pleased that the city of Jackson has researched ways that a creative economy could bring in financial revenue, but he does not think money is the primary focus in the Jackson creative culture.

"I don't think anyone is saying that we need to appreciate arts because arts bring in money. Art is an integral part of our community and culture, and that, I think, is what's important."

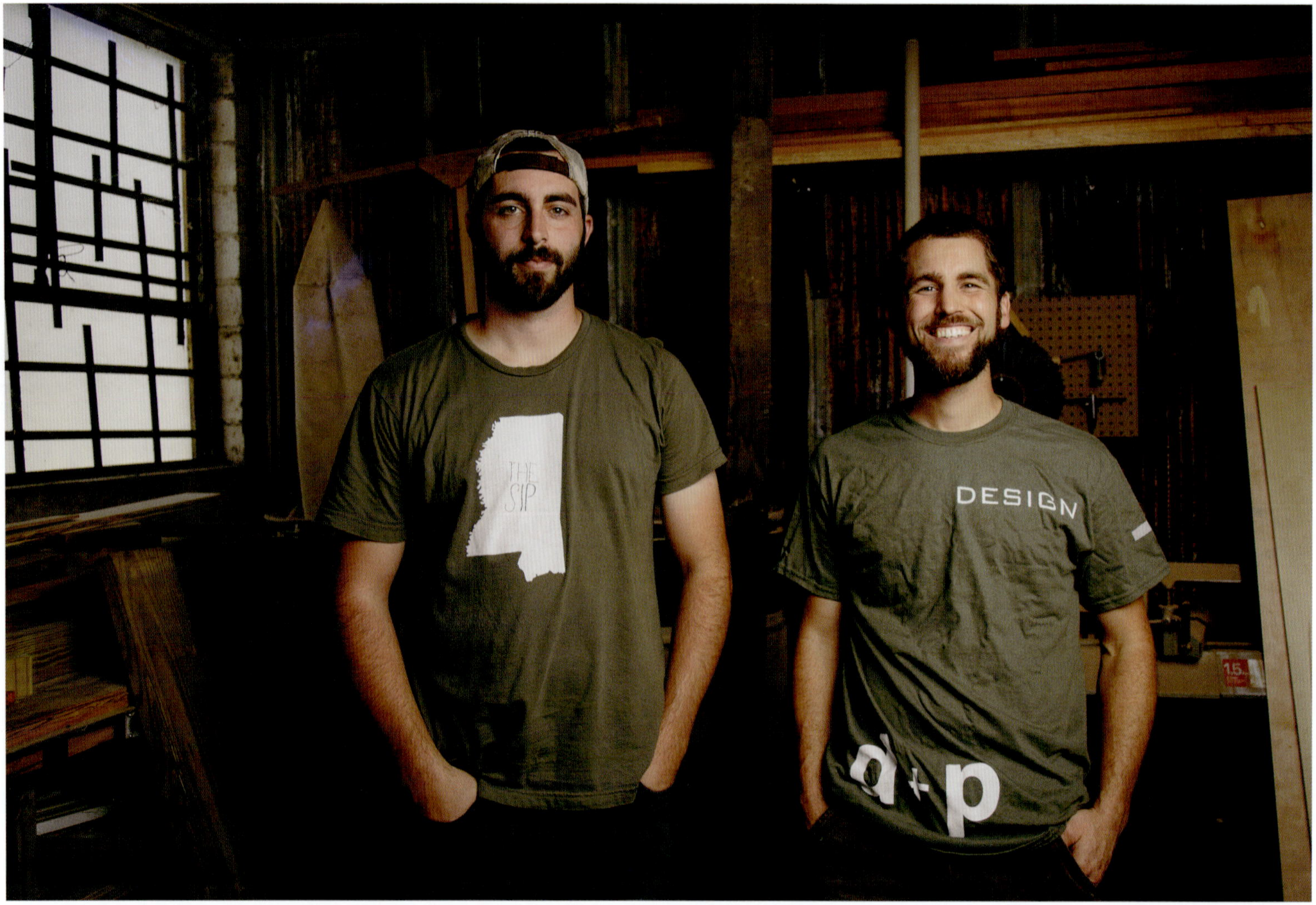

David Dill (left) and Paul Purser (right) are the architects who co-founded D+P Designs.

3
D+P DESIGNS

DAVID DILL AND PAUL PURSER

David Dill recalls visiting Jackson's Midtown neighborhood for the first time in 2012 and thinking, "This is such a great community. Why have I never heard of this area?"

David and Paul Purser rent a Midtown studio space in a warehouse owned by craftsman Andy Hilton, and together the three men have turned the warehouse from a "trashed" building to a community hub and modern furniture design studio. The warehouse is the home of D+P Designs, which is David and Paul's custom furniture and construction business.

"As architects, we have a desire to be part of our community, we have a sense of place," says David. "We have all worked on a variety of collaborations here in Midtown. We [all] feel that Midtown has been great for our business."

Architectural Alternatives

In 2010, Paul finished his degree in architecture at Mississippi State University (MSU). It was a bad time to be an architect, he says. He recalls the day his professors pulled the architecture students together for a meeting to inform them that employment prospects were grim.

"They sat us down and told us that none of us would have jobs," Paul says. At the time, Paul was living in Jackson and finishing his fifth year of school. He remembers feeling frozen. "I was disheartened and didn't want to move away from Jackson," he recalls.

Paul knew that his class was not the only group of young architects struggling to find work. David graduated from the MSU architecture school in 2009 and spent a year working with Engineering

Missions International in Uganda before returning to Jackson in 2010. Back in Jackson, David worked "odd construction jobs" to make ends meet, eventually calling in Paul when a project required additional assistance. Desperate to maintain an income, David and Paul began to take any job that came their way.

"We had this terrible job painting a 3,500-square-foot house," Paul recalls. "I never even met the owner face to face."

David and Paul discovered they had a mutual interest in furniture design that they both realize is influenced by their grandfathers: Paul's grandfather owned a furniture store on Farish Street in Jackson called Mississippi Furniture Company, and David's grandfather was a hobbyist woodworker who left David all his tools. Between construction jobs, David and Paul began building furniture, storing their tools in David's mother-in-law's garage and working in half of a two-car space. The work conditions were far from ideal.

"We had no money," Paul recalls. "We had a vision, but we needed a space."

David looked on Craigslist for an affordable space where they could house their woodworking tools and begin a custom furniture business. He found an ad for a warehouse space "owned by Andy Hilton and available for rent in Midtown." Hilton agreed to rent out a section of the warehouse to David and Paul, provided they help him fix up the building as part of their "rent." They agreed, and D+P Designs found a home in Midtown in 2011.

Since moving their business to Midtown, David and Paul have watched D+P Designs grow into a successful venture. In their studio, Paul fabricates the metal elements of their furniture, and the two men construct the wood elements together, meaning their products are completely made in Midtown. Like Hilton, David and Paul have made a point to use local woods, such as red oak, red gum, sassafras and maple. They have had some success harvesting their wood from fallen trees, a practice implemented by their icon, Fletcher Cox.

David and Paul have found that they are able to market themselves online to reach an audience far outside Mississippi. They use their personal website, as well as Etsy, Facebook, Instagram and the website custommade.com. The California-based company Tesla commissioned them after finding them online, but they have also achieved local acclaim; they have done commission work for Trim Salon in Jackson and Whole Foods in Jackson, and they helped build the wooden bridge featured prominently in the movie *As I Lay Dying* (2013), which was filmed in Mississippi.

"We have slowly learned what it actually costs to make something," jokes David, who asserts that they split their time evenly between commissions and building their own designs. The duo has created several original designs since moving into the Midtown studio, focusing on products that appeal to audiences in cities such as Atlanta, Nashville and Austin, where they think the creative economy is stronger. Their favorite designs include the Café Chair, which is inspired by the iconic look of retro children's school chairs, and the Soul Mate Chair, which features an asymmetrical back so that two chairs can fit together, meaning "they literally have a soul mate." They have also worked with Hilton on custom installations, doing cabinets when Hilton installs concrete countertops. David and Paul, like Hilton, are dedicated to the Midtown neighborhood. They are trying to make new connections in Midtown by participating in events such as the Midtown Holiday Studio tours, which they say "make the retail side of Midtown successful." Their long-term goal is to stay in Midtown, expand to a bigger warehouse and, one day, possibly rent out space to up-and-coming craftsmen as Hilton did for them.

This "Soul Mate" chair is an original design by David and Paul.

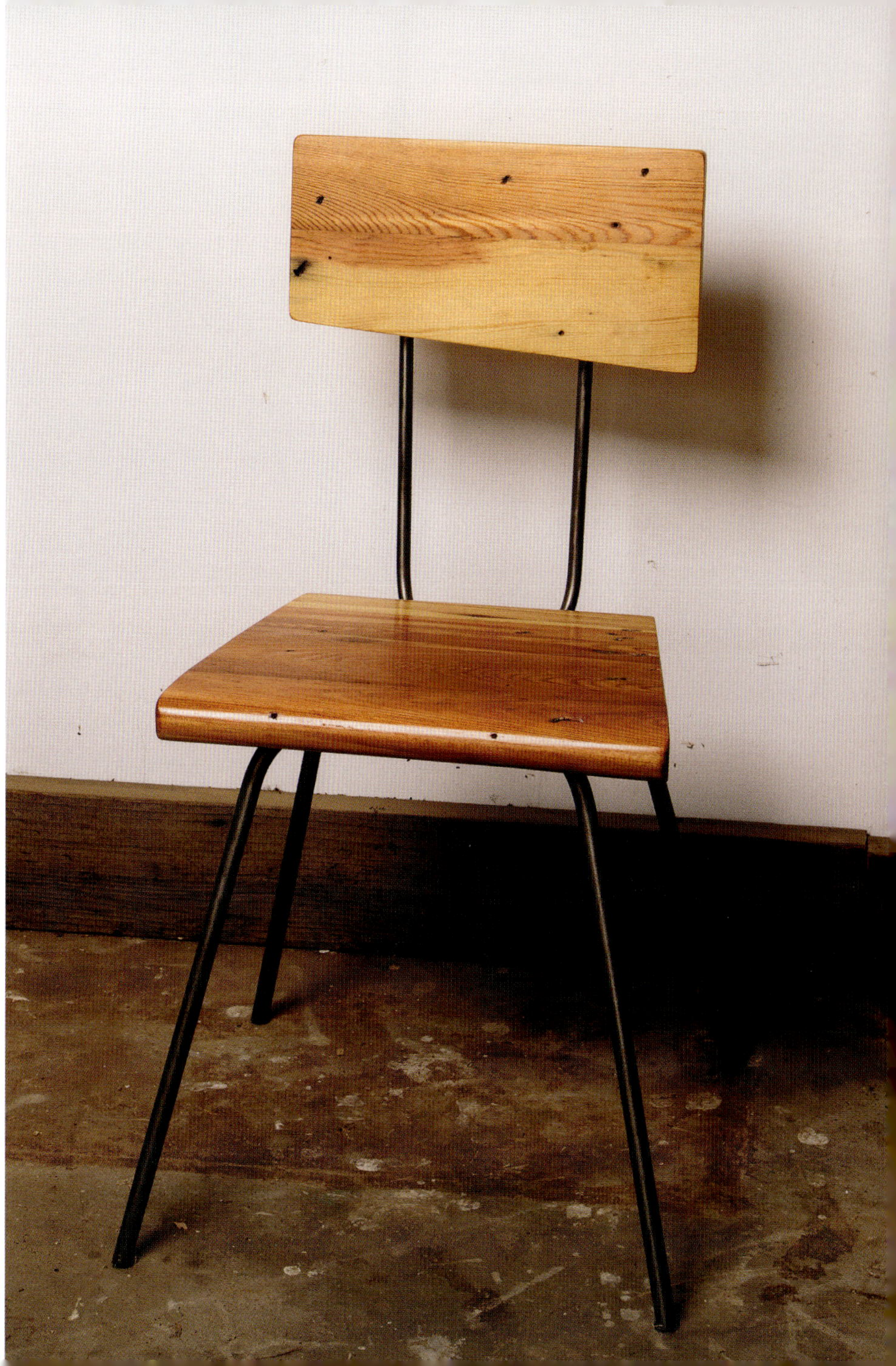

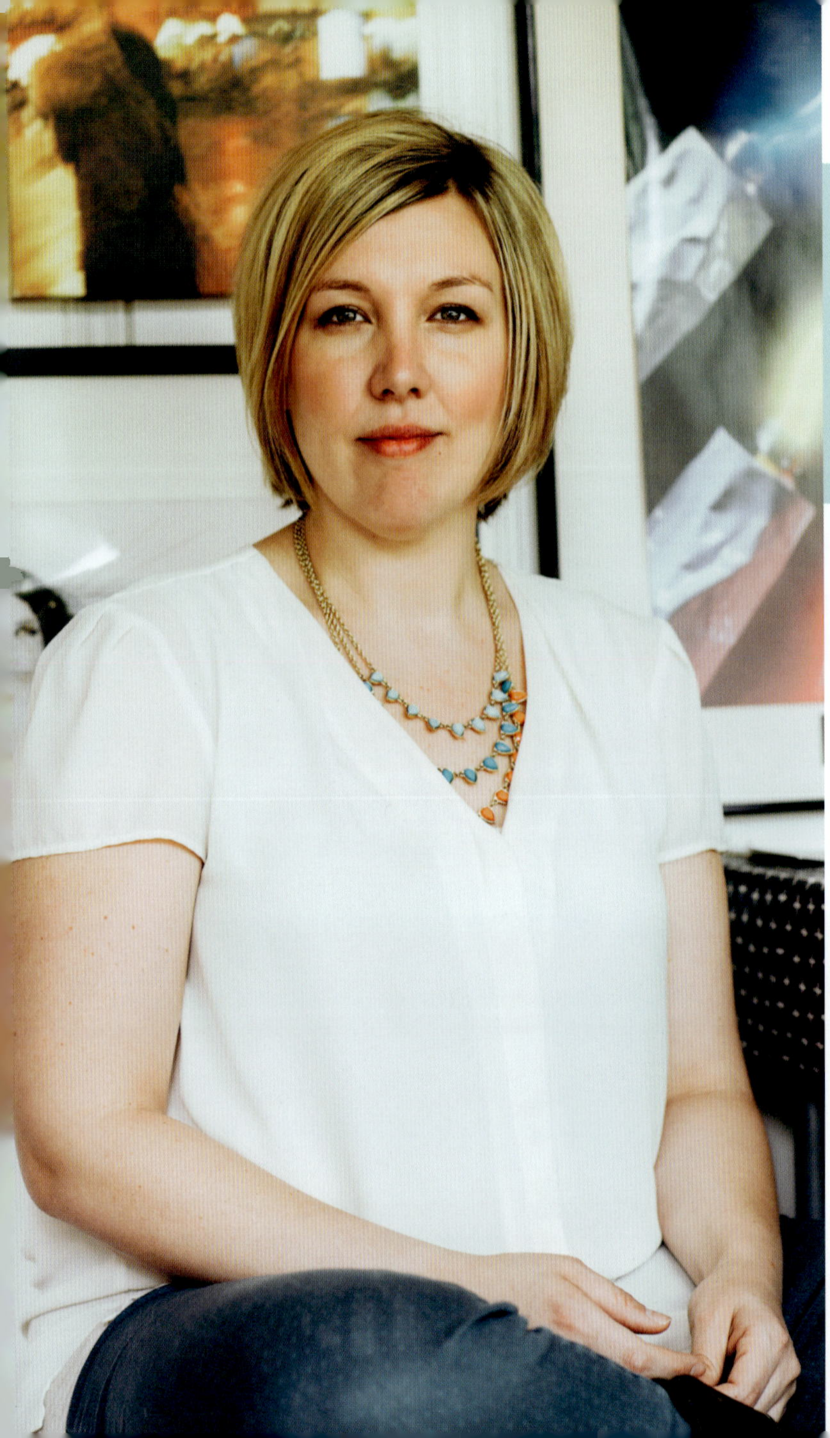

4

GINGER WILLIAMS-COOK

Ginger Williams-Cook was raised in South Jackson and decided early in life that she wanted to study either art or theater. She recalls making the choice to pursue art in the sixth grade. It was, by her account, "a big deal." After announcing to her family, "I am becoming an artist," Ginger began art programs for young students at the Mississippi Museum of Art in downtown Jackson. Her artistic gifts emerged; she possessed drawing skills and a fine technical ability that, coupled with the pluck and foresight to begin perfecting her art at a young age, have led to her commercial success.

Although art ultimately won the top tier in her hierarchy of interests, throughout the years Ginger has remained fascinated with improvisational theater,

Ginger Williams-Cook creates her illustrations in her Belhaven studio.

lending a theatrical, quirky, funny quality to her art. A prime example of such theatrical artwork is her collections of nesting dolls, which took off when she did a series inspired by *The Golden Girls*. Ginger created the *Golden Girls*–themed babushka set while trying to promote a solo show in 2010; she had experimented with Michael Jackson–themed nesting dolls when her husband, Justin, suggested she try *The Golden Girls*.

"I laughed nonstop as I was painting them," she says.

Her friend Will Simmons, a social media guru, asked to put the image of the completed nesting doll set on his popular blog. He warned Ginger that the image "could go viral," and within a day or two, Ginger was receiving national attention from media outlets such as *Good Day Sacramento*, *New*

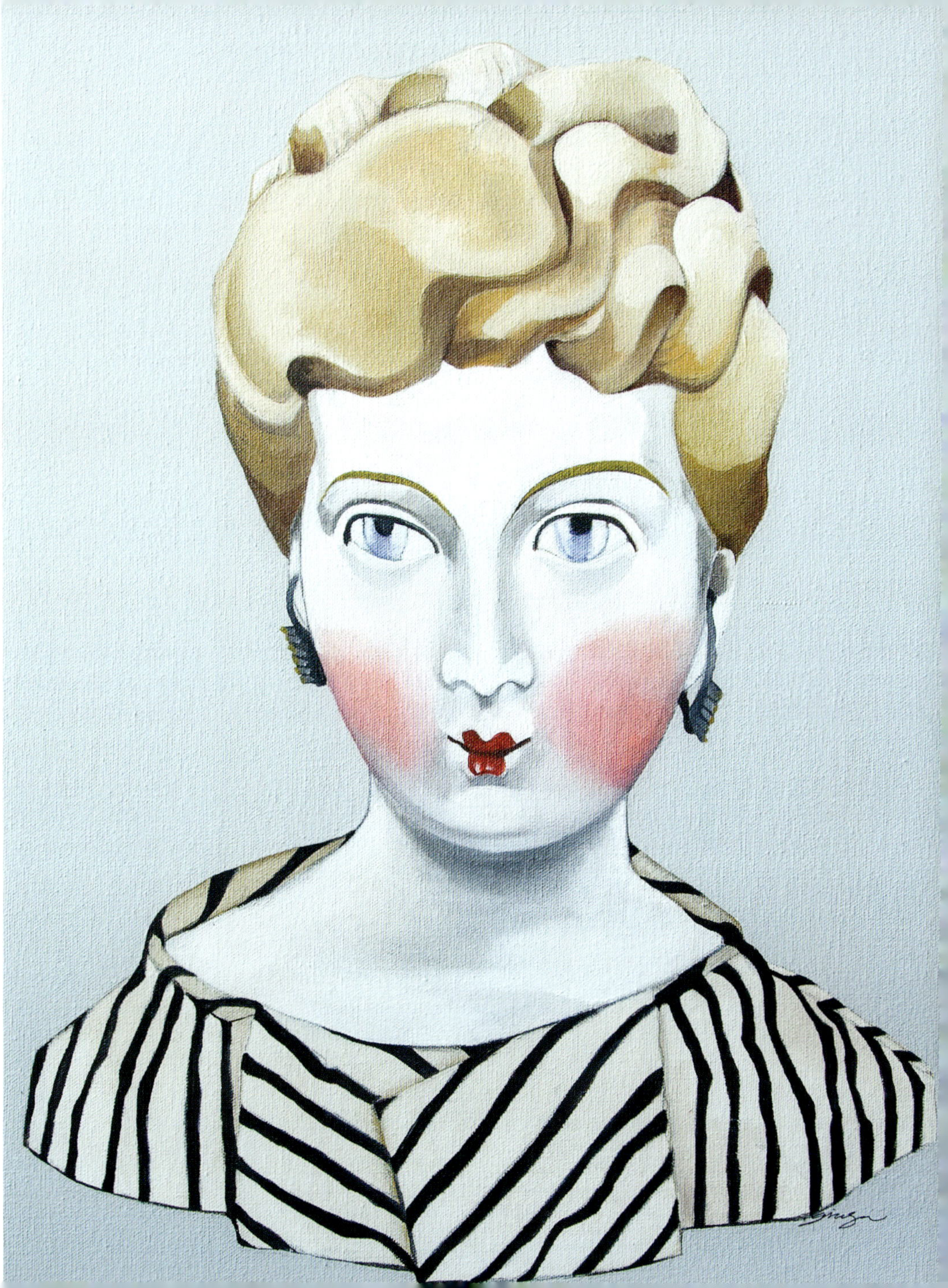

The Parian Doll of Dresden by Ginger Williams-Cook.

York Daily News, *Jezebel* and Buzzfeed. MSNBC asked to feature Ginger on "Around the World in 60 Seconds."

"Fan art can't be contained," Ginger shrugs, laughing. Still, she notes, "You can't prepare for sudden fame."

"It freaked me out," she admits. "I had an inbox full of messages and requests for commissions, and I had no idea what to charge."

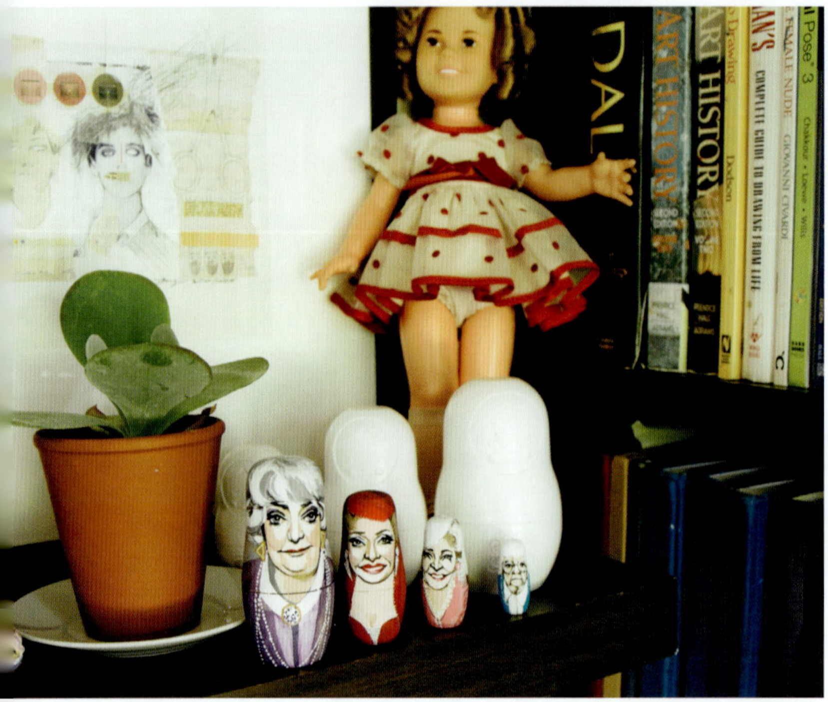

Ginger's famous *Golden Girls* nesting dolls and childhood Shirley Temple doll complete her inspiring studio space.

Ginger did a silent auction of the nesting dolls sets that she had available. Today, they retail at her online shop through Etsy.com.

"I want people to have my work," Ginger explains. "I went through such a long phase of time trying to figure out what was going to sell—you can't figure out your identity through that."

Ginger's identity as an artist is defined by her ability to capture many different subjects and emotions. Her artwork considers the boundary between lightheartedness and underlying grief drawn from experience: Ginger lost her mother to suicide when she was a teenager, and that inherent darkness permeates some of her work. One of her most treasured paintings is about the death of a parent, and it won a New American Talent award and was chosen for the cover image of the documentary film *The (Dead Mother's) Club*. Ginger, whose role in the documentary has been lauded by critics (she was a guest on Katie Couric's show), is proud that her work can show the duality of loving and missing her mother.

Ginger's ability to create a bridge between two sides of illustration—the hilarious and the grotesque—is a quality she shares with many creators and illustrators (she loves the worlds of Jim Henson and Dr. Suess) who use drawings that may appear lighthearted to convey a much deeper message. In fact, when Ginger sold her first piece of art, she cried. They were not happy tears. For Ginger, there are times when creating a piece of artwork is deeply therapeutic, and she develops a personal attachment to such paintings. Parting with the work is like giving a little bit of her heart away.

"I have a painful source of inspiration, but… when I am doing illustrations, I call it playing and having fun," Ginger explains. "Illustrations create a vehicle for what I love to do. It is rewarding to be working on illustrations that tell a visual story."

From Fondren to Paris and Back

As the Jackson art scene began to bloom with young talent in the early 2000s, Ginger connected with other artists who deeply inspired her work and remain some of her closest friends. She met Josh Hailey, a photographer, one summer while working at Camp Windhover in Crystal Springs, Mississippi. Hailey introduced her to William Goodman, who was one of the first young artists to establish an unofficial art colony in Jackson's Fondren community. The same night that Ginger met Goodman, she met her future husband, Justin Cook, and Goodman met Jason "Twiggy" Lott, whom Ginger knew from growing up in south Jackson. Ginger credits her friends with a good deal of her early success, adding, "We shaped one another's lives."

The group began collaborating on large projects, including murals. As they developed their personal styles, their reputations in the community began to take off. Some of her artist friends began moving to bigger cities to pursue their work, and Ginger struggled to decide if moving was the best choice for her art.

"I thought about moving to Austin, Texas, in 2006," she says. "I saw that once I moved to a major city, the cost of living would be a lot."

Instead of moving, Ginger saved up money for an extended trip to Paris, France, where she has family on her mother's side. She lived there for about six months in 2007 and was joined by William Goodman for part of her trip. Together, the two artists created a retrospective show featuring artwork created in Paris and inspired by their time there.

Like Goodman, Ginger was focused on creating large-scale works that sold for thousands of dollars each and appealed to national art collectors and jurors.

"People had these big loft apartments downtown and wanted large-scale paintings," she explains.

But the "bigger is better" mentality came to a halt when the economy tanked in 2008.

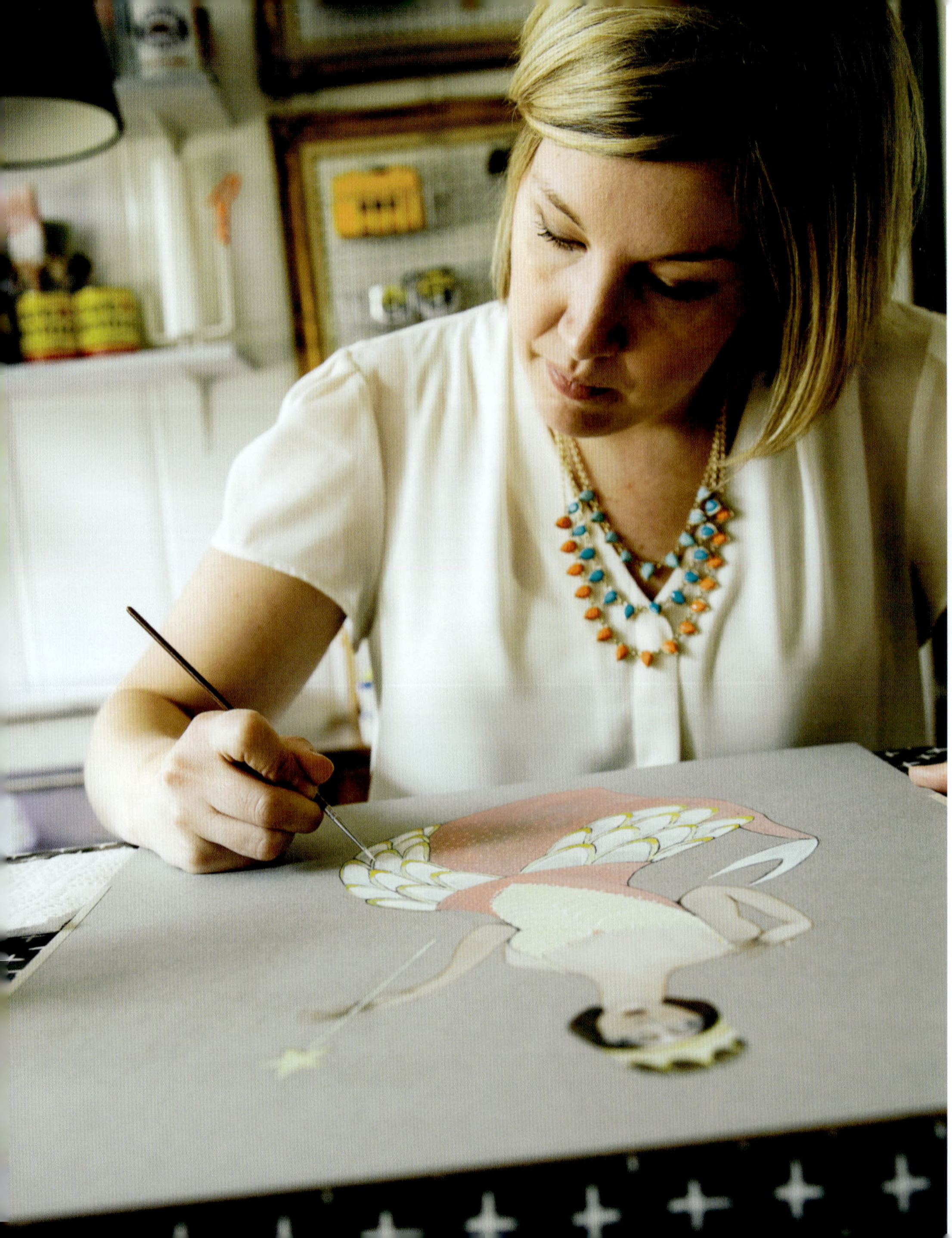

"The recession slowed everybody down and made everybody aware," Ginger notes. "I think artists were the first to notice the recession because art is a luxury."

To adapt, Ginger spent the recession years scaling back her work and focusing on what really mattered to her: connecting with her art and starting a family. Travel will always remain an important part of her personal exploration and growth, she says, but her focus now is on intuitive living, where "work and life decisions are all connected."

Ginger feels that the Jackson art community has always supported her, and lately she's been enthused to find fresh talent joining the scene. She recently

Ginger's paintings focus on small, detailed imagery.

worked with artist Kristen Ley, whose creative spirit and enthusiasm she found fun and refreshing.

She says, "There's a new wave of collaboration [in Jackson] that I haven't experienced since the early days in Fondren."

An Intentional Workspace

Ginger's studio is located in the back room of her home, located in Jackson's historic Belhaven community. Originally, the studio had dark, wood-paneled walls, which Ginger felt led to the accumulation of clutter and gave her a feeling of being "boxed in."

"Nothing was special about my space. I didn't want to be in here at night playing. I feel creative at night, but the darkness of the room made my skin crawl," she says.

After the birth of her daughter, Eloise, Ginger renovated her studio space, painting the walls a crisp white color. Mindfulness is important to Ginger, who "hates stress" and profoundly values developing her patience and eliminating clutter. Organized and perfectly maintained, her studio today is a reflection of where she is both creatively and emotionally.

"I have a two-year-old," she laughs. "At this point, I am always juggling, so working on a small scale and with print media is essential to where I am right now."

She is very interested in where her art is going and admits that "wanting something and not knowing where it's going is more frightening that anything."

Bright, cozy and decorative, her studio reflects her love of fashion, costumes, toys and dolls. For Ginger, books are a "quick way to get inspired," so her studio bookshelves are stocked with volumes on her favorite artists: Degas, Klimt, Picasso and Matisse, her "art idol."

During the renovation, Ginger carefully and intentionally planned to maximize her space, making a place for a long, narrow surface where she could lay out her paints and work, a place for her computer and a place where she could put her easel and then back up and view her work from a distance.

"The more stuff that's piled around, the less you can tell when things are clean," she theorizes.

Her workspace is so important that the renovation has dramatically altered her creative output.

"Since this room has been redone I've been making myself go to bed again," she says. "It has changed my world."

Looking at the future of her art, Ginger can see doing a book of her illustrations one day. She remains connected to social media and has also begun selling prints of her work, which, in her opinion, increases the values of the originals. Overall, she finds herself in a developmental stage.

"You have to maintain a balance between being busy and being busy enough," she notes, adding, "You're only going to keep improving."

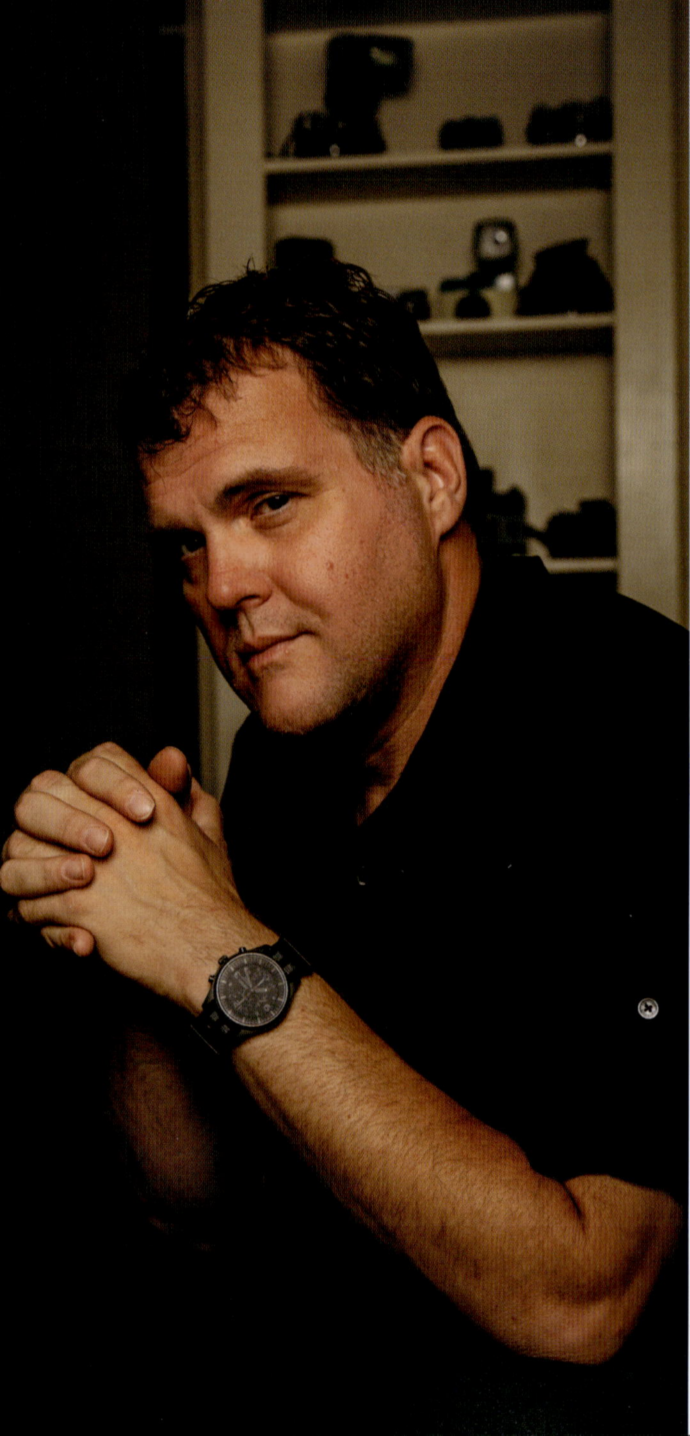

5

TOM BECK

Tom Beck has spent the past twelve years in Jackson, Mississippi, defining himself as a photographer and videographer specializing in editorial and commercial photography. Tom's clients include magazines, public relations firms, restaurants, modeling agencies and prominent Mississippi businesses. In addition to his commercial photography business, Beck Photographic, Tom co-owns Spot On Productions, a film production company he started with commercial and documentary filmmaker Philip Scarborough. Between running the two businesses, Tom jokes that it is harder to find time for fine art photography, his personal passion that brought him into the photography business in the first place.

Tom Beck works on location in Jackson.

"Running a business takes up more time than anything," Beck explains. "I've got personal projects that I haven't finished yet because I'm so busy with commercial work."

A great deal of Tom's commercial work is based out of Jackson, and despite his busy schedule, he and Philip found time to create the wildly popular "Happy MS" music video that features Mississippians dancing and singing to the Pharrell Williams hit song "Happy." The video was not created for any professional client; rather, Tom expresses his hopes that it will have a positive impact on the state. A Jackson native, Tom attended Forest Hill High School in south Jackson and studied at Ole Miss before returning to his hometown to work. Of living and working in Jackson, Tom says, "This is where I am, and it's where I've been. There are stories to be told here."

Despite commercial success, Tom has not considered leaving Jackson, noting that in the digital age the Internet is a useful tool for getting his name into larger cities without having to move.

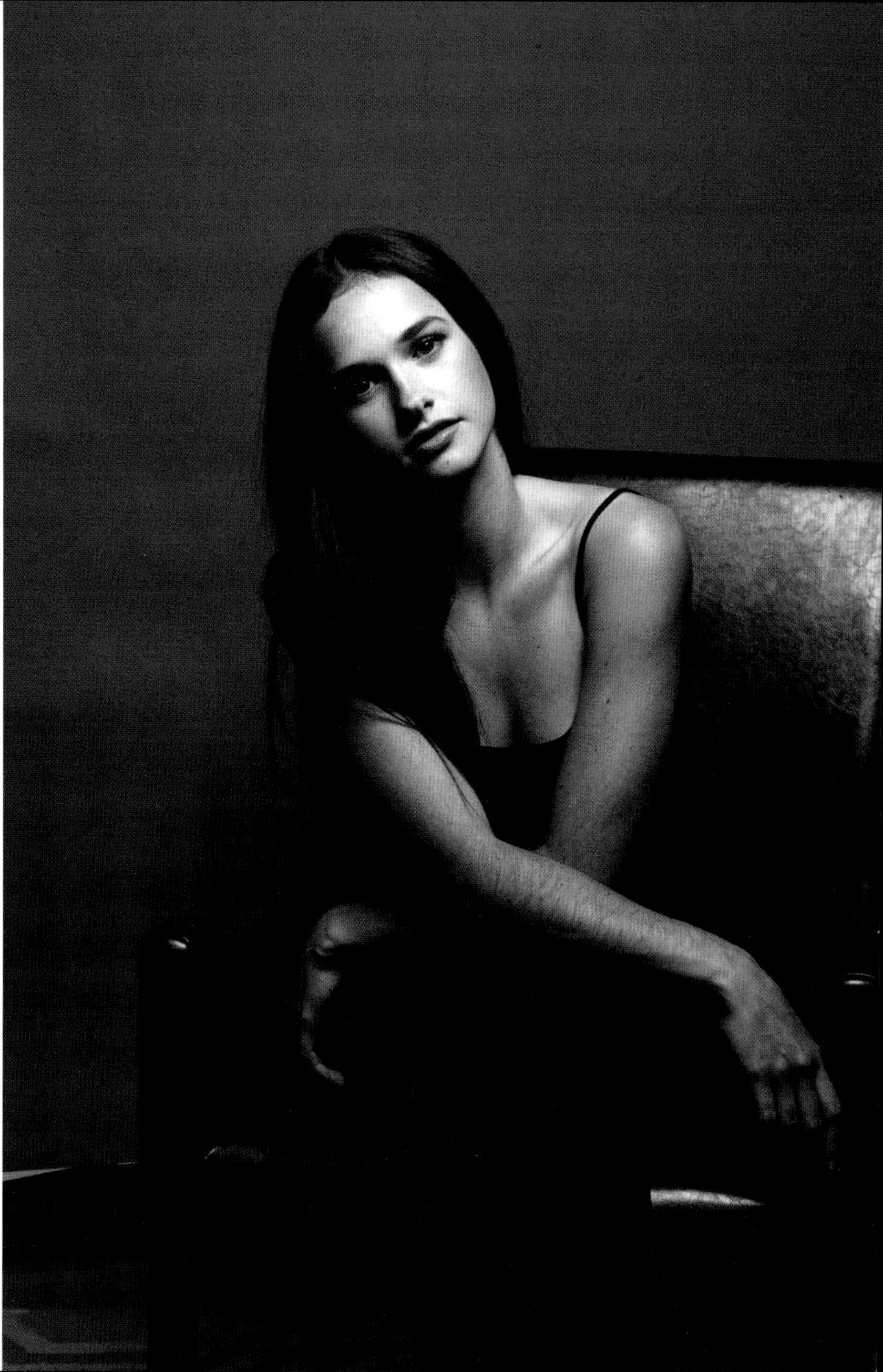

"Madeline." *Courtesy of Tom Beck.*

"You don't have to live in New York or LA to have your work seen all over the world," he explains. "The problem now is that it is easy to get it out there, but hard to cut through the rest of the noise and get noticed."

The Business of Taking a Picture

For Tom, the most important part of editorial photography is telling the story. He started his commercial photography business because he enjoyed the challenge of interpreting the creative visions of other businesses and making their stories a reality and because earning a living exclusively as a fine art photographer has become increasingly difficult. Gone are the days when people would eagerly shell out money for a photograph the way that they might for a sculpture or painting. At one time, photographers had a monopoly on a certain market and could charge for whatever their time and art was worth. Now, Tom says, it has become impossible to truly make a living as a fine art photographer or even as a portrait studio owner.

"It's a tough market and a tough crowd as far as being a fine art photographer," Tom laments. "People don't appreciate it. They think it's just pushing a button—everyone with a cellphone is a photographer now. It's hard to convince people that what you've done is worth what you have to charge to make a living."

Instead of working exclusively from a studio, Tom prides himself on his ability to use the city as his workspace. He conducts his digital editing and production work out of his downtown Jackson apartment while his gear and his camera travel with him from one location to the next, allowing him the mobility to create a studio wherever his work requires him to go. Instead of using a darkroom, Tom sends his film to be professionally developed, noting that the economics of owning a darkroom are exceedingly frustrating as fewer and fewer photographers shoot exclusively with film.

"The day of the photography studio is somewhat dead and gone, which is kind of sad," Tom asserts. "There are things you can do in the studio that you can never do in the field, but economically, it's hard to do it."

At any given point, Tom could be shooting a variety of different scenes. For a fashion editorial, for example, he might travel to various locations to shoot models. To make his work efficient, he says, the key is scouting out locations beforehand.

"I don't want to shoot 300 photographs to get one. I want to shoot 24 photographs to get one," he says.

He jokes that he is something of a "visual raconteur," noting that each location presents its own unique challenges, and he has invested in lights and equipment to enable him to shoot the way he wants to in any circumstance. For Tom, this is the only logical way to run a photography business.

"The business of photography has changed so much; the overhead of the business has changed so much," he points out. "It's cheaper to become a photographer now than it ever has been, so photographers are not getting paid what they used to. It's become democratized—which is fantastic, but it's also much harder to make it," Tom explains.

During the economic recession in 2008, Tom says he watched as commercial advertising and editorial budgets dried up. If companies could do without photography expenses, such as new portraits of all the executives, they would. In recent years, as the economy has started making a turnaround, Tom has noticed a new attitude toward hiring commercial photographers: everyone wants—even demands—photography

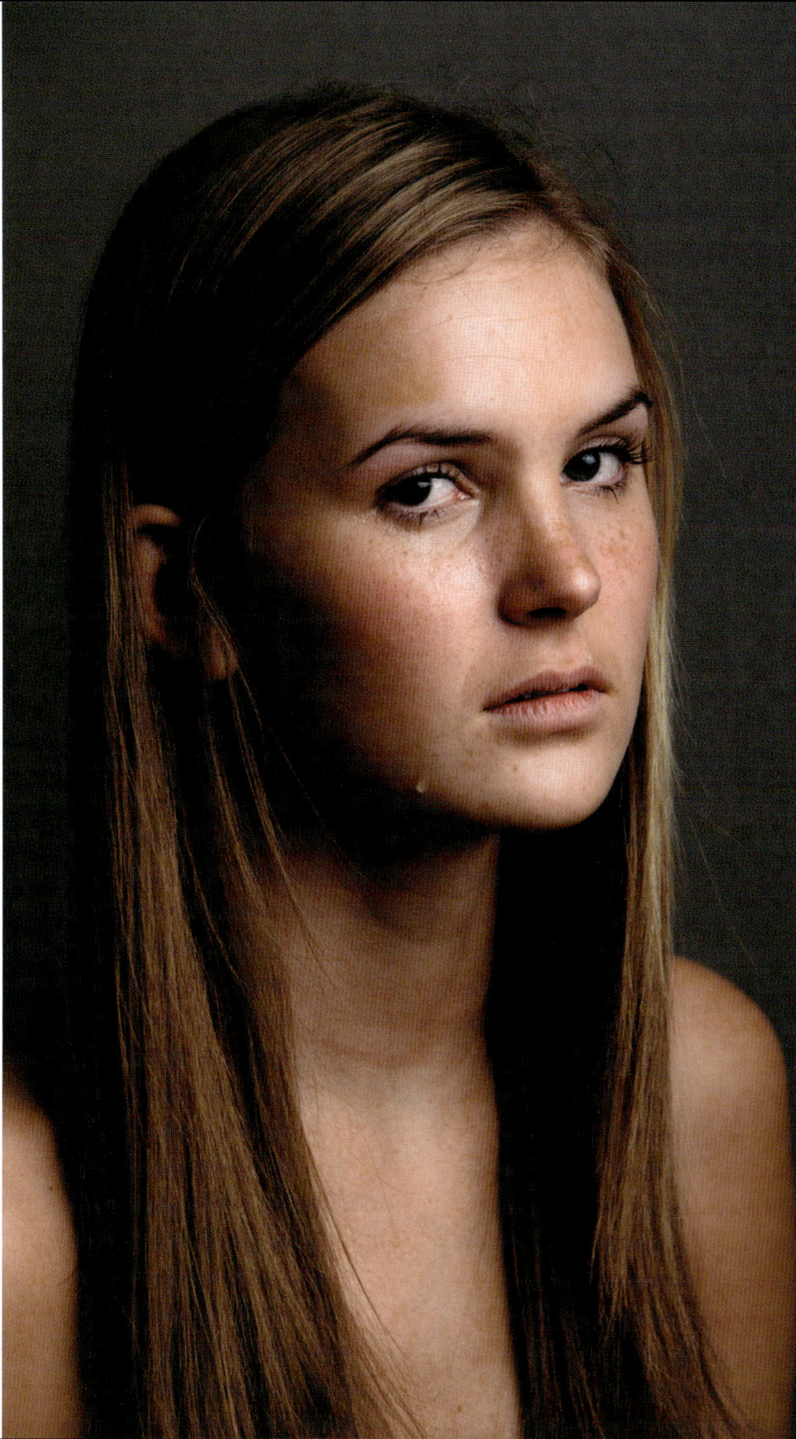

"Avery." *Courtesy of Tom Beck.*

and video, but now businesses shop around for photographers, trying to find the cheapest options. To this, Tom chuckles, noting, "You pay for what you get."

Photography in a Digital World

It seems that the way that photographers understand their craft seems to be shifting just as the way that the world understands photography seems to be shifting. When using photo-sharing applications such as Instagram, Tom has observed what he refers to as the younger generation's "obsession" with photography. Ironically, Tom has also noticed that as photography continues to become a currency of social media, there is a renewed interest in the older photography processes, such as wet plate.

"You can't make digital look analog," Tom states, adding that young people interested in photography as an art form struggle to replicate what they see in old film prints. "Analog film grains are round. Pixels are square."

And while fine art photography may have lost some value with the digitalization of the medium, commercial and editorial photography depend on it. Take advertising, for example. Not too long ago, many ads were created using drawings and cartoons instead of photographs because photography posed a challenge and an expense. Now, photography is an essential part of advertising. What would an advertisement for a restaurant be without a picture of the delicious food that it serves? As Tom puts it, "The photograph is the currency of the digital age... We don't have time to sit and process things. A picture is worth way more than 1,000 words."

6
RICHARD KELSO

For almost three decades, Richard Kelso has been creating oil paintings in his studio above Hal and Mal's restaurant in downtown Jackson. Kelso is known for his landscape and still-life paintings. Kelso's primary goal with his paintings is to capture light, atmosphere and color. Raised in the Mississippi Delta town of Cleveland, Kelso paid his own way through Delta State University, where his professors encouraged him to study art.

"I'd never seen a real painting before," Kelso recalls of his early years. "All I knew was my girlfriend, TV and sports. I just knew I drew all the time."

After he finished at Delta State, Kelso taught community college in Meridian, Mississippi, where he had a steady

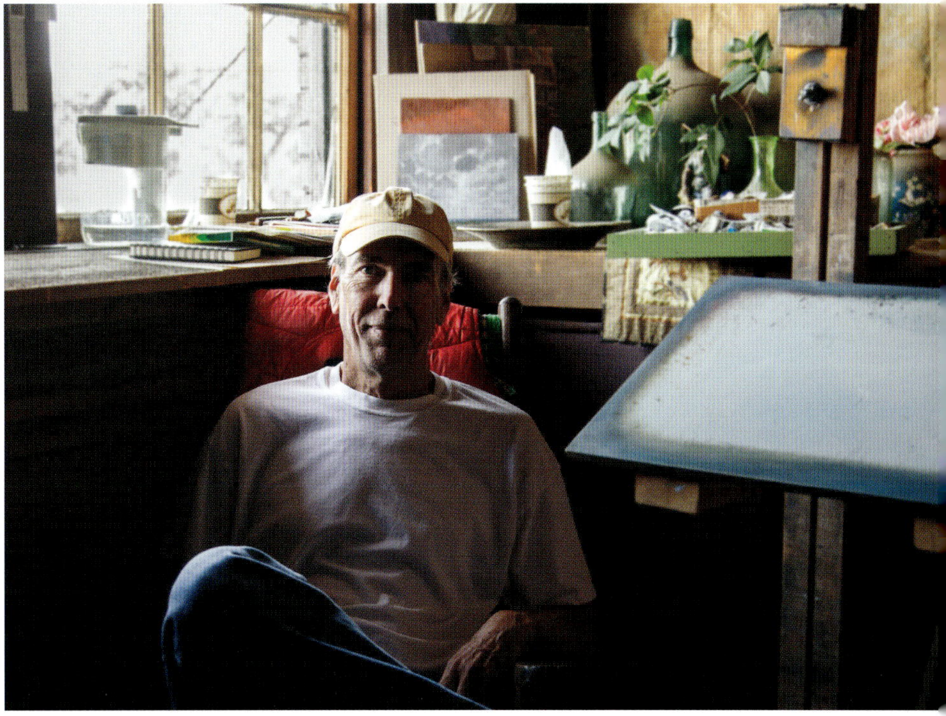

Richard Kelso is pictured here in his studio.

income but little time or inspiration to paint. He found himself wondering again and again how many paintings he would have to sell a month to make enough money to live on. Finally, he realized that he could never deal with growing old and wondering, "What could you have been if you had decided to be a painter?" The thought of striking out on his own as a painter excited him in a way that teaching never would.

"Something deep down in my gut told me I was doing the right thing," he remembers. "There are rarely such clear decisions. I've never had that feeling before or since. It was the most liberating and wonderful thought: I am going to be a painter."

Kelso left Meridian for Jackson, assuming that, in a bigger city, he would have a better chance of selling his work. However, he is the first to admit that after moving to Jackson he did very little to promote his work, instead focusing on perfecting his craft. He looks back on those early years and wonders how he sold enough work to keep going.

"I guess little by little people saw my work," he muses.

Friends in Atlanta helped Kelso connect with Lagerquist Gallery in Buckhead, where he sold his work for a time. Eventually, Kelso's fame as a painter grew. Today, Kelso shows his work primarily at Fischer Gallery in Jackson, Mississippi. He has had a solo show every December for the past sixteen years.

For Kelso, the key to financial success as an artist has been to keep things simple. He does not communicate by text message or e-mail, eschewing technology for the benefits of a lost era. By his own admission, his success may well be the result of his dedication to a simpler way of life. He enjoys running marathons, and he finds pleasure in the ascetic nature of his existence.

"The quickest way to drive yourself crazy is to think about something you don't have and want," he explains. "I'm like a kid. I appreciate what I've got. I've lived close to the ground for so long...a lot of it is in my DNA."

An avid runner, he cites his most important personal achievement as the time he finished the Chicago marathon in less than three and a half hours.

"That is the greatest thing I ever did," he declares. "I ran under that big Seiko clock, and it was the best feeling...I don't care what I do in the art world. That was my finest hour."

Kelso finds inspiration for his artwork in literature (he prefers to read American history and world literature) and music. One of his greatest memories is seeing the Beatles perform in Memphis, Tennessee, in 1966. His concert ticket was $5.50; the band performed two full sets. Kelso remembers seeing Ringo's drum kit on the stage, the iconic Beatles logo stenciled on the drum. The crowd waited breathlessly, and then

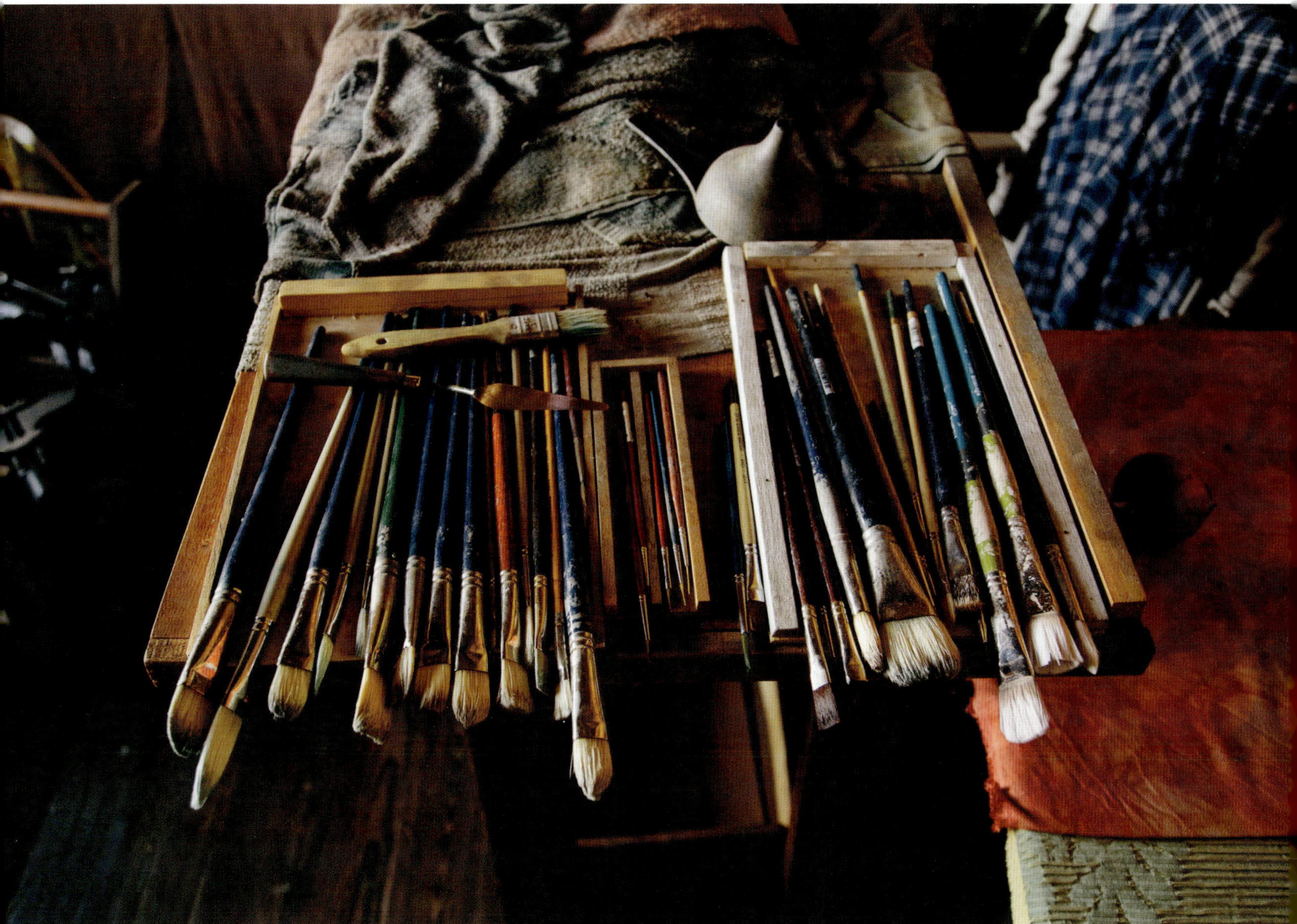

Oil paints are Richard's medium of choice.

the Beatles emerged in chartreuse-green suits and ties.

"All of the sudden without any warning they break into 'Rock and Roll Music,'" Kelso remembers. "I thought, 'I have arrived.' It was absolutely wonderful."

In the Studio

On a mild morning in March, Kelso's studio is finally shedding its winter chill, reaching a comfortable temperature before it is doused in summer heat. The studio is only accessible by an elevator original to the early twentieth-century construction of the Hal and Mal's building. The elevator is a point of consternation for everyone who frequents the second floor because, in order to operate properly, the elevator gates must be pulled back up after exiting. Failure to close the gates results in the elevator getting stuck on whichever floor where it last stopped, meaning that Kelso has been trapped upstairs and downstairs multiple times. For the most part, it seems that Kelso finds these experiences mildly amusing, although he has made a point to tape signs to the elevator alerting passengers to the importance of closing the gates.

Kelso makes a point to live a simple life that is utterly focused on his artwork, and his studio reflects his focus. His studio is composed of two simple rooms, which are neither heated nor cooled. The second-floor space was an open attic loft for years; there were no rooms or doors until 1989—for the first two years that Kelso occupied the building, he painted in an open attic space. The rooms that he has occupied since their construction retain the attic feeling. The walls are lined with his collection of objects for use in still-life paintings: dusty glass jars and bottles, dried flowers, figurines, busts and old books. The high, slanted ceiling beams are hung with empty frames, and an old rocking chair is situated next to his easel by the window. Some of Kelso's beautiful paintings adorn the walls, but the space is largely undecorated and geared toward functionality over comfort. It is clear that this is a studio of a focused, passionate artist.

Surveying his studio, Kelso remarks, "People will say something to me like 'You're so disciplined,' and I think, 'No, I am just doing what I love to do. It's a lot easier to just keep it going.'"

Kelso once read something that struck him as profound: the secret to success is believing that you can achieve something while simultaneously believing that what you had done so far is not good enough. This line of thinking struck a chord with him, as he admittedly possesses a decidedly self-deprecating sense of humor that many people may mistake, upon first meeting him, as self-doubt.

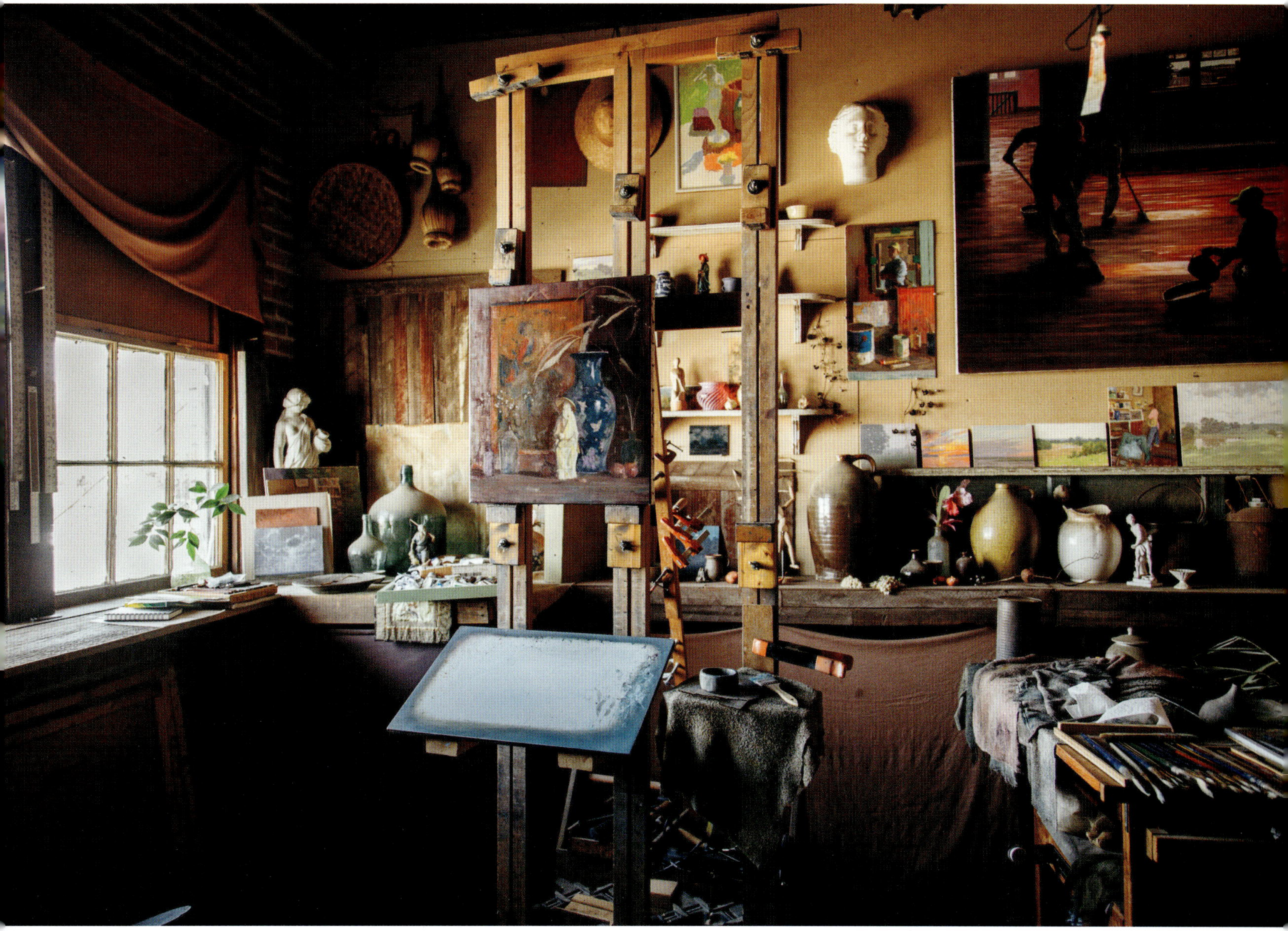

Richard's studio is located in the Hal and Mal's building in downtown Jackson.

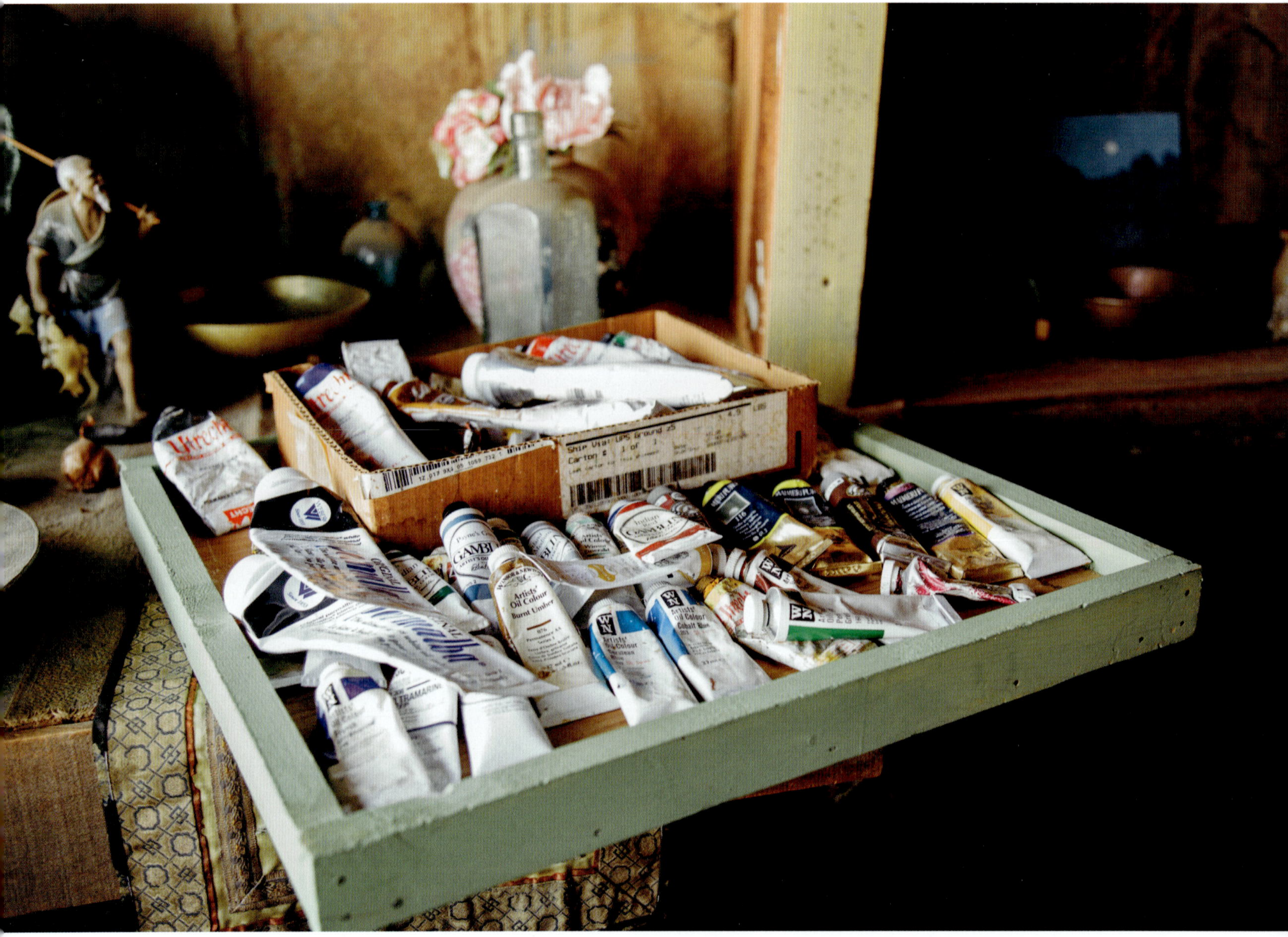

In addition to paints, Richard's studio is filled with objects he arranges for still-life paintings.

"If I had to describe myself in one word, I would say 'inept,'" he chuckles.

Richard Kelso is not concerned about popularity or that anyone agree with his line of thinking because his primary focus was and will always be creating the best possible artwork that he can create, which is precisely what makes him such a skilled artist. Here is a painter who lives and breathes his art. Instead of letting self-doubt keep him from discovering who he could be as a painter, he uses self-doubt as a tool to better his work. Kelso has kept going for so many years, not in spite of a cold or hot studio, or a broken elevator, or a paycheck he desperately needs, but *because* of those things. The same resolve and willpower required to finish a marathon allow Kelso to keep improving his paintings because he embraces the fact that a successful artist is one who knows the power of not only dedication but also determination.

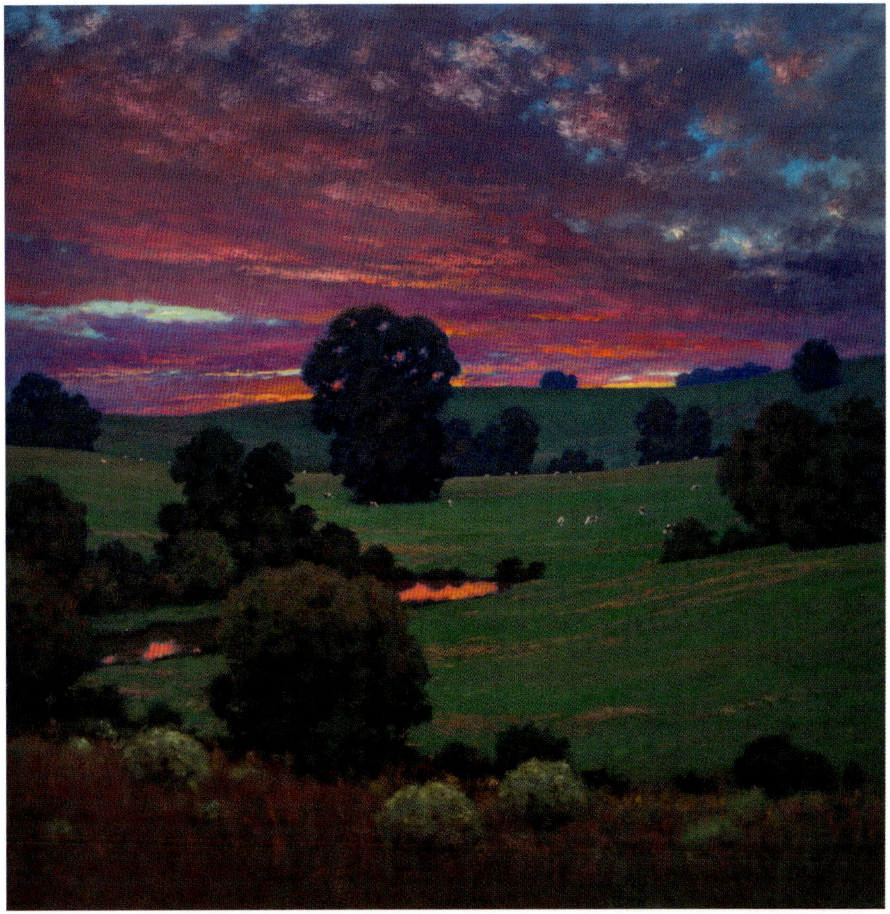

Late Summer, Sunrise by Richard Kelso.

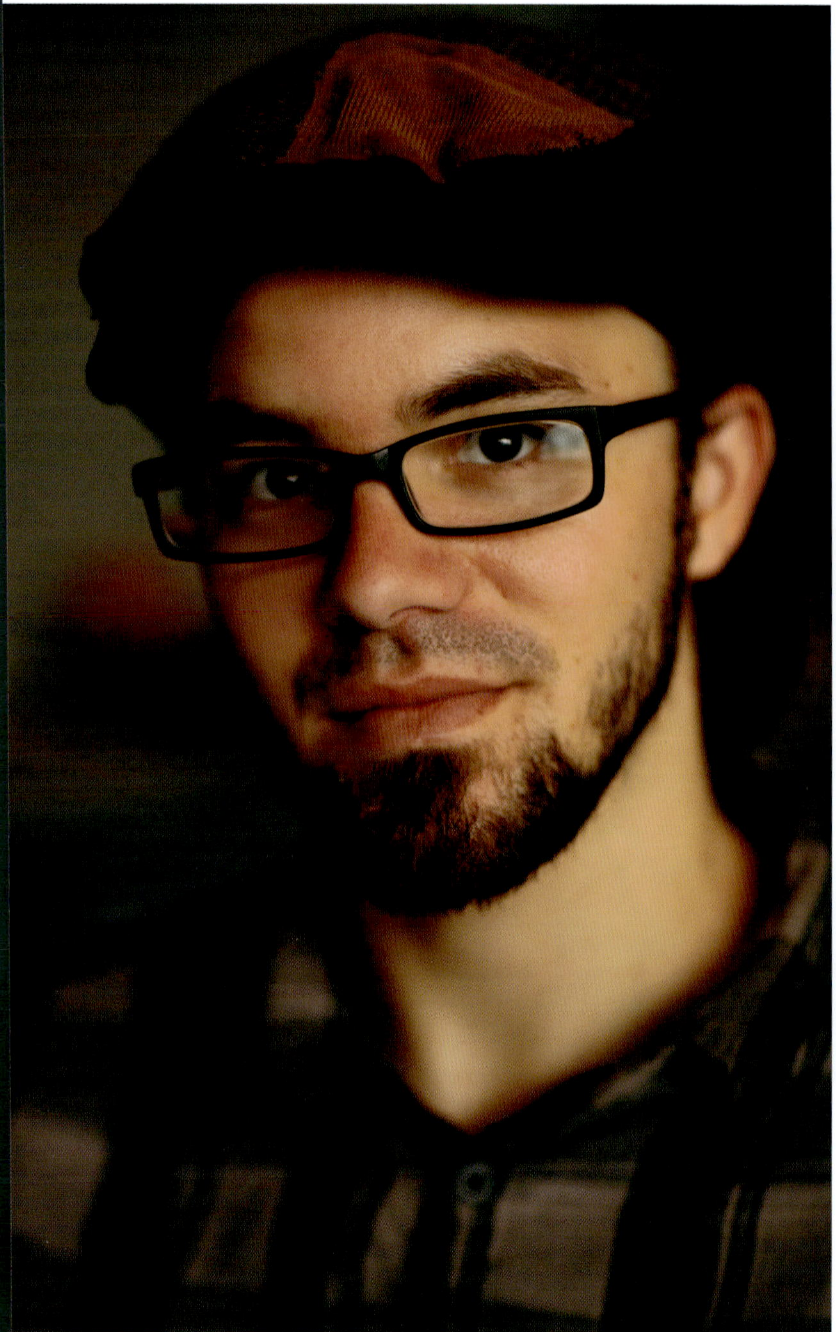

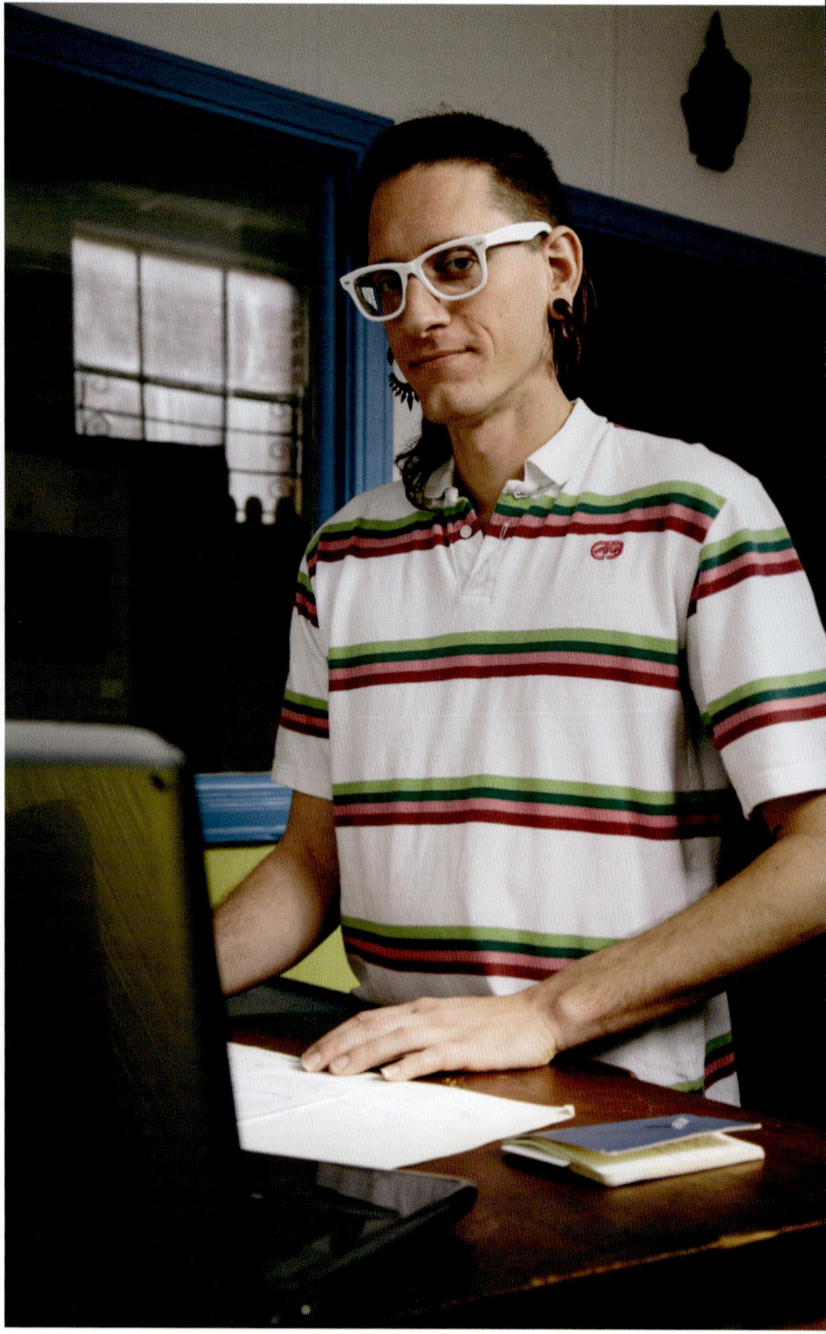

7
TURNUP STUDIO

CLAY HARDWICK, DANIEL JOHNSON AND JAMIE WEEMS

TurnUp is a studio space shared by Clay Hardwick, a videographer and painter; Daniel Johnson, founder of Significant Developments, LLC; and Jamie Weems, a musician. The group of friends and creators always knew that they wanted to base their work out of Jackson's Midtown community, and when craftsman Andy Young told them about a vacant space in Midtown, the three men worked to transform it into the creative workspace it is today. Founded in

Opposite, left: Clay Hardwick is a co-founder of TurnUp Studio in Midtown.

Opposite, right: Daniel Johnson is a co-founder of TurnUp Studio in Midtown and owner of Significant Developments, LLC.

Right: Jamie Weems is a co-founder of TurnUp Studio in Midtown.

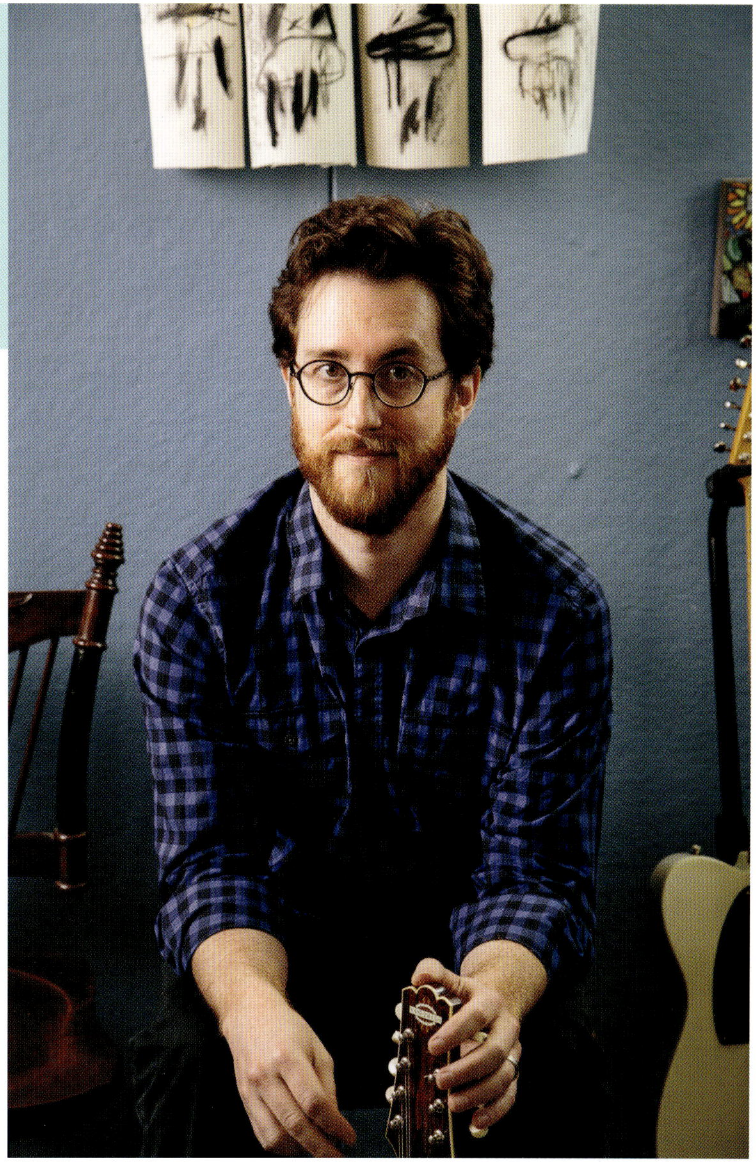

2013, TurnUp Studio's creators are representative of a growing group of entrepreneurs in Jackson who are recolonizing the Midtown neighborhood, aided in part by the efforts of Young, who led the movement of creative businesses moving to Midtown in the 1980s.

Turning It Up in Midtown

Together, Hardwick, Johnson and Weems form an element of the emerging social visage of the Midtown neighborhood: the cooperative studio space. While they each pursue their own creative endeavors, Johnson notes, "This studio allows us to spin off our individual identities."

Hardwick, who attended Millsaps College in Jackson, began his art career as a visual artist. He says that to survive economically he has to spend about 80 percent of his time focused on video production, but he finds the Jackson art world to be accepting and "broad." At one point early in his career, Harwick moved to Portland in an attempt to expand his work. In Portland, he found that building a new base was difficult in a large city: he found that he only met "about two people" and could not establish the connections he craved. He moved back to Jackson, where he has found a like-minded community of artists who support one another. Now, he views Jackson as a solid hub and home base. He lives in the back of the TurnUp studio space and is delighted by the buzz of activity in Midtown.

"On the surface, it seems kind of dead down here, but living down here, I've learned there's a lot going on inside," he explains.

Hardwick sees Midtown as the preeminent emerging arts district; he wants TurnUp Studio to grow into a community space that offers events for the public. Hardwick is also interested in job creation and is currently pushing the "TurnUp Sessions" at the studio, where Mississippi musicians looking for exposure can record short videos, which Hardwick edits and promotes on the TurnUp Studio website. Hardwick relishes the fact that Jackson artists have an open canvas, noting, "Other people have already made up their minds about what art is. Jackson hasn't."

"In Jackson, there is so much awesome stuff that's untapped that no one knows about. I want to go through and find these beautiful things and then share that with the outside world," Hardwick says.

Johnson is also particularly attuned to changes taking place in Midtown. Like Hardwick, he attended Millsaps College on the edge of the Midtown neighborhood. Johnson experienced the creative economy firsthand working for craftsman Bebe Wolfe at Wolfe Studios, and now his business employs artists and craftsmen, furthering the pattern of job creation.

Johnson has personally acted as an agent of that change: in 2011, he spearheaded an art project called "Debris Organization" in which he and other artists gathered and organized trash found on the streets of Midtown, displaying their collection in an abandoned Midtown building.

"I see Midtown developing more mixed-use buildings with living spaces integrated," Johnson says. "We are part of the cultural conversation in the Jackson community."

Weems, who has found it difficult to live off his earnings as a musician, sees Midtown cooperative studios like TurnUp as a new hope. Weems, who has supplemented his music income doing IT work, is in the process of searching for new ways to pursue his music as a full-time career and is excited to curate TurnUp Studio as an event space.

For Hardwick, Johnson and Weems, sharing a workspace allows for collaboration and creative freedom. Weems believes that "lots of interweaving of thoughts" is key to any artistic success, and Johnson proclaims that collaboration is essential to every part of his business. Johnson's business, Significant Developments, LLC, is a "strategic advancement agency specializing in the use of relational art experiences." For Johnson, it is all about connecting people through art, and like Hardwick, he has found that Jackson is the perfect home base. Johnson has worked with local businesses such as the Rainbow Co-op, the Museum of Natural Science, the Jackson Chamber of Commerce and the Mississippi Museum of Art (MMA) to create "socially engaged artwork."

"In Jackson, I am able to get access that could not happen elsewhere," Johnson explains, adding that a mid-sized city allows him to integrate his work with a cross-section of people who are thinking the same way he does and are aware of the work that he is doing. Combined with the 2014 push for a creative economy in Mississippi, Johnson has watched his business grow.

Hardwick agrees, with one caveat: "We have a creative culture here and a progressive city," he says. "[But] we may never have a creative economy because we [as a state] are poor. We have that creative culture though."

Weems points out that a lot of his contemporaries grew up in Mississippi and left as adults, but in recent years, he has witnessed many of them, like Hardwick, return, bringing pieces of other places and new ideas home.

Johnson adds, "Ten years ago, anyone who wanted to be an artist and musician wanted to get out [of Jackson] as quickly as they could, whereas now we are already seeing the slowdown of the diaspora."

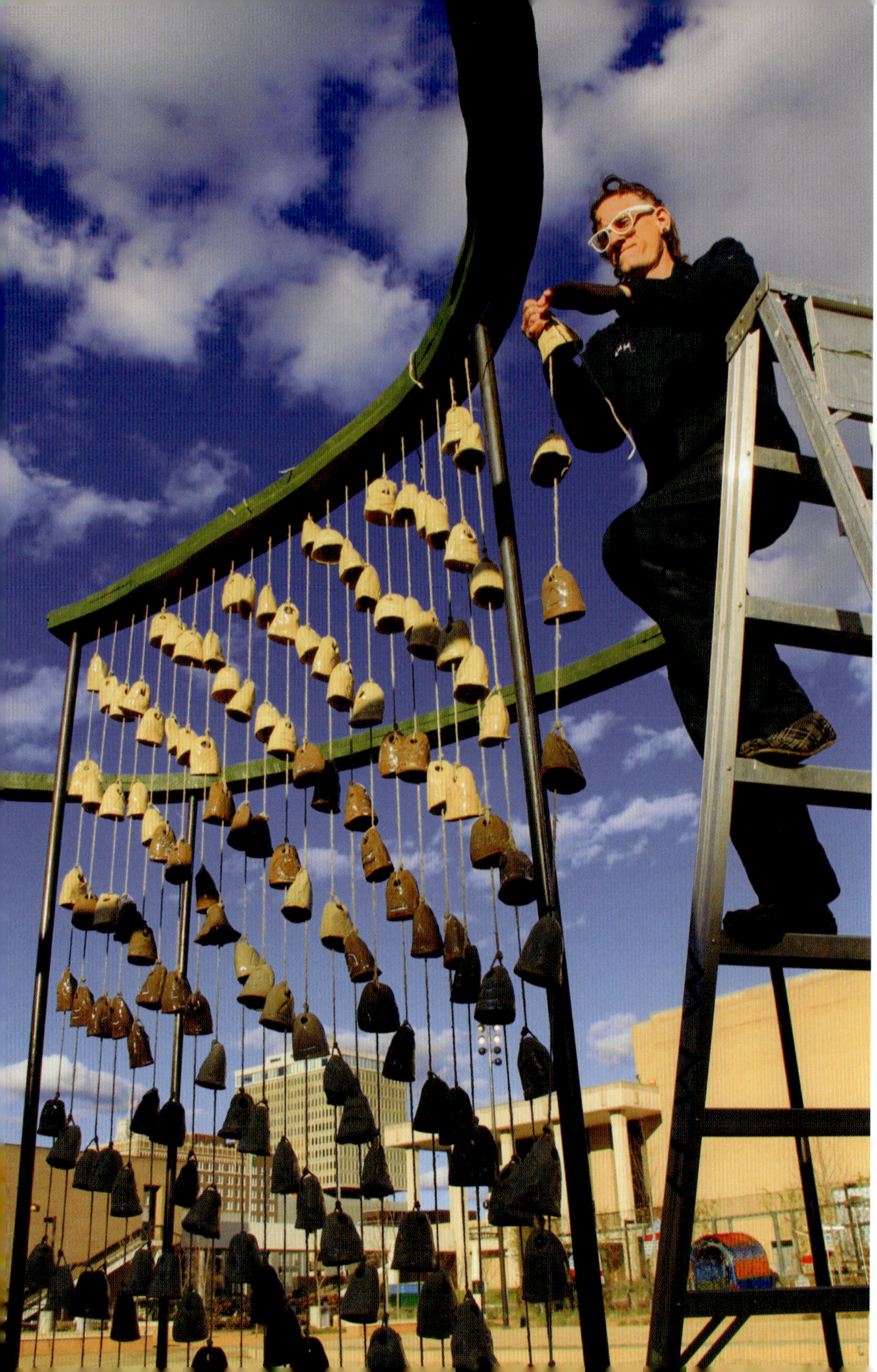

Significant Developments in Action

TurnUp Studio witnessed a convergence of its ideals in late March 2014 in the garden at the Mississippi Museum of Art in Jackson. A crowd gathered to view the unveiling of a public art installation, "Core Sample," created by Significant Developments, LLC.

The installation, commissioned by the Mississippi Museum of Art, was essentially a giant wind chime constructed from 2,222 handmade clay bells. The bells hung on ropes arranged in rows on a spiral-shaped metal frame, and occasionally a member of the Significant Developments, LLC team would grab the outer pole of the frame and give the whole installation a tug, eliciting a resounding ripple of chimes from all 2,222 bells.

Inside the spiral, Johnson and his team stood together in navy-blue jumpsuits, their names embroidered on the front like the uniforms of a delivery crew. Two of his team members were his sons, Vesper and Wiley; another was his wife, Amber. Other team members whom Johnson hired to help with the task were present, along with

Hardwick, who moved throughout the bells with his video camera, recording the scene. Weems was in the audience, along with many other Jackson artists, including William Goodman, Roy Adkins, Jerri Shearer and Bebe Wolfe. The gathering was indicative of the community that Jackson creatives share, supporting one another and celebrating individual achievements as a collective success.

As Johnson spoke into a microphone from within the spiral, he shared that he and his team handmade each bell, inscribing a symbol on both sides. The symbols were submitted to the MMA specifically for use in this project: Mississippians were asked to draw a symbol that was meaningful to them; each symbol is now part of a whole. According to Johnson, "Core Sample" is "meant to resemble a core sample rising from the ground" and shows a sample of what is meaningful to Mississippians today.

What many in the crowd may not have realized is that core sampling is a geological phrase that refers to taking a deep sample of a natural substance to study. The beauty of Johnson's work with the "Core Sample" installation and many of his other public art displays is that beneath the exquisite craftsmanship lie multiple layers of meaning that linger with viewers and leave them wondering about the deeper meaning of the project.

Daniel shared that "Core Sample" took weeks to construct and would only be on display for a month, during which time museum guests were urged to come and admire the bells and notice the different symbols that make up the state of Mississippi. Hearts, stars and Celtic symbols appeared on many bells, as well as the triangle, which Johnson informed the crowd stood for the mathematical symbol for change. He encouraged viewers to consider meditating on that subject.

Opposite: Here, Daniel Johnson is at work on the art installation "Core Sample." *Courtesy of Julian Rankin.*

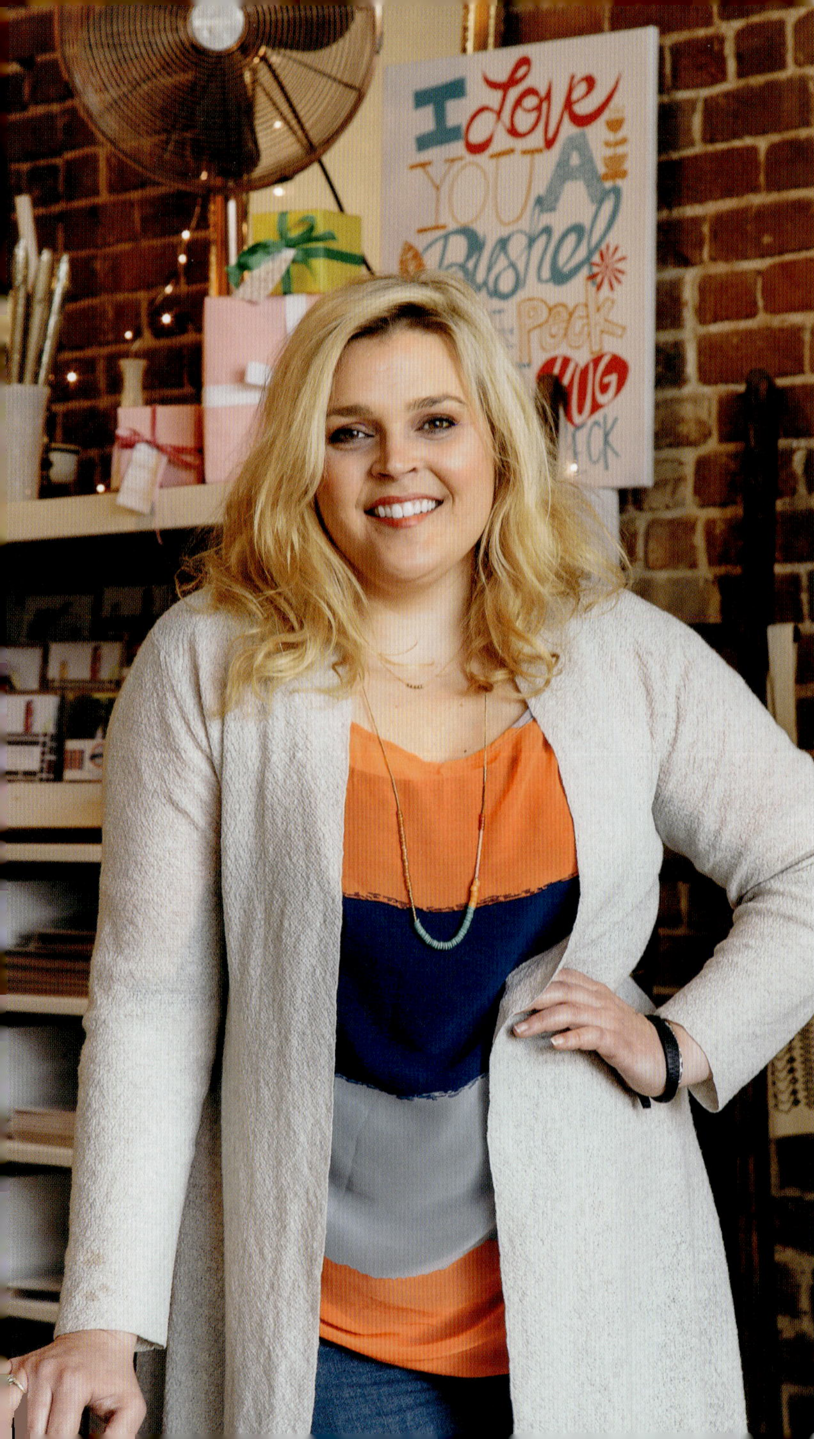

8
THIMBLEPRESS

KRISTEN LEY

Kristen Ley is a painter and designer best known for her multihued letterpress greeting cards, which she markets under the brand name Thimblepress. Her work has been featured in dozens of popular magazines, and she has created custom products for a range of national clients. She has a thriving wholesale business and attends art shows and fairs throughout the year, but she is most at home when she is at her charming store on North State Street, located in the heart of downtown Jackson.

"Jackson is a great place to be because it is a big enough city and yet also small enough to make an impact," Kristen explains. "The city of Jackson is so supportive of any new creative developments. I have a heart for Jackson."

Kristen Ley has a heart for downtown Jackson.

Background

Originally from Houston, Texas, Kristen's family moved to Jackson when she was thirteen. She graduated from Jackson Academy in 2003 and majored in art at Mississippi State University.

"I wanted to be a graphic designer before I even knew what that was," she recalls of her childhood aspirations.

Kristen grew up with a family who encouraged her love of the arts, helping her develop her seamstress skills and ever-growing thimble collection. When she acquired her first letterpress machine, she kept it in her mother's garage. Kristen worked on her letterpress designs after college while teaching full time at her old high school. In 2012, she began to hunt for a space to move her letterpress machine and focus on her art as a career.

"A garage is hard because you're not really working with stable temperatures," Kristen jokes. "But a lot of businesses start in a garage."

Kristen had noticed the storefronts on North State Street in downtown Jackson across from the Old Capitol Building, and she made inquiries into leasing the spaces with no luck. In February 2013, Kristen received a phone call from Lesley Frascogna, owner of Tulip Floral. Lesley had learned that Kristen was looking for a space to rent downtown and offered Kristen part of her downtown studio. Coincidentally, the space Lesley was renting was one of the storefronts that Kristen had already researched. Taking that as a "sign from God," Kristen met with Lesley and discovered that although the studio was too small to share, the location next door was available. The space was in terrible shape, but Kristen was not daunted.

"I've always been one to look past and see the potential in something," she says. "I saw the place and I prayed. God just started opening doors for me. God is my rock in everything—everything I take to prayer, and he has blessed my business from the start."

Business Developments

Recognizing the appearance of a one-time opportunity, Kristen took a leap of faith and decided to turn Thimblepress into a full-time business. She moved her personal possessions into a smaller house with three roommates so that she could afford to rent the downtown shop. She retired from her teaching position at Jackson Academy and began the process of renovating her space, prepping for the National Stationery Show in New York City and learning how to run her own business.

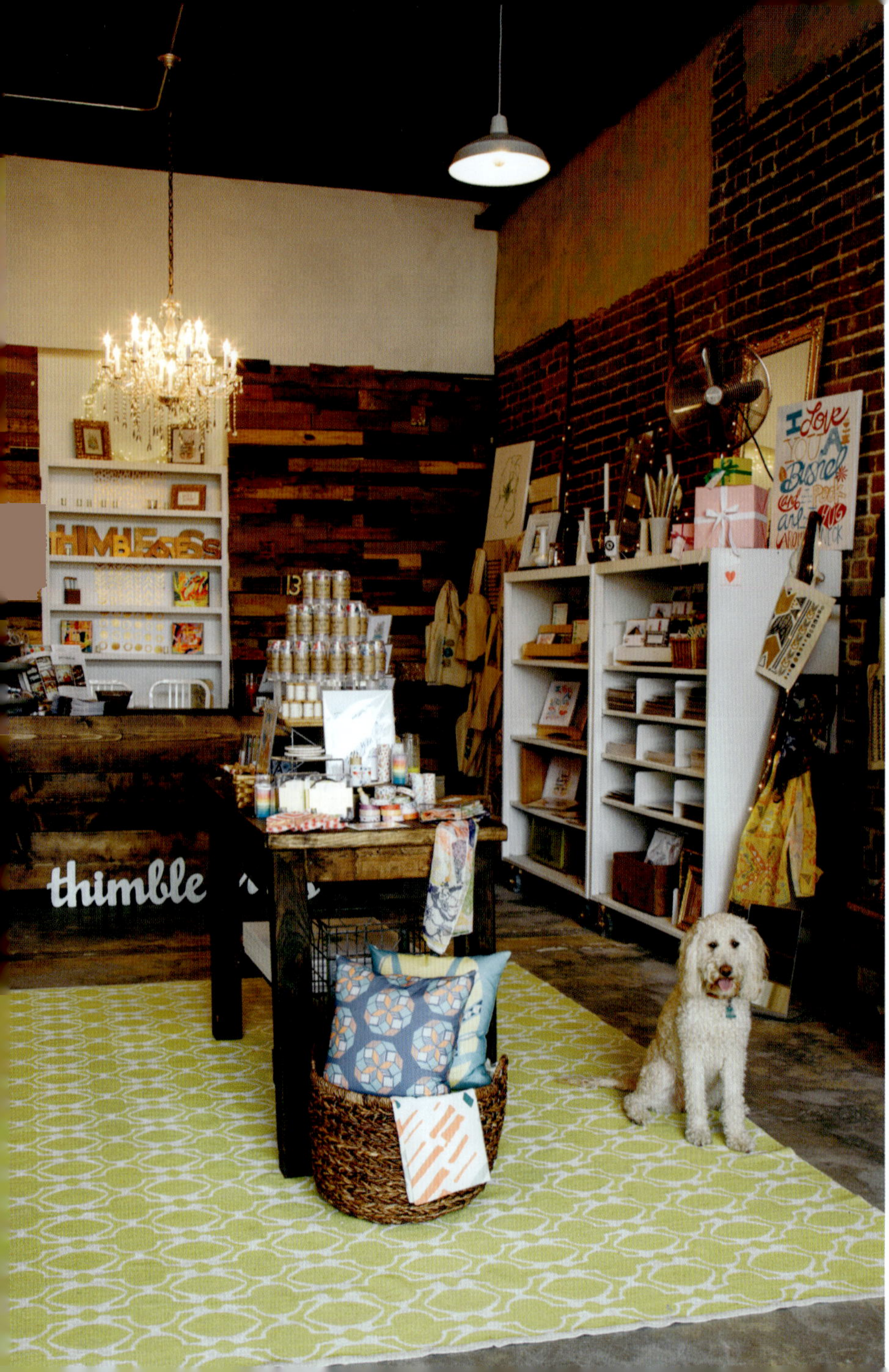
thimble

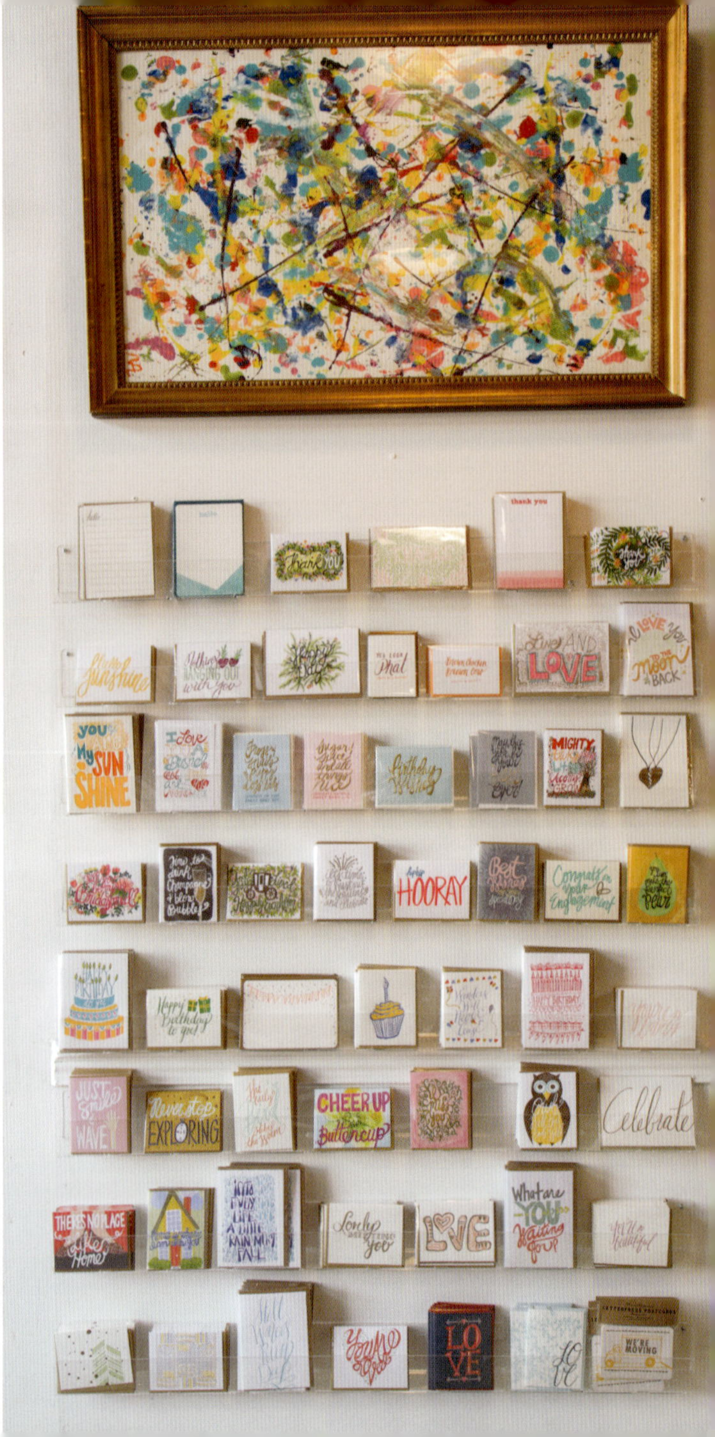
HOORAY
CHEER UP
Buttercup
EXPLORING
Celebrate
LOVE

"It was an absolutely crazy time," she says, looking back at the formation. Over the course of a single summer, Kristen completed a transformation on her shop, doing most of the renovation work by herself. Although she hired her friend Neil Polan to sand down the concrete floors of what would become the shop front, she personally painted the walls and organized her office, her stockroom and the production room that houses her letterpress machine. It was not until after her success at the National Stationery Show that Kristen was able to afford to hire an employee. Dani Griffin, who had volunteered with Neil to help Kristen early on, joined Kristen's team. Currently, Dani is director of operations and handles all wholesale orders, which make up the bulk of Thimblepress's business. Since hiring Dani, Kristen has been able to add multiple employees to her payroll, including a paid intern.

"I don't believe in unpaid internships," she states simply.

Kristen remains in control of the creative end of her business, which centers on reproductions of her original designs via letterpress. Only Kristen runs the letterpress machine, and although she accepts custom orders and commissions, she is adamant about only printing her own designs. All of her letterpress designs begin as black-and-white drawings. She keeps all of her originals in a vintage X-ray case that she inherited from her father, a physician.

"All of my artwork is created by hand," she explains.

Watching Kristen work is mesmerizing. Donning rubber gloves, she cranks up the letterpress machine, which she has prepared with inks that she mixes herself. She is nonchalant operating the mass of wheels and belts of the device that resembles something from the seventeenth century. As she deftly slips cards in and out of the rapidly churning press, she explains over the noise of the machine that inspiration is the key to artistic growth.

"I keep a running list of my inspirations, and I am always expanding my frame of reference," she says.

Kristen cites vintage book illustrators and the Disney illustrator Mary Blair among her favorite artists, but her influences are truly diverse; Kristen's "Small World" collection is inspired by her love of the song and ride at Disneyworld, and her series of state flowers is inspired by a quote by Ladybird Johnson. Kristen loves Shel Silverstein's books, Gray Malin's photography, Kandinsky's use of color and the graphic designs of Saul Bass. She

Opposite, left: Kristen's dog, Willow, plays inside the Thimblepress shop on North State Street in downtown Jackson.

Opposite, right: A display of Thimblepress cards, packaged and ready to sell, is available in her shop.

admires the artwork of fellow Jackson artists Ellen Langford, William Goodman and Ginger Williams-Cook, as well as the watercolor paintings of Wyatt Waters of Clinton, Mississippi.

In addition to running the letterpress machine and creating original artwork, Kristen designs and runs her own website, where customers can place wholesale and custom orders. A company in Atlanta represents her work, and she continues to attend craft festivals and wholesale shows. She is an active social media presence, where enthusiastic fans keep up with her work. She has been featured in magazines, on craft blogs and on other websites, but she remains grounded in Jackson, which she declares will remain the home base of her business.

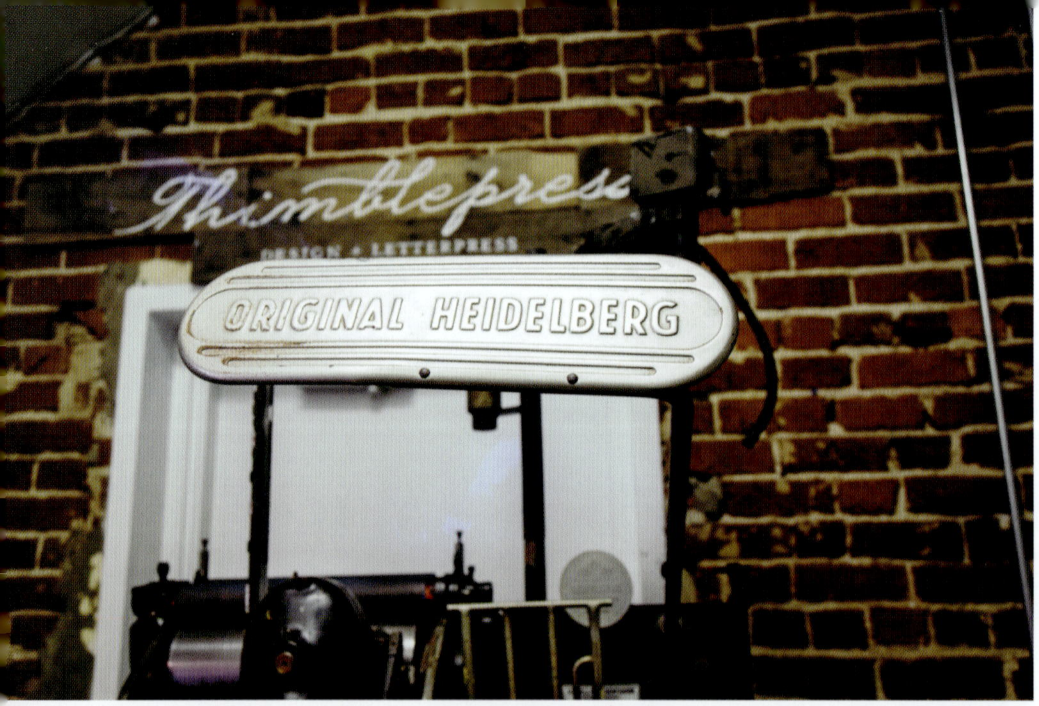

Top: Kristen works on the letterpress machine.

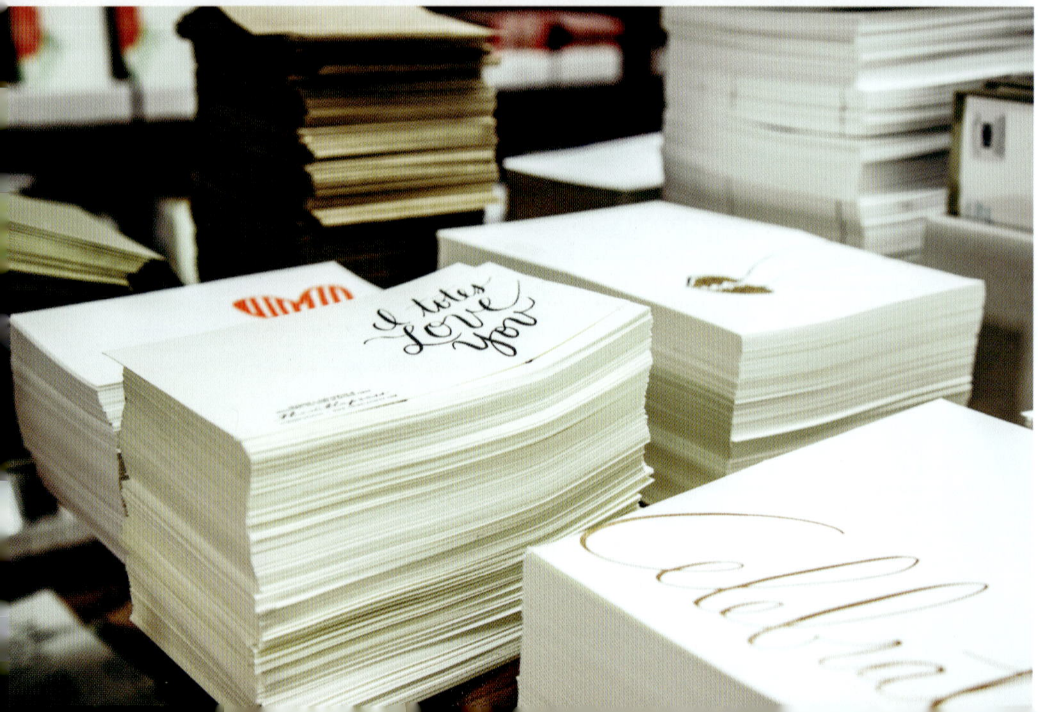

Left: Stacks of letterpress cards are hot off the press.

"When I was working at Jackson Academy, I participated in a program called Leadership Jackson," Kristen explains. "I have a heart for this city, which is constantly evolving and changing. It's all about attitude. We have to be able to have good things to say about Jackson."

Kristen thinks it is important to have cheerful storefronts in downtown Jackson.

"If you lose your downtown, you lose your identity. I do not want to see that happen to this city," she says.

The Thimblepress storefront is filled with Kristen's merry designs and inhabited by her dog, a golden doodle named Willow who is something of a mascot for her business. Kristen sells her original letterpress cards and designs out of her shop, which a vast array of merchandise, such as greeting cards, T-shirts, tote bags, stationery, banners, coasters and prints of her artwork.

Kristen sees the state of Mississippi as one big community of storytellers,

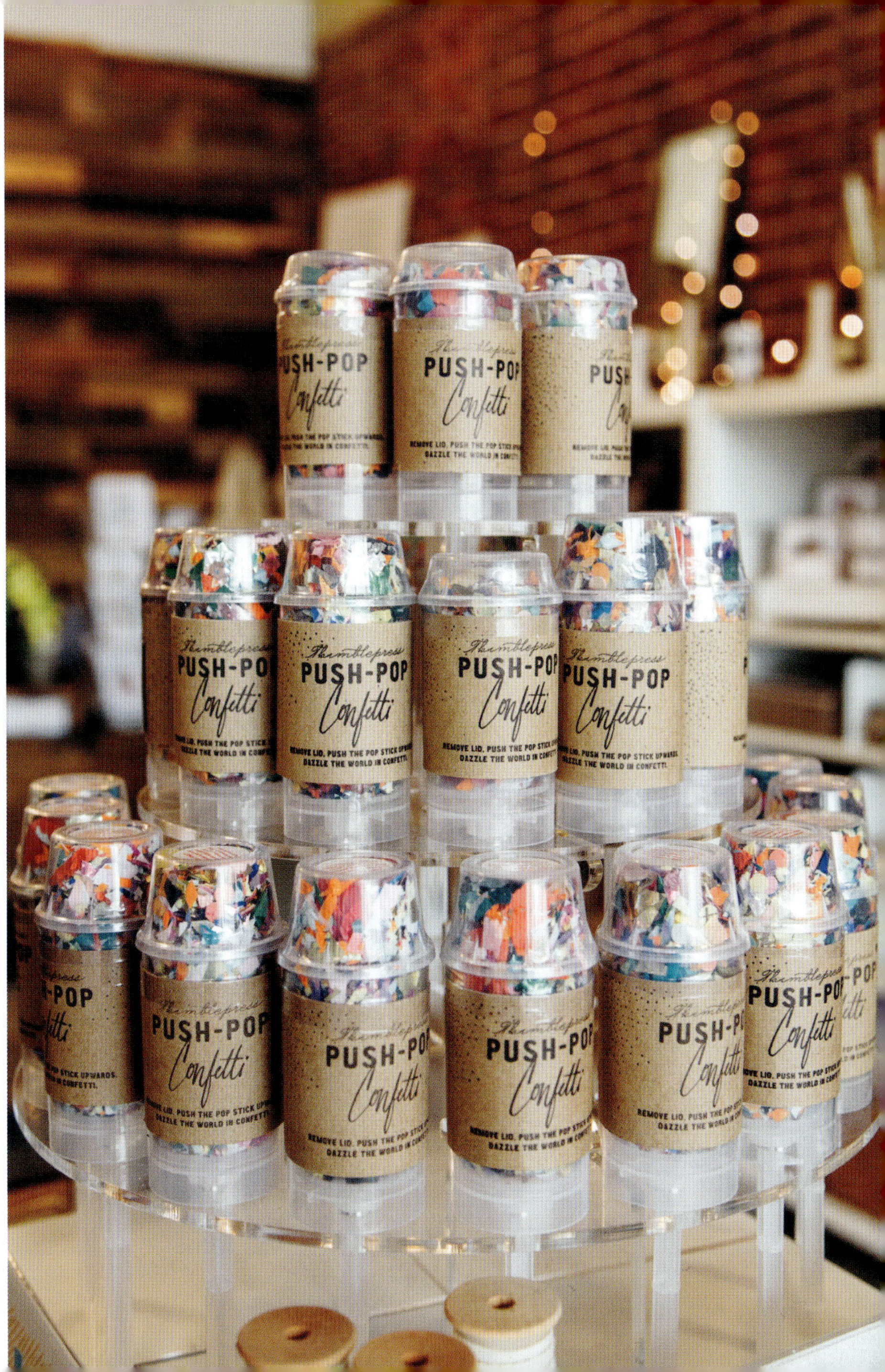

Kristen assembles her customizable confetti push-pops by hand. She has a patent pending on the product, which is popular at weddings and parties.

and she considers herself a part of the evolving and changing story. She acknowledges that the city of Jackson has many problems but remains encouraged by the growth she is witnessing, especially downtown.

"You can see development downtown," she enthuses. "It's not happening overnight, but in ten years, we are going to look up and say, 'Wow, this happened so quickly!'"

9

DAVAINE LIGHTING

STEPHEN BARNETTE

Stephen Barnette is the first to admit that he is an unusual type of artist.

"I'm not a visual artist in the traditional sense," he explains. "I see surfaces. I paint with light."

A Jackson native, Stephen studied performing arts at the University of Southern Mississippi, where he focused on theatrical production, lighting and special effects. He worked for the local newspaper, the *Jackson Free Press*, for five years before leaving to pursue his interest in lighting full time. His business, Davaine Lighting, provides lighting for special events, including weddings, galas and fundraisers—what he calls "theatrical design in the nontheatrical setting." His

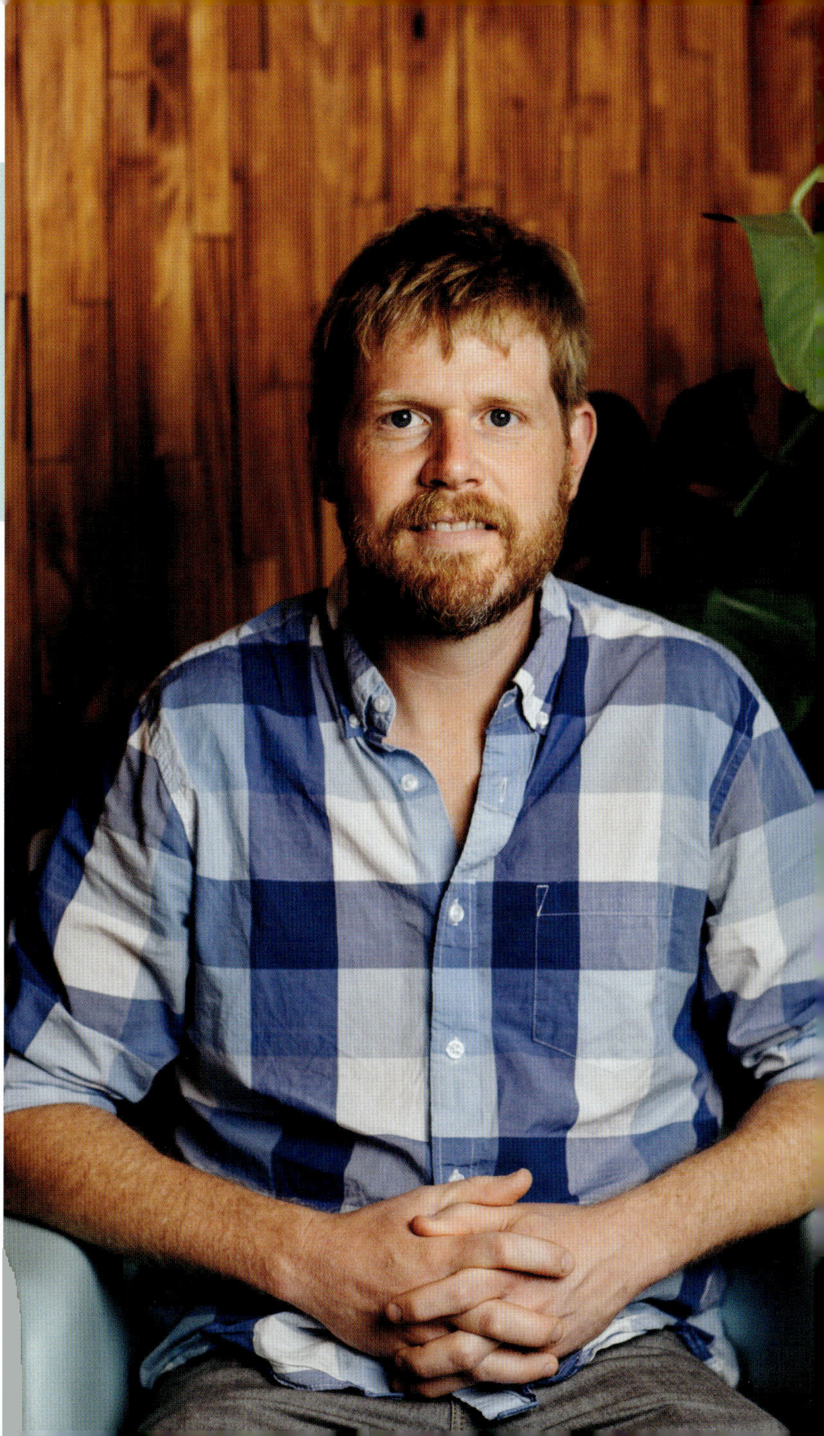

Stephen Barnette owns Davaine Lighting in Midtown.

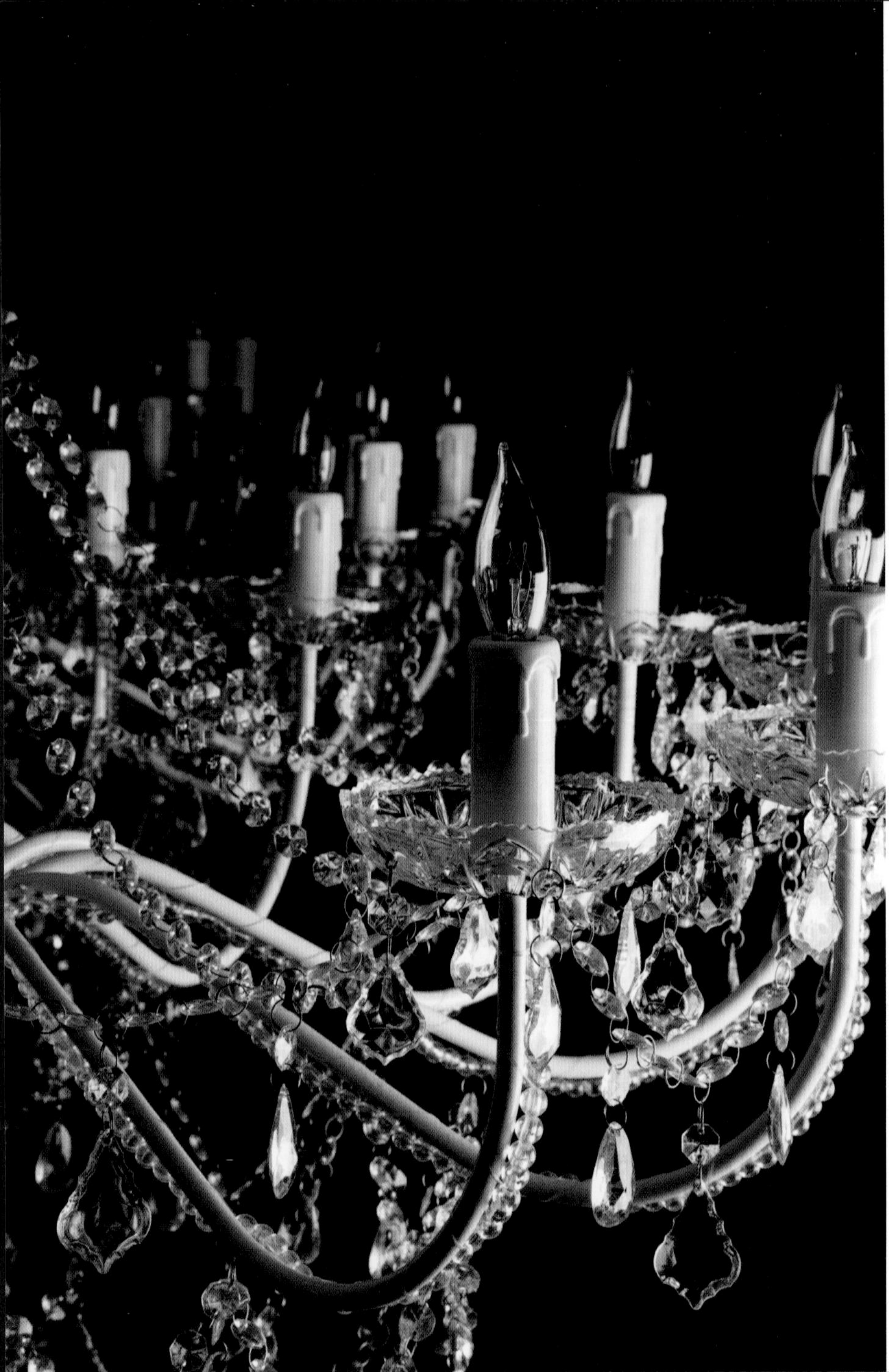

passion, however, is creating "interactive light sculptures" by lighting up buildings at night and effectively transforming them into pieces of art.

"The color spectrum is a different palette," he relates. "The visual art is live—it's in the room, or tent space, and that becomes the canvas."

Stephen is invested in the science behind lighting, including the power distribution, cabling and technical details.

"I pride myself on 'hiding the junk,'" he jokes. "When approaching a job, I ask myself, 'How do we create the look without giving it all away?' I want to be as unobtrusive as possible."

Stephen loves to collaborate with florists and sculptors to add a new dimension to their designs. He was instrumental in lighting up Fletcher Cox's "noodle" at the Mississippi Museum of Art, a sculpture that Fletcher created to frame the stage in the Art Garden.

"The moment the lights turn on is the masterpiece," Stephen declares. For him, that is when the light becomes art.

Some of Stephen's commercial clients include local restaurants, such as the historic Iron Horse Grill.

Choosing Jackson

For Stephen, moving out of Jackson is not an option. In a bigger city, he says, you can be a participant; in Jackson, you can be a leader. Stephen's desire to lead drew him to the Midtown community. Like many artists who have chosen to base their studios and business out of Midtown, Stephen is invested in the neighborhood. He lives downtown but says he has always viewed Midtown as a "connector" for Jackson. He was fascinated by the cyclical nature of the neighborhood, which began as a working-class one, then fell into poverty and now is once again becoming a stomping ground for the working class, particularly creative businesses. When he found an affordable warehouse for sale in Midtown, he moved his business out of the basement space he was renting downtown and set up shop in what he calls a "hub of like-minded creative professionals." When he purchased the building, he says, it was "trashed, but manageable."

Stephen divides his studio into two spaces. He has a reception area and a front office, where he can meet with clients, and a large warehouse in the back of the building with a separate entrance for trucks and cargo. Aside from ample space, Midtown offers Stephen a place to be creative and run a business without the need of a separate studio. In his opinion, buying a building in Midtown was a decision that broadcasts a message to greater Jackson: artists are prepared to invest in Midtown.

"The past of Midtown is becoming the future of Midtown," he muses. "A few creatives can be a catalyst for change"

As a "postindustrial area," Midtown "won't appeal to real estate developers because Jackson is already so sparse," Stephen theorizes. Success, he postulates, can begin in Midtown and bloom out into the rest of Jackson.

Stephen has witnessed positive changes in Midtown as creatives flock to the area, and although he believes that Midtown has a long way to go, he finds the phrase "Save Midtown" very derogatory.

"It will be a sad day when someone comes in and tries to force change to 'save' Midtown," he declares. "It's not the Wild West here."

He wants to see Midtown increase in density, with families moving into functional, urban-style housing in favor of some of the derelict homes that line the streets of Midtown today. He would like to see artists given exhibit spaces, where they can live in small apartments behind galleries facing the streets. Stephen is very aware, however, of the paradoxes brought about as a neighborhood gentrifies.

"Jackson has flown under the radar from a commercial perspective," he observes. "Whole Foods has made other businesses better, and competition is great, but national brands tend not to come here until later, and by that time, local businesses are already well established. It's like corporate brands that usually move in have forgotten Jackson exists. Where are you, American Apparel? Chipotle?"

In the same vein, Stephen appreciates the nod to the creative economy but notes that while something about Mississippi drives the creative spirit, broadcasting that spirit to the world can be a dangerous thing when laws still exist that "discriminate against the creative class" and make it harder for creative businesses and artists to survive.

"We [members the creative economy] are creating jobs and tax dollars. We aren't Microsoft, but the taxpayers were not asked for money to create the jobs that we create. You give people power and freedom to be creative and use their craft, and they will create jobs," Stephen says.

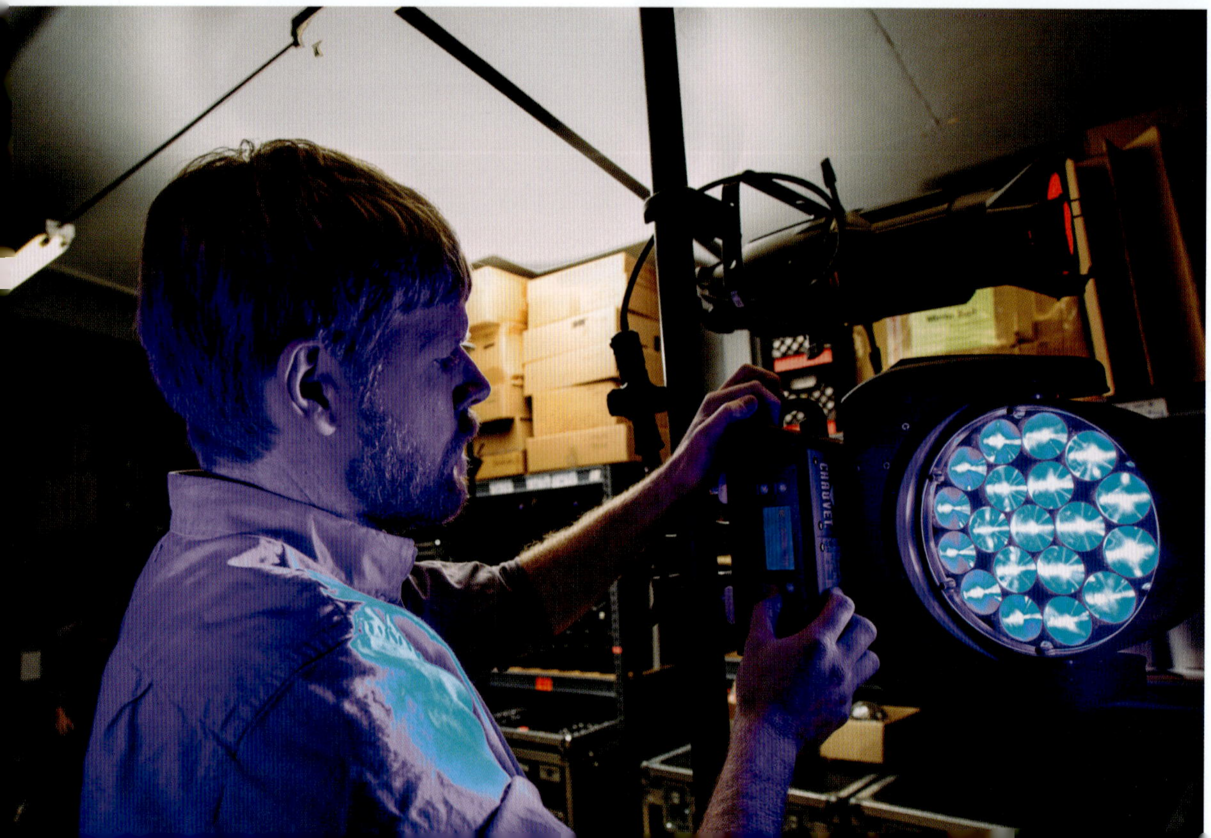

Stephen divides his time between creative personal projects using light as art and commercial lighting projects. His Midtown studio is also the location of his business, Davaine Lighting.

10

ROZ ROY

Roz Roy's studio is located in an older home on North State Street in the heart of the Fondren neighborhood, where rezoning has allowed artists to colonize the area in homes converted to studios. When Roz is open for business, she puts a big sign in the front yard welcoming customers, whom she greets with a hug when they stop by to view her artwork or take an art lesson. Inside her studio, Roz has transformed the first floor of the space into a gallery showcasing her work, which spans many different mediums, including clay sculptures, paintings on paper and canvas, clothes that she has made and prints of digital creations that she has designed on her computer.

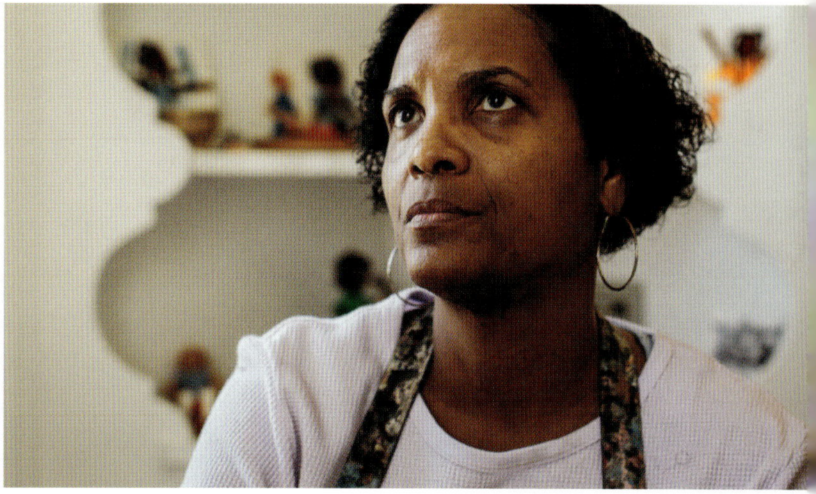

Roz Roy, a Jackson native, creates art that celebrates the history of African Americans in the South.

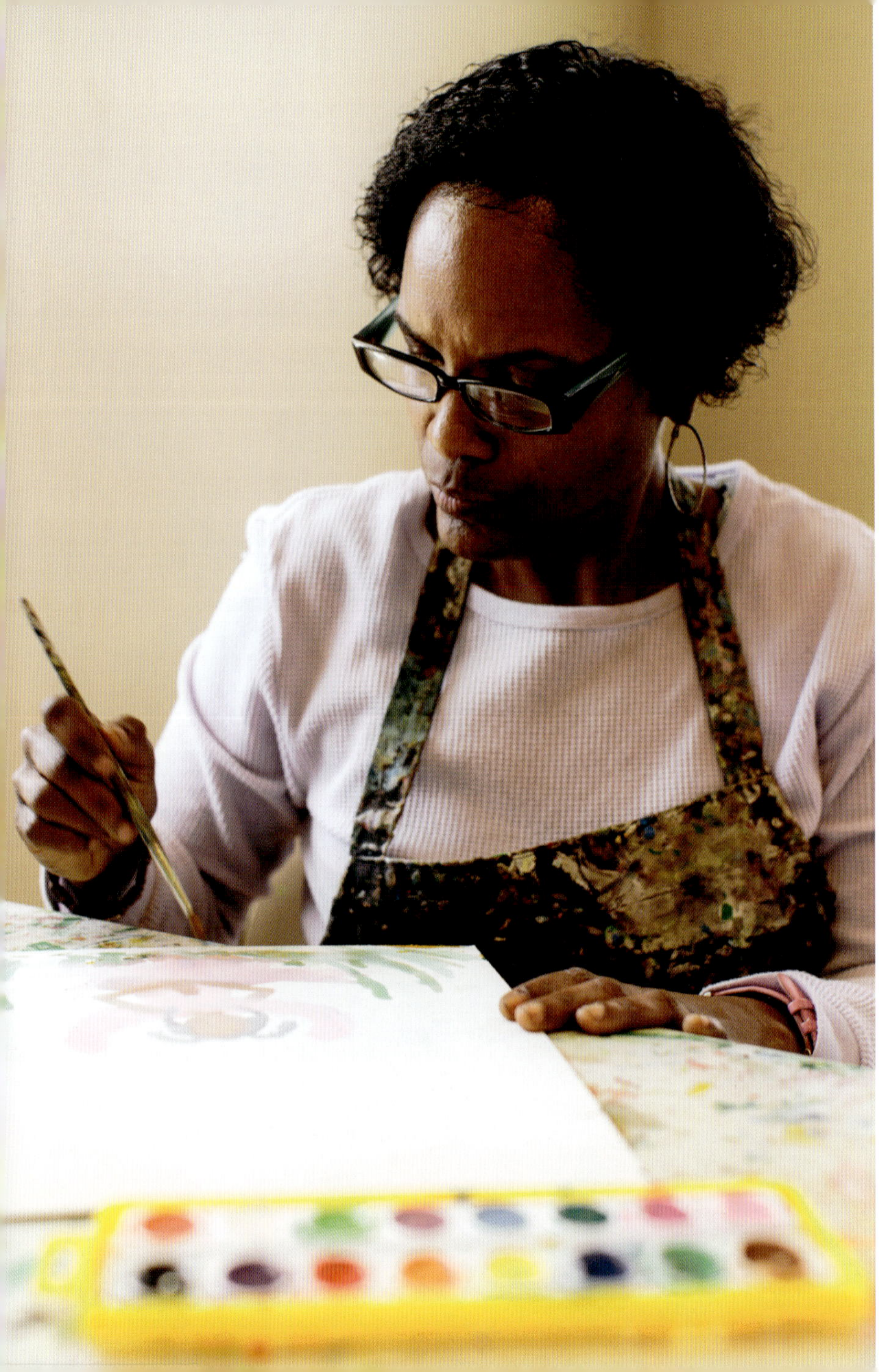

Upstairs is her workspace, filled with her paints, brushes and other supplies. Roz spends her days painting and teaching art lessons with her little dog Sam by her side.

Folk Art in Fondren

The location of Roz's studio is, by her account, a small miracle. Growing up in Jackson, Roz knew Fondren and the adjoining community of Woodland Hills as a place where white people lived. She remembers riding through the neighborhood as a child, seeing black women lined up for the bus with their garters loosened and stockings down after a long workday and realizing that the only black women in Fondren were domestic employees. Today, she realizes the cultural implications of her position as a black female artist running her own business in the Fondren community.

"I believe, now, as an artist, I see why

Roz works in her Fondren studio.

God put me over here in Fondren," she muses. "I have seen the flip side of *The Help*," Roz explains. "Prejudice is a taught behavior. I know black men and women who were domestic workers and have *always* been cared for by their white families."

When the movie version of Kathryn Stockett's bestselling novel *The Help* was filmed in Jackson in 2011, it brought back Roz's memories of a friend who had worked for a prominent white family in Jackson and had loved their little boy like he was her own son. Roz has a series of paintings of black women holding white children. These paintings, she realizes, bring back sentimental memories for certain people.

"White women love black art," she asserts. "I have white women who tell me they had a black friend as a child, and their white families put a stop to it."

Roz admits that white people purchase the majority of her paintings, a fact that initially caused her great pain.

"I cried because I created this work for black people, and they asked me, 'Why are you stereotyping us like that?' But now I see how God has blessed me," she says, looking around her studio. "I tell my white friends, 'I'm a black woman who keeps it real.'"

"Keeping It Real"

When Roz was eighteen months old, she contracted polio from a bad batch of vaccines, permanently damaging her legs. Doctors told her parents that Roz needed to be put in a home for crippled children, but Roz's mother and father were determined to give Roz a chance at a normal life. Instead of isolating her, Roz's parents educated her about the disease, telling her that she should live without shame and be whoever she wanted to be.

"As a kid, I didn't see myself as being beautiful with a brace on my leg," she admits. "But my mother told me I could do things in this world."

Roz's mother encouraged her daughter's artistic temperament, buying her coloring books. Roz designed clothes for her paper dolls. She was always aware of her surroundings, and her fascination with "doo dads" and trinkets is evident in her detailed sculptures.

Roz grew up in a world of changes in Jackson. Until third grade, Roz attended a segregated school. Her family attended Holy Ghost Catholic Church, where around the age of twelve or thirteen, Roz became close with a nun named Sister Linette. Her father told Sister Linette how much Roz liked to make art, and Roz recalls that Sister Linette said, "You will be a great artist." Roz was skeptical.

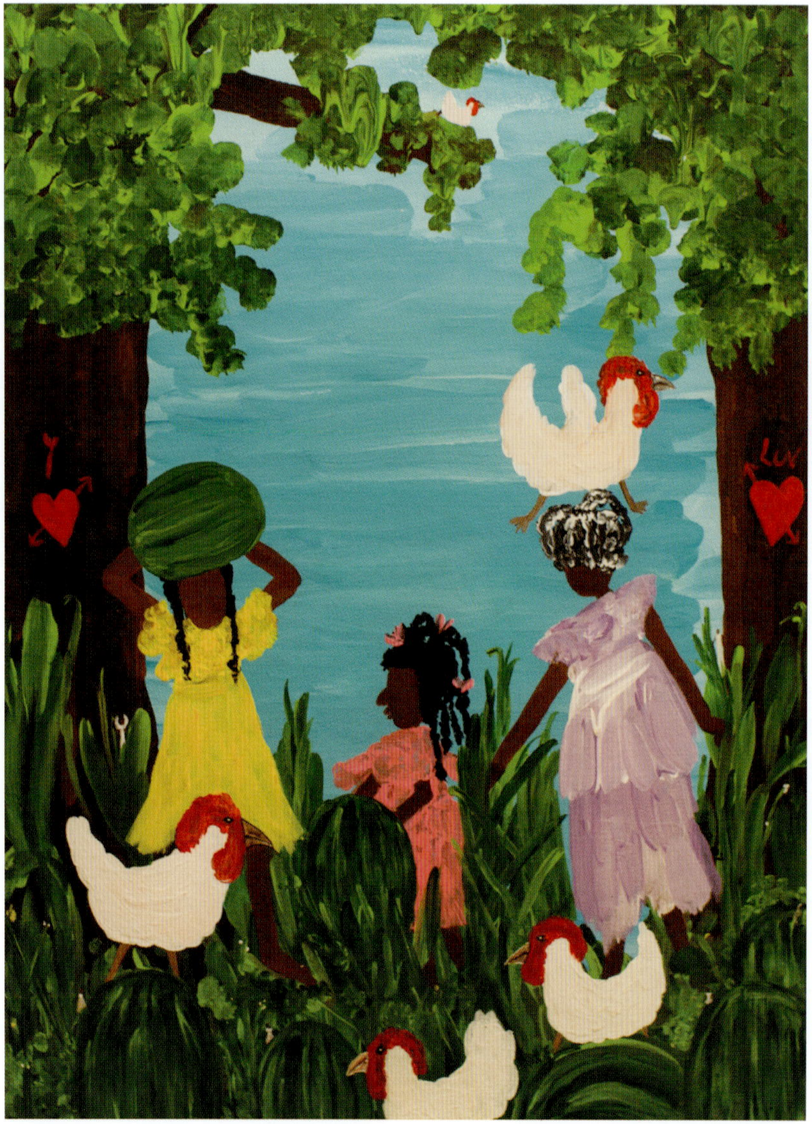

"I never imagined as an artist that things would turn out for me," she says.

Roz took art in high school but says she really wanted to take woodworking instead. She studied art at Tougaloo College in Jackson, where she says she felt like a rebel because she wanted to create her own way and "not do something for someone else." At times, she wondered why she was even in school. Rarely, she encountered a professor who appreciated her art for what it was, helping her realize that beauty does not have to be neat and tidy—it can be complex and "sloppy."

"I'm not a competitive artist," she professes. "My art was never for bragging. It was part of my relaxation."

For a long time, Roz held temporary jobs while taking care of her aging father for over a decade. When she lost her father in 2003, she pondered her next step. In 2005, Roz lost her brother, "the brother who gave me the nickname Roz," she says. Her grief quickly made its way into her paintings.

"All this art is my cussing, crying and praising Jesus," she says. "Believe it or not,

Them Chickens Keep Flying Over My Head by Roz Roy.

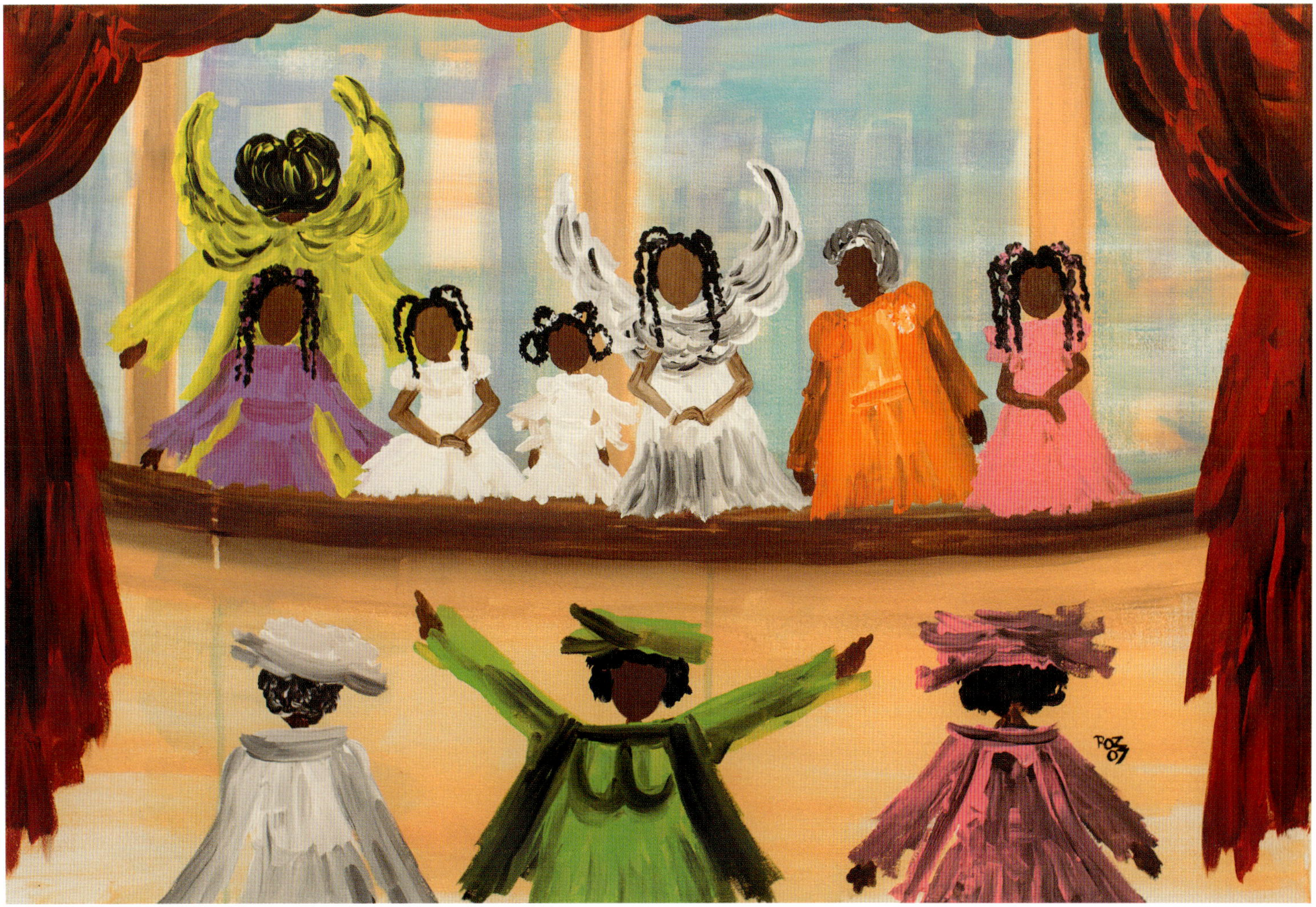

Hold Up—Let the Church Say Amen by Roz Roy.

most of my art has come out of pain—but I have been blessed."

To cope with her sadness, Roz focused on her artwork with a renewed zeal, setting up a booth at the Belhaven Market on Saturdays. At the market, she met a local interior designer named Tommie Goodman, who was intrigued with Roz's art. Tommie, who owned MAX furniture store in Fondren, introduced Roz to her stepson, artist William Goodman, and told her friends and clients about Roz's art. As her popularity grew, Roz remained true to herself and kept painting in her own folksy style. She did a series of paintings called *Preacher Man* that was a commentary on her observations about corruption in black churches.

"'For where your treasure is, there your heart will be,'" she quotes. "My art is praying to God, asking, 'What is going on with our black preachers?'"

Much of Roz's artwork is tinged with religious elements—baptism scenes, crosses, church choirs and angels permeate—but she despises people who argue about the right way to worship.

"There's always going to be controversy until man stops looking at man," she bemoans. "While you're here on earth you can be a blessing and a witness to one another."

Roz is passionate about exposing children to art, and she has a heart for children with disabilities. Like her parents taught her, she wants children with disabilities to know that they can still achieve great things. Roz, an active member of the Craftsman's Guild, teaches art classes at the Mississippi Children's Museum and at her studio, where she accepts students by referrals, which often come from public school teachers who recognize a talented student who is languishing because his or her school does not have enough funding for the arts. Still, she worries when parents ask her how their child can become a professional artist. Not one to mince words, Roz answers honestly.

"I told them, 'Why do you think I'm teaching art lessons? I'm a broke professional artist!'" she laughs.

Instead of pushing children one way or another, she says, it's important that parents of artistic children deal with the facts.

"To make art, you have to love it," she says. "I'm happy that as a woman and a black artist I am able to sell my work."

11

DAN PIERSOL AND MAUREEN DONNELLEY

Dan Piersol and Maureen Donnelly have been together for thirty-four years. Partners in creativity and marriage, their presence evokes the romances of movies and novels.

"We adore each other," Maureen says, and Dan adds, "We're really lucky."

Their history together, which they profess is "mostly sunshine and rainbows," began in New Orleans. They met in the basement of Tulane University in New Orleans through mutual friends. At the time, Dan, who holds two degrees from Bowling Green State University in Ohio, was employed as a house painter, and Maureen was studying ceramics. Maureen's early ceramics are covered in abstract

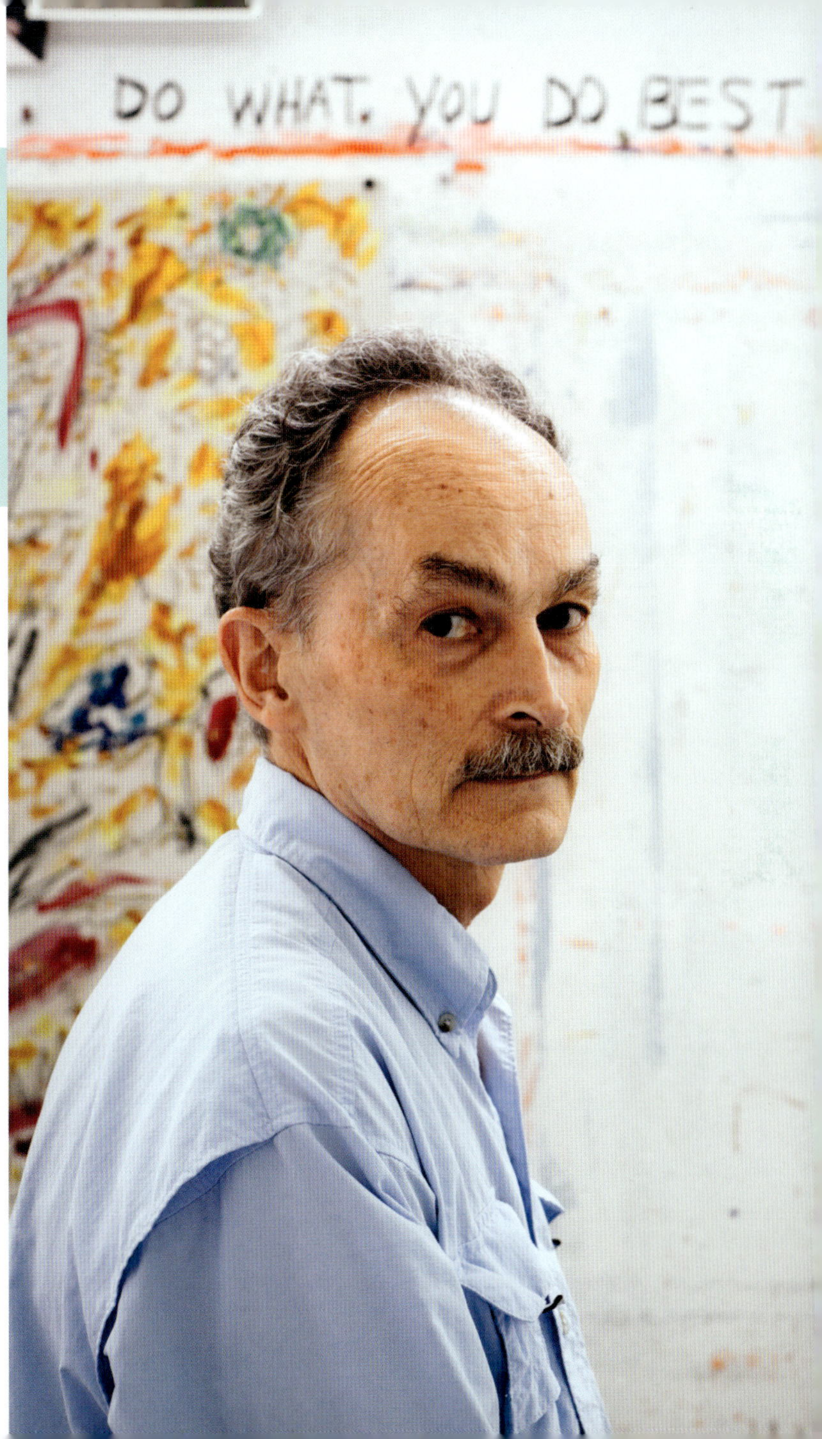

Dan Piersol and his wife, Maureen, moved to Jackson from New Orleans after Katrina.

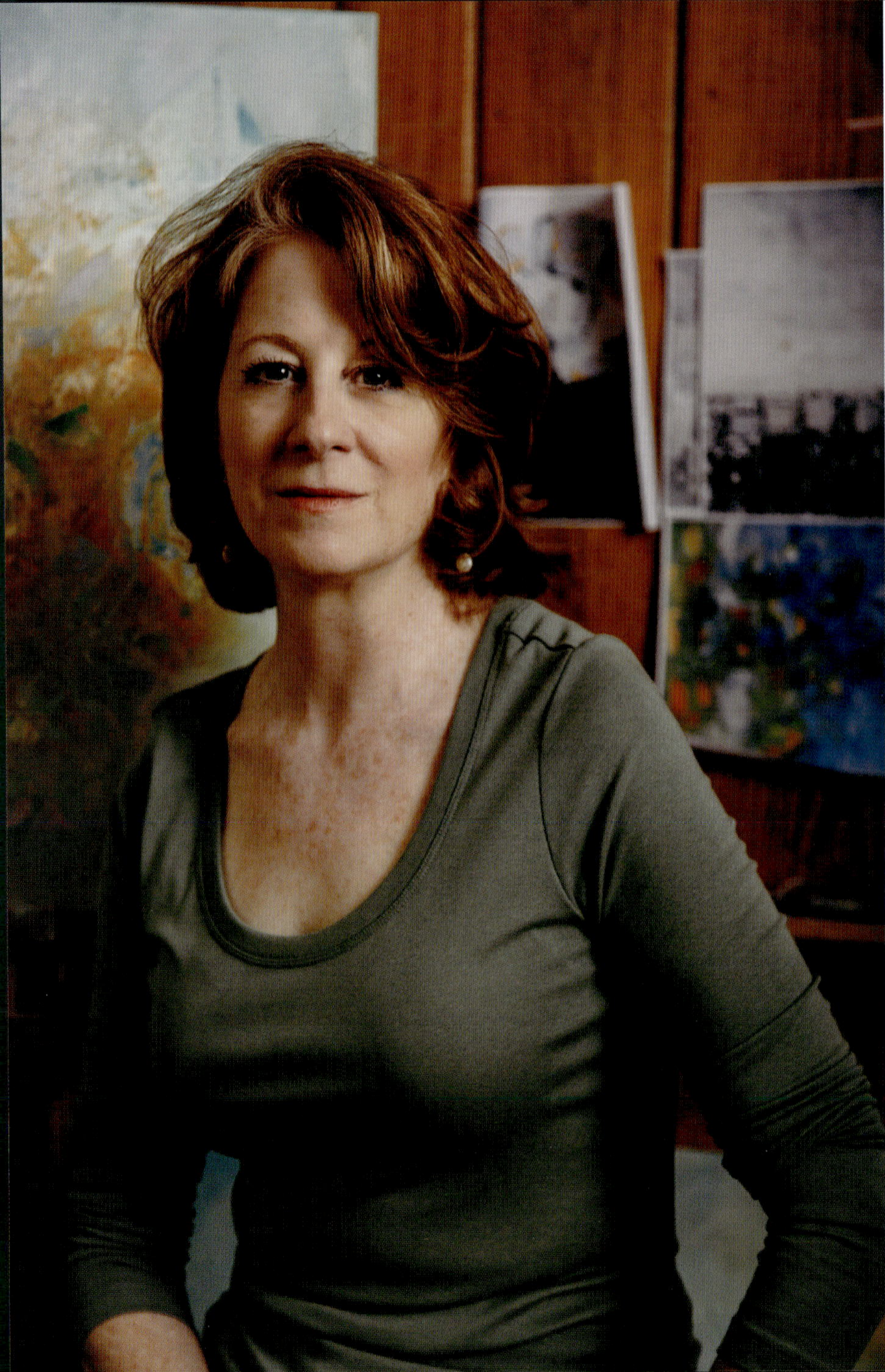

designs, and she remembers, "It was the first thing that I did that I thought, 'I could do this forever.' I loved clay, I really did."

Life for the two was, by both of their accounts, blissful. They moved into a shotgun house built in the 1890s and converted half of it to a studio for Dan, who pursued his visual art in addition to working for the New Orleans Museum of Art as curator of prints and drawings. Maureen worked for Neal Auction in New Orleans; for a while, she was the only accredited art appraiser in the state of Louisiana. Career driven from the start, Maureen recalls how she was constantly observing and assessing art.

"We both pretty much had the same path," Maureen observes. "It was really and truly what we both wanted to do: work with art—collect, observe, exhibit. Dan used to come home from work and go to the studio every night."

There were trials, sure. But in the end, Dan and Maureen had each other, and they had their art. They were happy to be settled. In August 2005, they remember celebrating because, as they saw it, "Everything was

Maureen Donnelly worked as an art appraiser before pursuing her painting full time.

right in the world." Then Katrina hit, and their life was ripped apart. Today, Dan still recoils at the memory of the storm and "the trauma of having twenty-five years of your life dashed in seconds."

"We had a couple of hours to pack everything and get out," he recalls. Dan lost a lot of his artwork and temporarily lost his job, since museums were not open for months following the storm. Dan was promised another job when the city was restored, but he began to look for work outside New Orleans. He heard about a job opening at the Mississippi Museum of Art in Jackson, and museum director Betsey Bradley hired him on the spot.

"Jackson was extremely appealing," says Maureen. "We were so happy to have landed here. New Orleans was so special, but we had thirty years there."

"Everything has changed there," says Dan.

Maureen agrees. "It's very different. We always feel like we're home when we're there. But we would never move back. [Jackson] is home now."

Before moving to Jackson, Maureen researched different neighborhoods. Since they both love old houses, Maureen began looking for the oldest house she could find. Happy to find a house in Fondren built in the 1930s, they researched the neighborhood, which Dan says turned out to be "interesting." Attracted to the neighborhood's mixed history (Fondren was home to the Mississippi Lunatic Aslyum, which Maureen and Dan found fascinating), the couple slept on an air mattress while renovating their house.

"We were giddy to be here," Maureen recalls. "We found this great house—well, it had no heat," she admits. "But it's a great house."

Dan immediately noticed the creative culture in Jackson, especially in the Fondren neighborhood at that time. He sensed a great group of people interested in the arts and was pleased when Betsey Bradley and the trustees at the MMA were determined to keep the museum downtown instead of moving it to a more suburban area.

"I saw the potential of downtown Jackson ending up like the Warehouse District in New Orleans," Dan explains. "Betsey had a vision for that museum."

Dan has been able to see that vision come true over the years. He retired in 2012 and now pursues his art full time; both he and Maureen have achieved their ultimate dream of becoming full-time artists, and they operate in home studios on their Fondren property. Dan's studio is in a freestanding structure in their backyard that also serves as his personal archive—months after Katrina, he and Maureen were able to return to their New Orleans home and salvage what was left of his artwork and supplies. Dan is one of the "messy artists," and thus his workspace reflects exactly where he is mentally at any given point. The walls of Dan's backyard studio are cluttered with notes, photos, inspiration

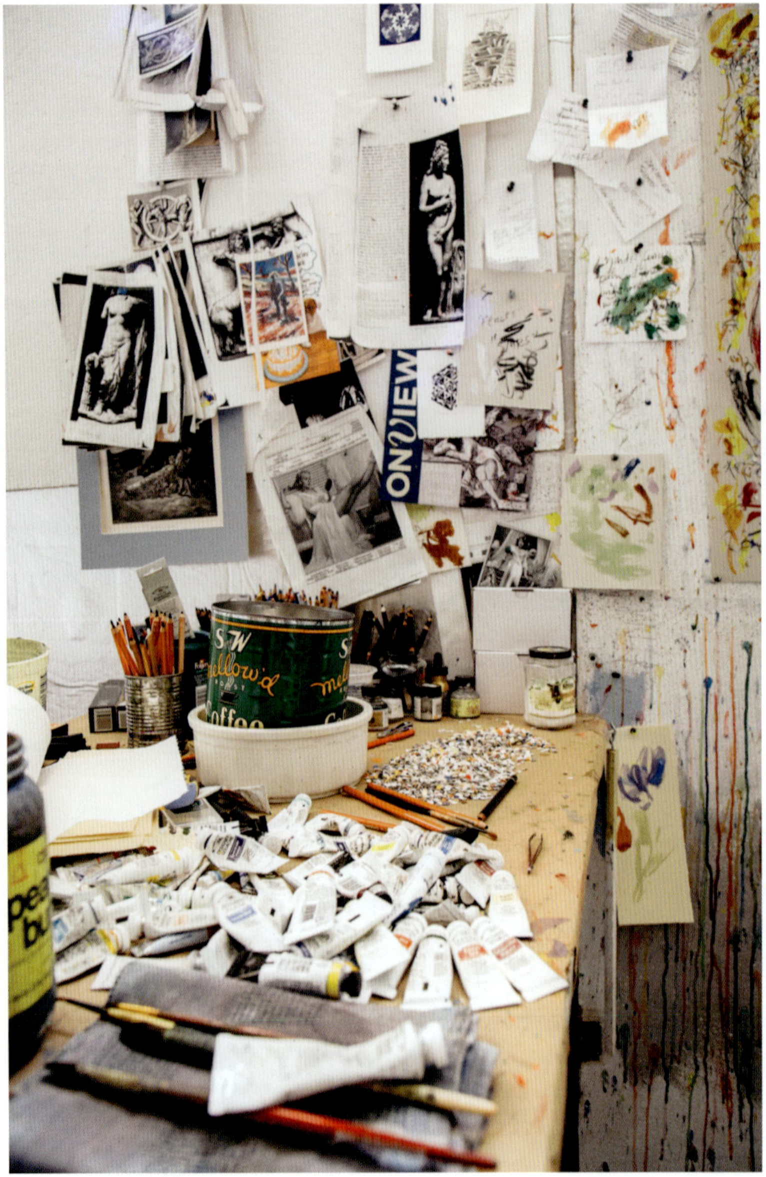
ONVIEW
mellow'd
Coffee

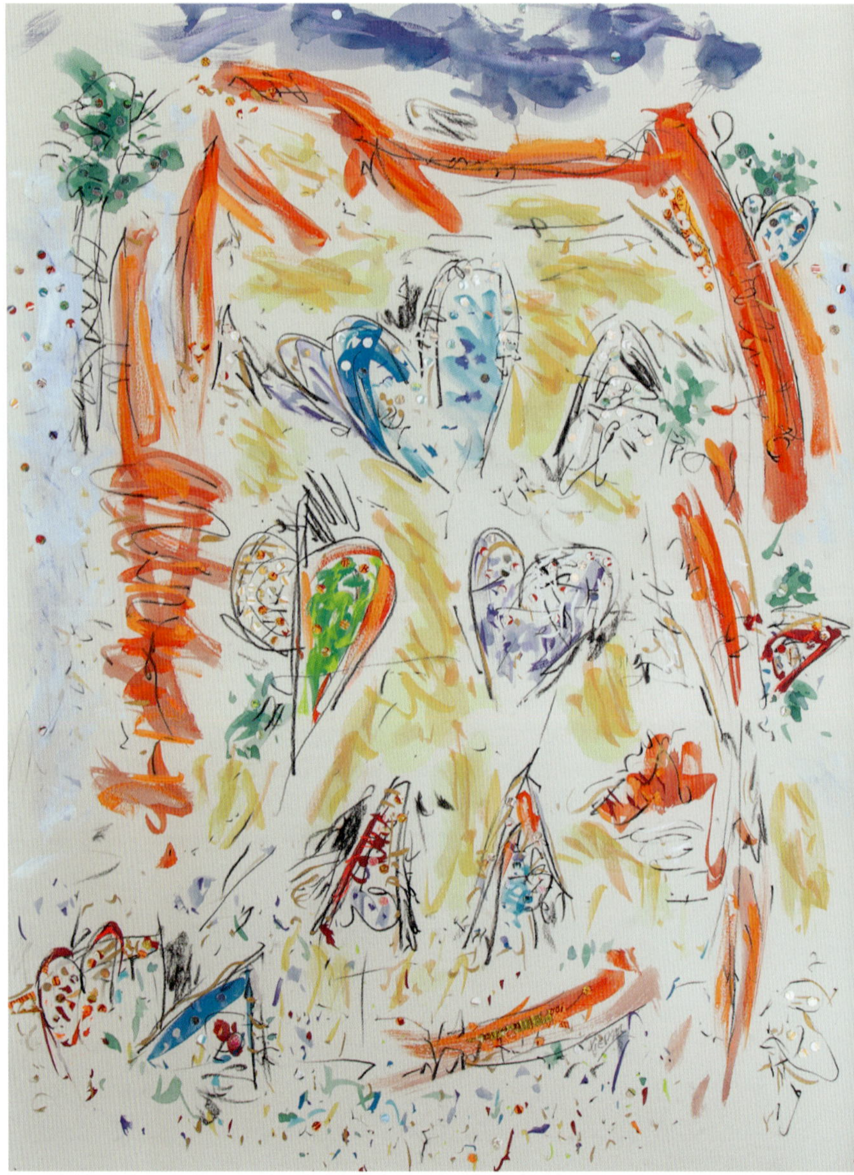

and bits of paintings. He has painted motivational slogans on the walls, including "Do what you do best" and "It's not rocket science."

In contrast, Maureen's studio is a converted wood-paneled bedroom on the second floor of their house, where she makes her art using palette knives and oil paints, which she keeps in organized lines on a table by the window. Maureen retired from making ceramics after hand problems kept her from continuing her pottery, but in the spirit of art, she passed her wheel and kiln along to a young artist who she believes in. Sculpture, she says, is a community endeavor whereas painting is a more solitary work.

Dan and Maureen have made the effort to ingratiate themselves in the

Opposite, left: Dan's studio is located in a separate building in the couple's backyard.

Opposite, right: *Corralled* by Dan Piersol.

Right, top: Maureen applies her paint to canvas with palette knives.

Right, bottom: Marueen's palette knives rest on a ledge alongside a photo of Dan.

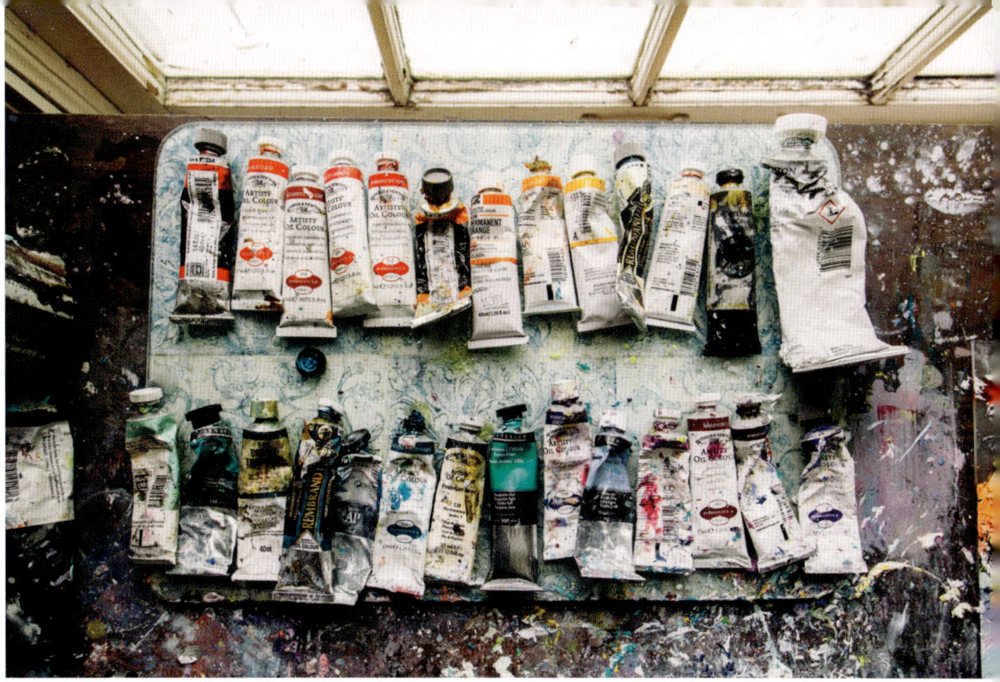

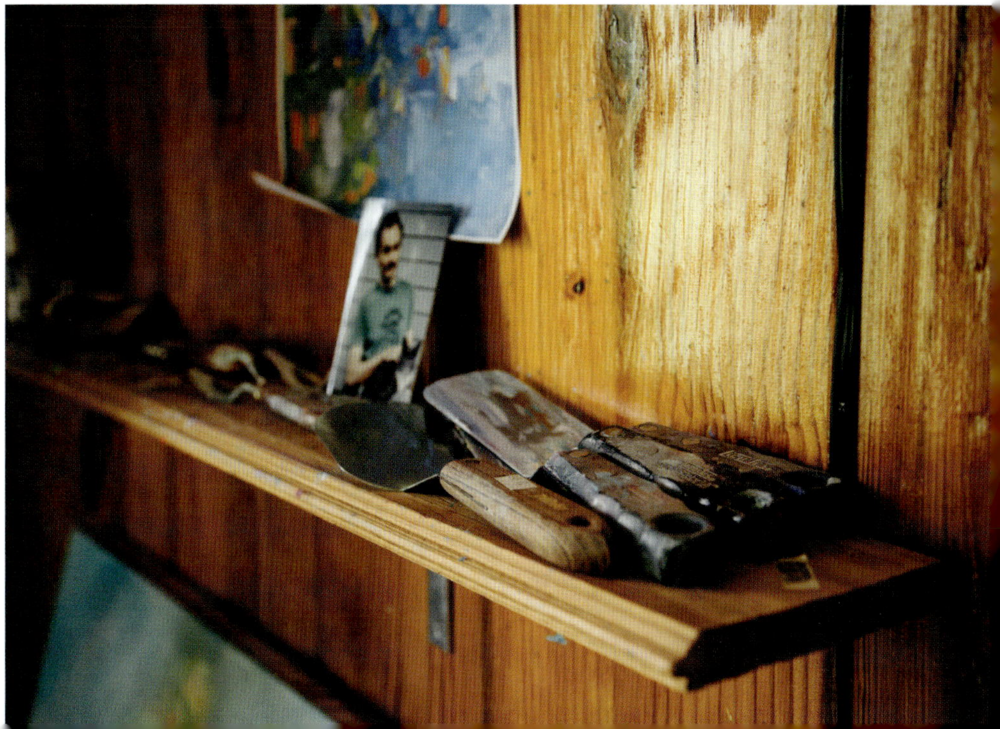

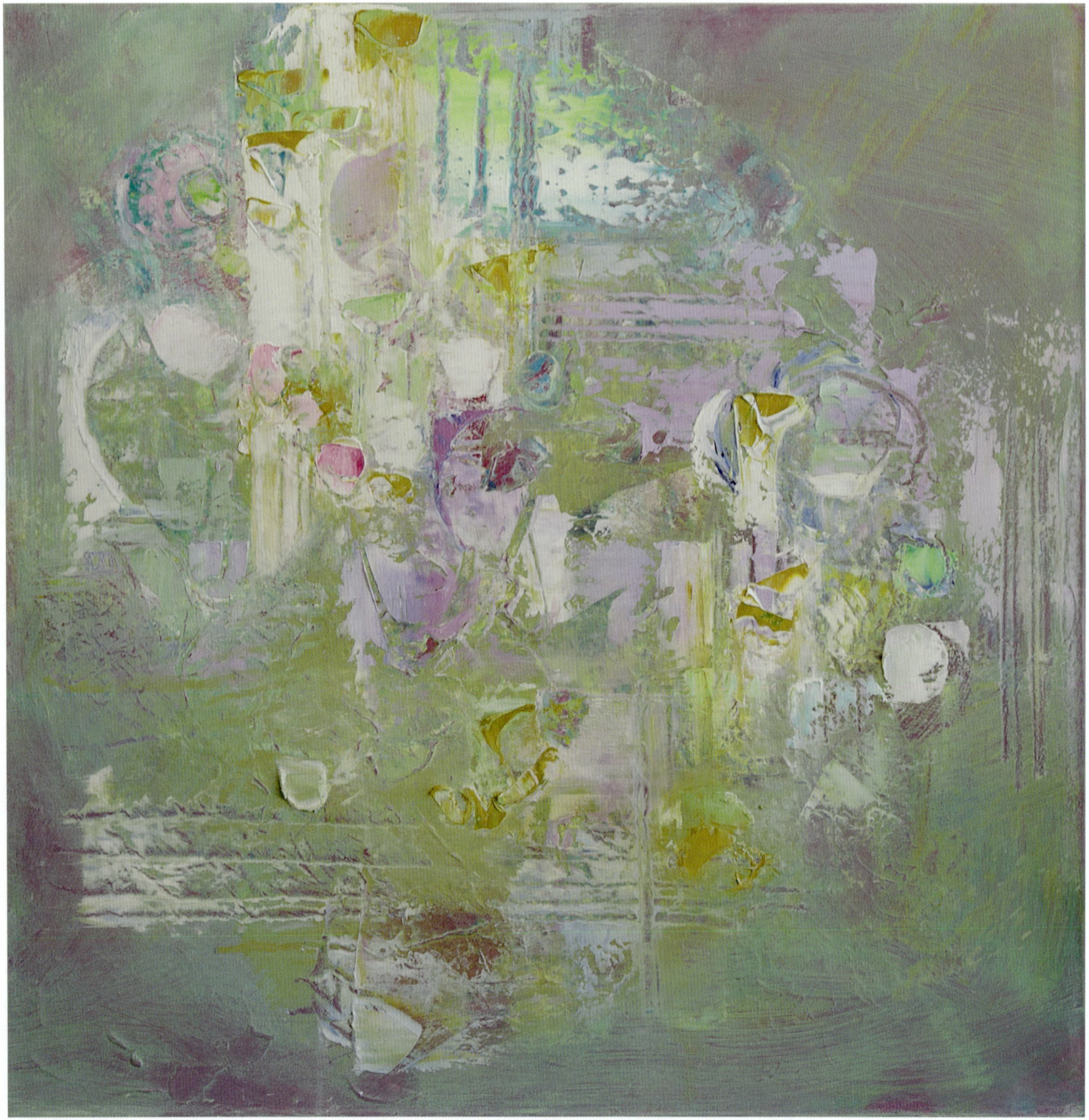

Bolla Rosa
by Maureen
Donnelley.

Jackson art community, with fantastic results. As Dan puts it, "You can't just stay home and paint. You have to make connections with other artists." Dan and Maureen both currently show their paintings at Fischer Gallery in Jackson, and their work is part of many corporate and private collections. Dan's work is part of the permanent collection at many notable museums, and he is the recipient of a National Endowment for the Arts Fellowship. Still, Dan jokes, "Great reviews doesn't always translate into sales." The economics of the art world are always in flux, and Maureen and Dan have watched the ebb and flow of the art world with considerable interest.

"It's hard to be a full-time artist anywhere," Dan notes. "I don't think it's any different today. One of the only differences that I am aware of is that artists now have the ability, through the Internet, to promote themselves."

The Internet is no substitution for the camaraderie artists require to survive, which Dan says Jackson possesses "like a magnet."

"There's a pull here," he notices. "I felt accepted right away."

Dan and Maureen were interested to hear that Governor Phil Bryant had declared 2014 the "Year of the Creative Economy."

"I think it's a great idea," Dan says, noting his admiration of former Mississippi Arts Commission director Malcolm White. White was an early champion of the Year of the Creative Economy, and his current work for the Mississippi Development Authority promotes the arts in Mississippi from a tourism perspective. "It's remarkable how creative this community is. Malcolm is a really great person who sees so much in Mississippi. And this state is terrific. It has the arts, the symphony, such history, so much going for it."

In fact, Dan believes that along with an impressive literary history, Mississippi is home to true American artistic genius, citing George Ohr and Walter Anderson.

"Human creativity is always there, and that's the ace in the hole. Try to pull the rug out from under humanity—it won't happen," Dan says. "There are always artists coming up. Creativity is nurtured in progressive circles here. And I think that's very wise."

Maureen agrees, adding, "We are always blown away by the people we meet here."

"New Orleans is known for crazy people, and it was great to come here and see there's no drop off," Dan says, smiling.

Maureen adds, "The South embraces its eccentrics."

12

ANDY HILTON

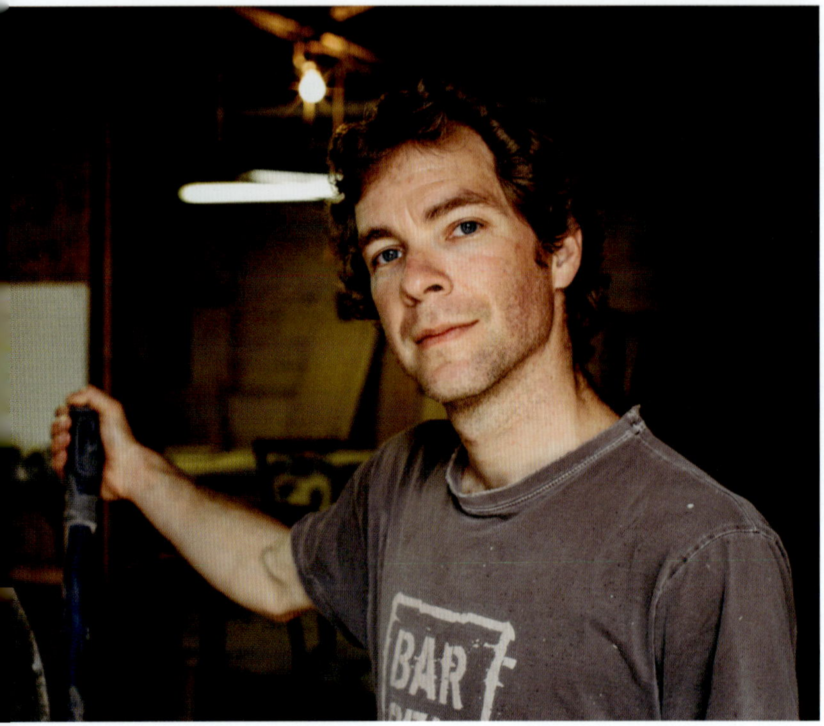

Andy Hilton is a concrete artist who has gained recent fame for his creation of designer swings.

Andy Hilton, a Jackson native, bought a warehouse in Midtown in 2010 because he needed square footage to grow his business and was hard pressed to find a large space that he could afford. At the time, Andy was working primarily with concrete, building countertops, sculptures, benches and whatever other commissions came his way. Andy is currently studying civil engineering at Jackson State University and has also studied industrial design at Auburn University. He has always been attracted to the distinction of modern design.

"Something [modern] is different, is always more challenging," Andy explains. "A different type of person wants concrete countertops."

Andy's concrete designs are undoubtedly successful. In 2013, he received his biggest commission to date with Spectrum Capital, which hired Andy to construct a monument for display at the outlet malls in Pearl, Mississippi. Still, after years of working with concrete, Andy realized that "the medium isn't as important as the fact that I like to design products."

"Sometimes, building the molds for the concrete was more fun than working with the concrete," he explains.

Andy is very connected to the Jackson community. He uses only a moderate-sized section of his warehouse as a personal studio; he is passionate about providing a space where emerging craftsmen can afford the rent. He rents a portion of his studio space to David Dill and Paul Purser, owners of the furniture design company D+P Designs.

SwingLab

A little over a year ago, Andy developed the idea for a swing that blended comfort with the appeal of modern design. With the backing of a grant from the Mississippi Arts Commission (MAC), he began producing midcentury, modern-inspired swings with a modular design

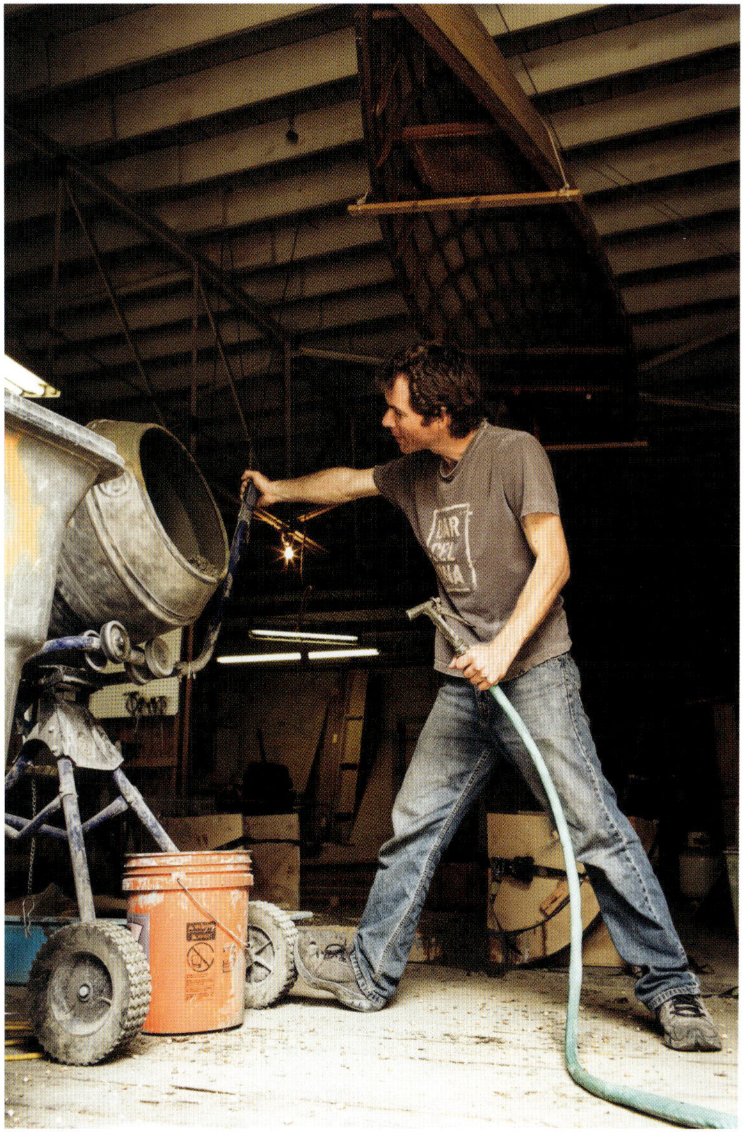

Andy mixes concrete in his Midtown studio.

that allows the owner to switch up the positions of the two backrests. In marketing the swings, Andy hoped they would appeal to the styles of "urbanites and hipsters" but wanted his design to be functional and ecologically sourced. Andy gets his wood (he prefers bald cypress) from Follen Wood Preserving Company in Jackson, Mississippi, and sources his aluminum from a welder in Gluckstadt, Mississippi. On his website, SwingLab.com, an entire page is devoted to the history of his craftsmanship and design, noting that each swing is entirely "handmade in Jackson, Mississippi." Since launching his product, Andy has sold "about one swing a month," with most of his sales coming from out of state.

"I sell pretty much zero swings in Mississippi," he laughs. The Mississippi Museum of Art bought one of his swings for its porch, and the swings are known throughout Jackson. But Andy thinks that there are people who admire the modern design of the swings who might not be able to afford one.

"Jackson is very emotionally supportive," he explains. "But younger people who might like to buy my swings just don't have the cash."

The swings, which currently retail for about $900, are gaining popularity nationally through the Internet community, where they have been featured on multiple design blogs, including the very popular blog Apartment Therapy. Through online sales, Andy is able

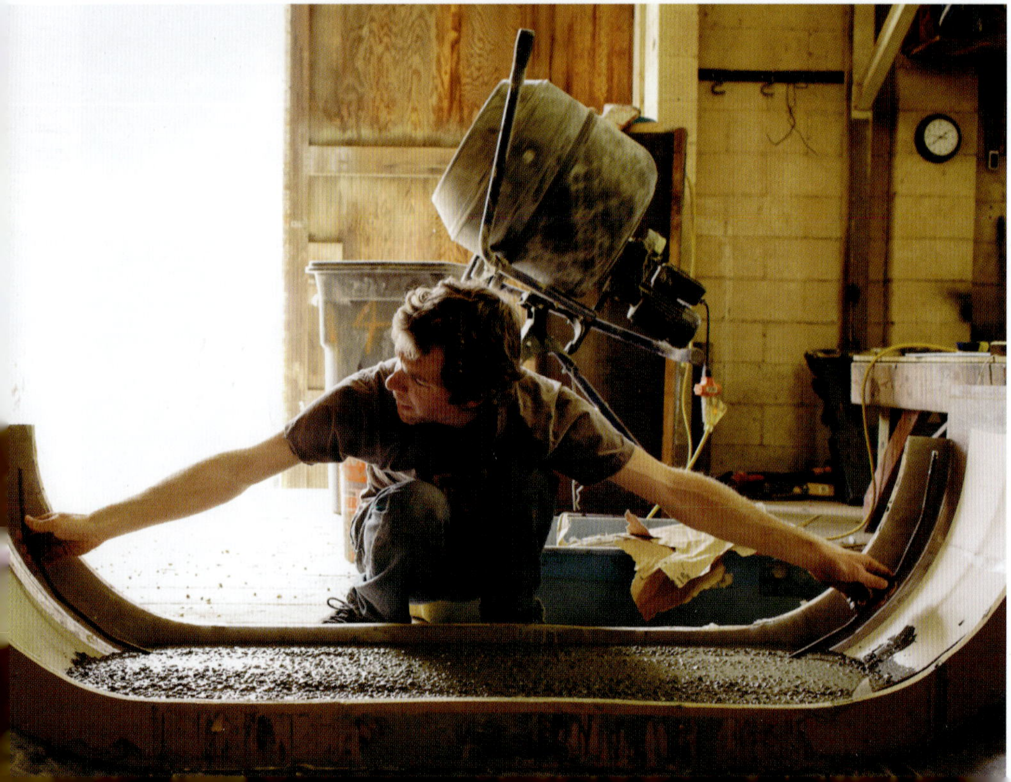

Left: Building his own concrete molds inspired Andy to start building swings.

Opposite: A Swinglab swing hangs in Andy's workshop.

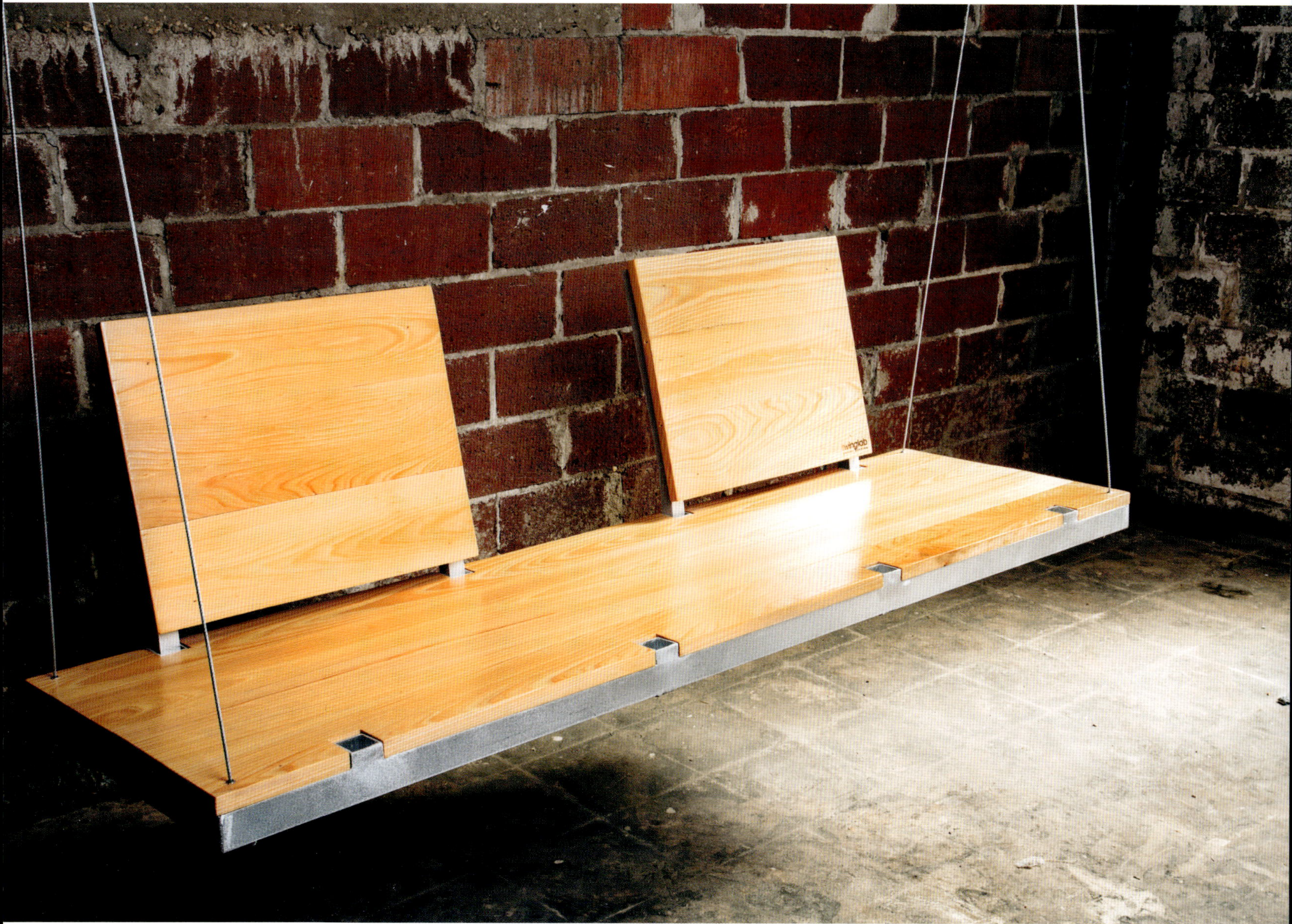

to reach a market in larger cities, where there is more disposable income for luxury handmade goods, without having to leave his hometown.

"My goal is to keep living in Jackson, where everything is cheap—and fun," he says.

13
PEARL RIVER GLASS

ANDY YOUNG

In 1975, Andy Young opened his first glass studio on North State Street in Jackson. He was twenty-three years old and had recently completed a degree in landscape architecture at Louisiana State University, winning a Frederick Law Olmsted award for excellence in preservation and landscape work. His desire to work with glass was born from a simple idea: "I wanted to work with cool stuff, and glass is really cool because it's transmitted light, not reflected light. Anytime you look at a window, it's going to be different."

Andy is interested in the concept of understanding the nature of the material you are working with. "If you are attuned to the orderly

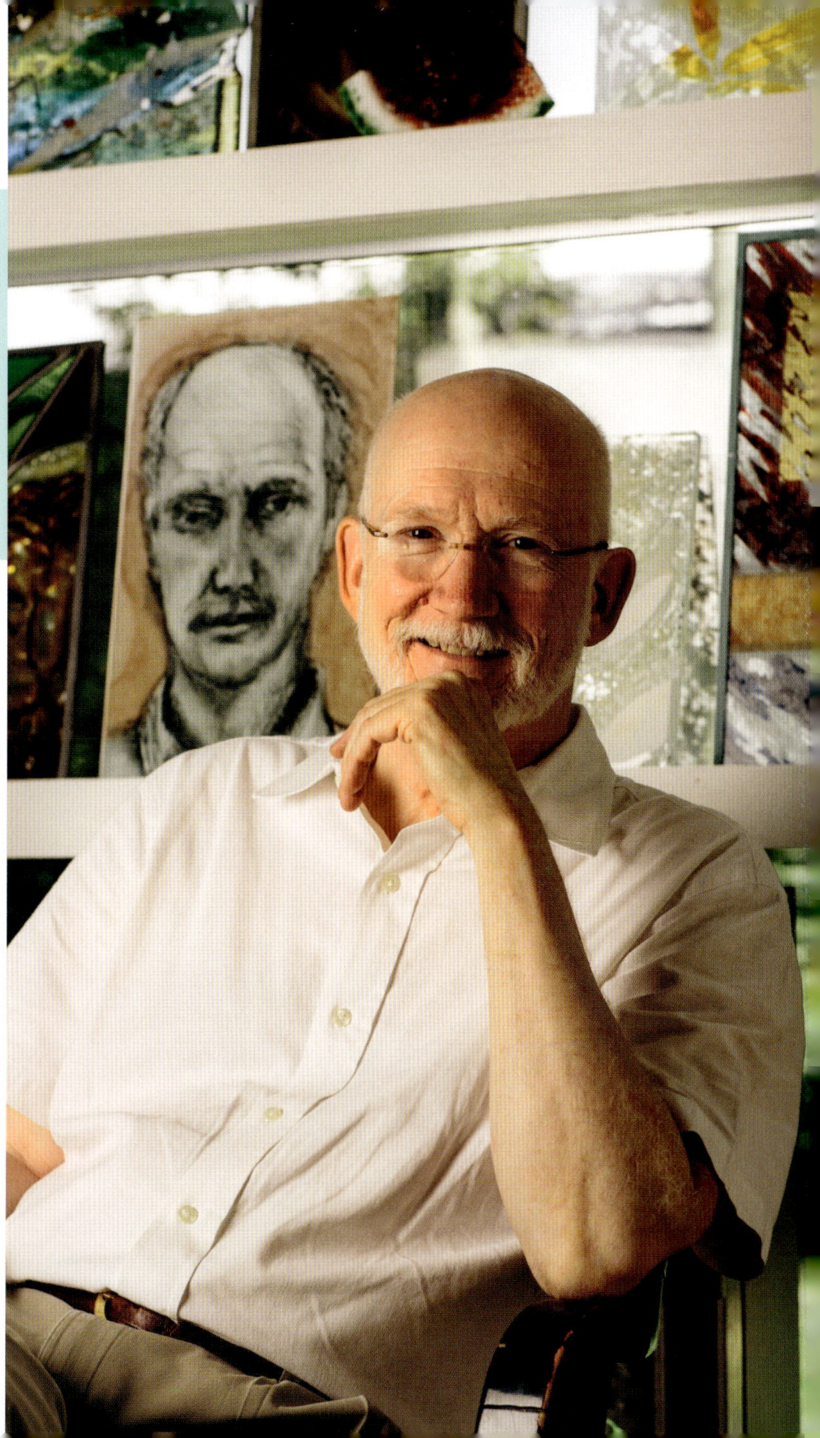

Andy Young is the founder and owner of Pearl River Glass.

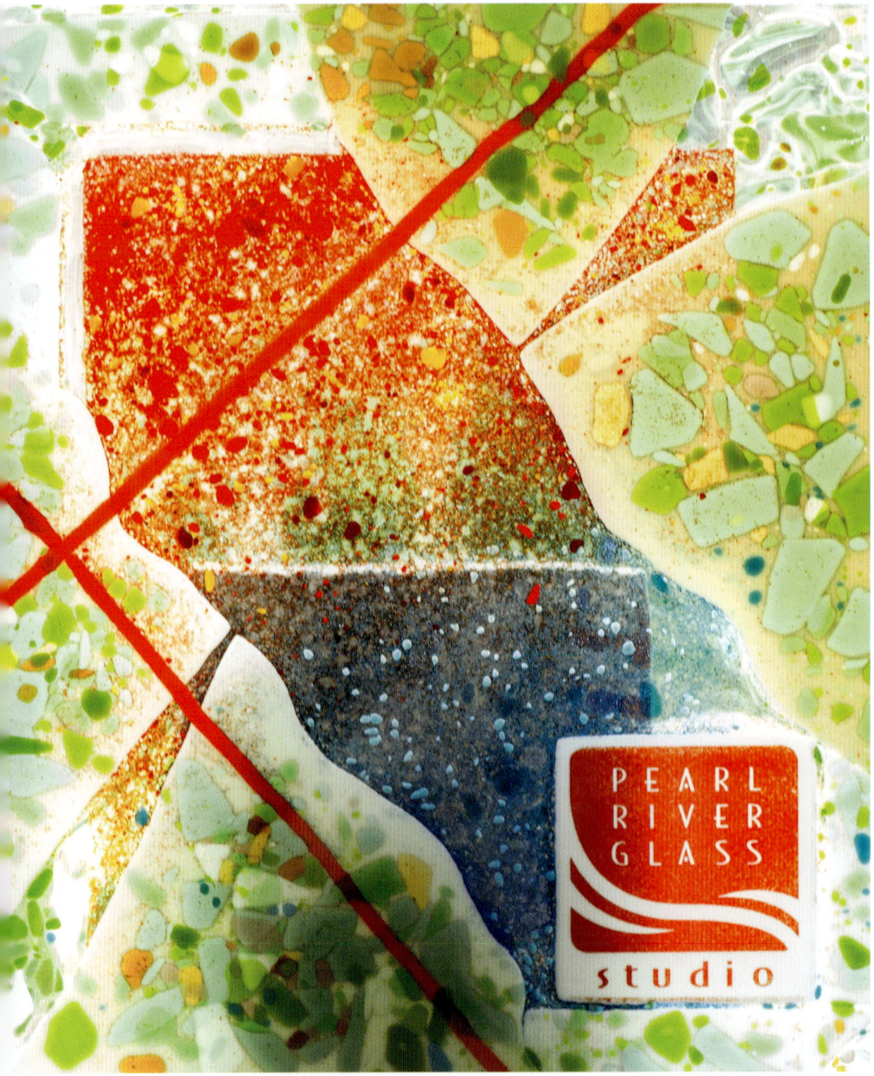

ways of materials, you can extrapolate the truth to other things. If you concentrate on one thing for a long time, it will eventually reveal the truth," he asserts.

Studio History

In 1976, Andy moved his studio to a 2,000-square-foot warehouse on Millsaps Avenue in Jackson's Midtown neighborhood. At that point, he recalls, Midtown was still largely residential, though by 1980, Andy did a few calculations and came to a shocking realization. There was over 100,000 square feet of empty space in Jackson's Midtown neighborhood, composed of vacant lots and unoccupied or abandoned buildings and warehouses. Andy began spreading the word of the abundance of space to work in Midtown. The rent was cheap, he explained, and with low rent, you could keep the overhead costs down. Other artists and craftsmen began to join him there. In 1981, Susan Ford, another glass artist, moved her

You can admire this window at the Pearl River Glass studio.

studio to Midtown, and an enterprising couple, Debra and Chip Billups, seeing the potential for an art district in Jackson, began buying up Midtown property. Over the years, as Midtown has experienced ups and downs, Pearl River Glass has remained a neighborhood fixture. Never once has Andy considered a move.

"My theory on all of this is that the reality is that artists are going to be where they want to be, not where they're told to be," Andy explains.

Today, Andy owns a solid block of property in Midtown, over seventeen thousand square feet of studio space. His space stretches from Millsaps Avenue to a storefront at 151 Wesley. He currently rents the Wesley space out by the month using a 50/50 deal in which artists have one month to use the space for free, and at the end of the month, they do a show of their work and split the profits with Andy. It is one of many ways that Andy is encouraging artists to move to Midtown.

"I don't think Midtown will ever be Fondren," Andy theorizes. "I really don't see it gentrifying that much. It's always going to be an artist's space."

As far as Pearl River Glass goes, Andy plans to keep expanding. A recent loan has allowed him to purchase even more high-tech equipment, including a glass-cutting machine that currently occupies its own warehouse, and multiple new kilns. He has plans to build a classroom space, which he calls a "permanent alternative studio space," and to continue expanding his square footage; he has considered "going vertical" and has looked into using shipping containers or boxcars on the roof to form a second story.

Art, Philosophy and the Mississippi Narrative

Andy's family has lived in Mississippi for over 150 years, and he believes that the tradition of oral narrative is crucial to understanding Mississippians today.

"People in Mississippi want to know the story," Andy elucidates. "There's a narrative structure to everything."

The southern tradition has profoundly influenced his life philosophy and kept him grounded. Andy has never had doubts that an artist or craftsman can make a living in Mississippi. Of his early reasoning, he remembers thinking, "If I stayed here and really got to know who I was, I could develop. Why would I go somewhere and get lost when I can stay here and get to influence a community?"

Andy has made a point to divide his personal artistic life and his work at Pearl River Glass.

"I've always tried to sustain a separate body of work completely independent from the glass," he relates.

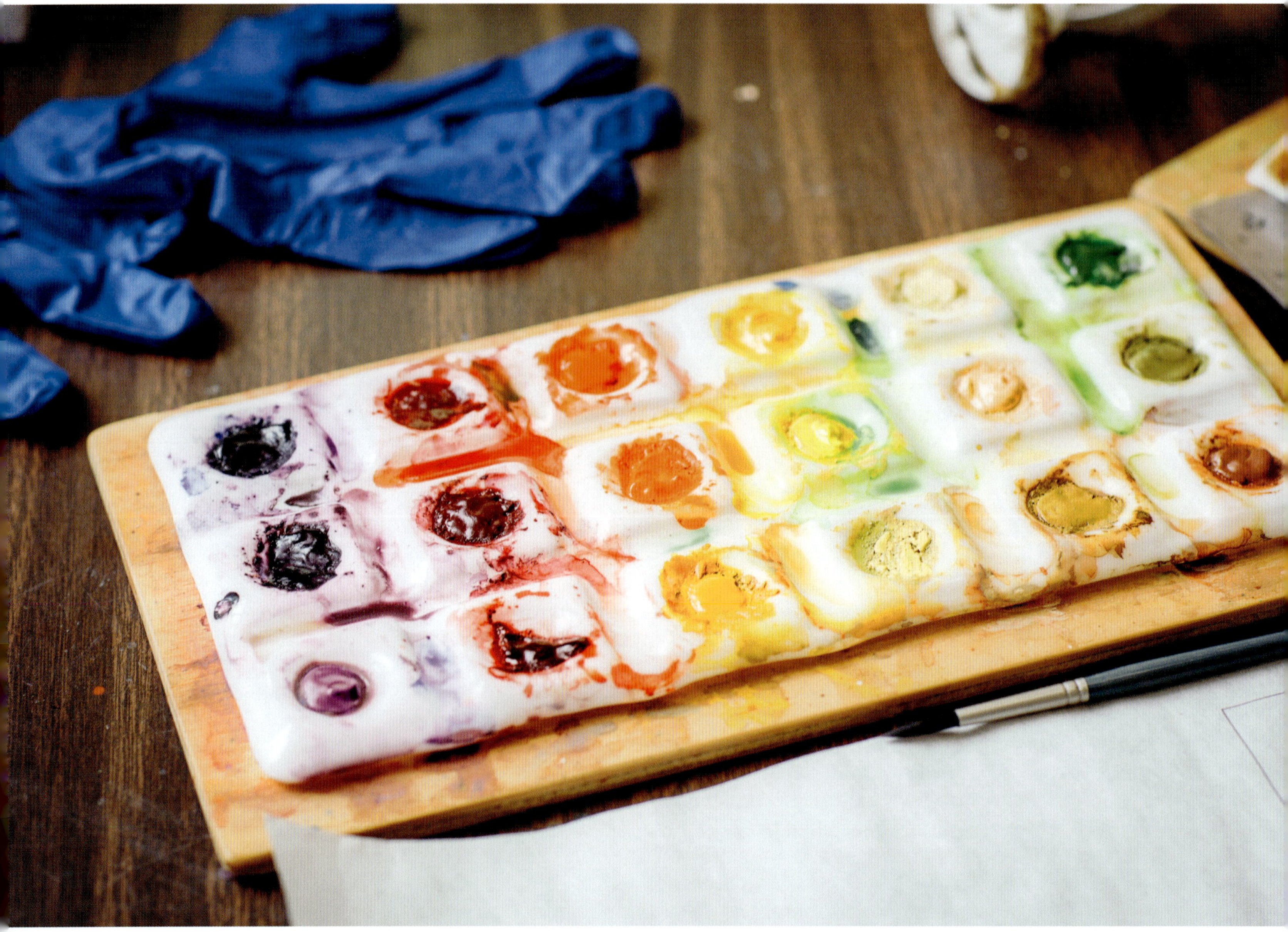

Andy has made a point to continue pursing his personal art in addition to creating and running Pearl River Glass Studio.

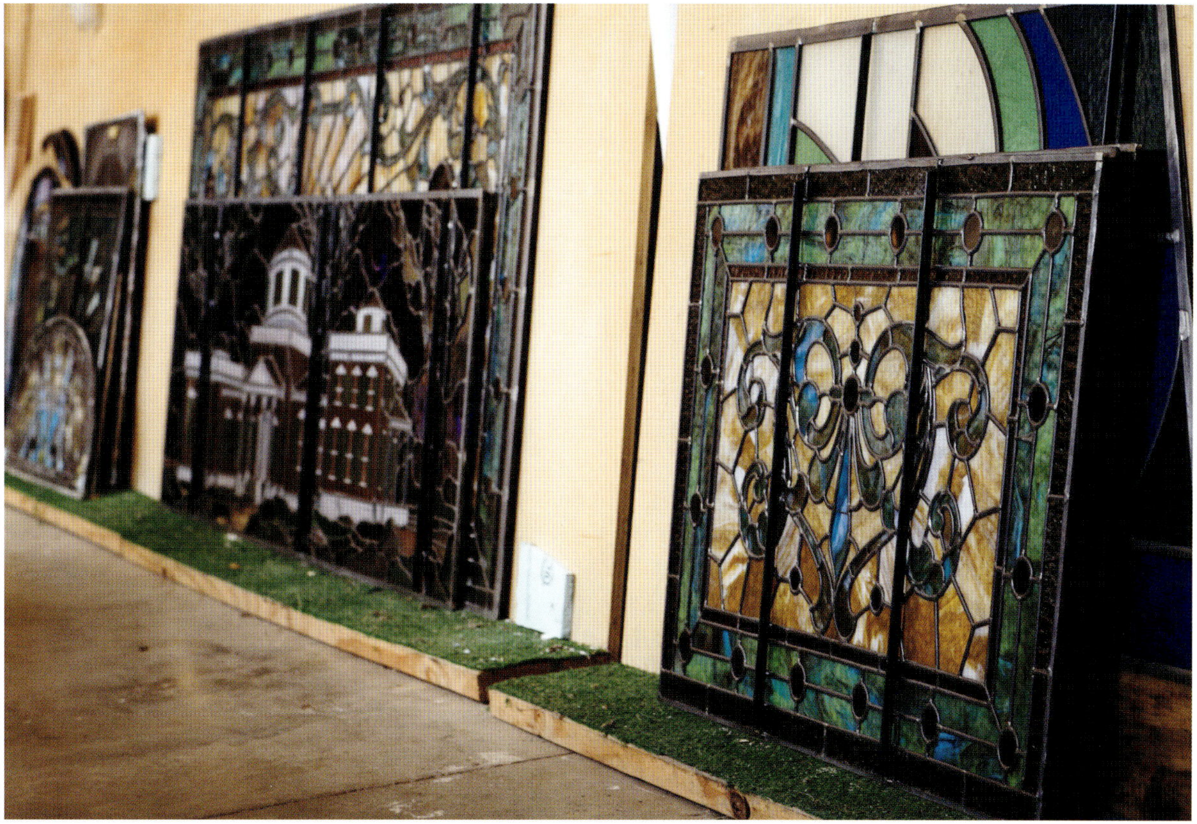

The Pearl River Glass team not only creates stained glass but also restores old stained-glass pieces.

Part of separating his artistic interests requires that he use a home studio space to focus on his other creative works, which include figure drawings, paintings and poetry (his personal hero is William Blake). He took figure-drawing classes at LSU and has maintained his interest in the subject, periodically practicing the craft and showing his work in galleries.

An integral part of Andy's character is his faith. Stained glass, of course, is traditionally a focal point of churches, and Andy, a devout Episcopalian, is acutely aware of the link between art and religion.

"One of the joys that I have is that my artwork enhances worship," he says. "I take that seriously. If I'm going to be creating artwork for the Christian church, it damn well better mean something."

He spent his early years studying many esoteric traditions, which his family encouraged, and he is keenly aware of deep spiritual connections that he does not profess to understand but rather accepts with admiration. His grandmother, for example, spent many years volunteering in a local B'hai chapter office in Jackson. Andy remembers going to lunch with his mother and her when he was only two or three years old. Years later, Andy had a personal studio downtown in the same building.

"I would walk up the stairs adjacent to where the B'hai office used to be," he marvels. "It still amazes me."

For a while, Andy lived in a second-story walk-up apartment on Minerva Street in downtown Jackson. He vividly recollects moving into the apartment, which had bright pink walls and was surprisingly peaceful for such an urban area. The quiet weekends inspired his poetry and drawings, invoking a very innovative period in his life that led to the creation of an entire body of personal artwork that he refers to as the "Minerva Street series." His close friends Fletcher Cox, Bebe Wolfe and Patty Hinson encouraged his work, and although there have been rough patches in Andy's personal life, he has tried to work them to his advantage in every case, even when such an outcome seems unlikely. Andy is not a man who fears the future.

"The next ten years could be the best ten years of my life," he says emphatically. "I'm always interested in what-ifs."

The Economics of Creativity

Like many artists, Andy has grappled with the concept of sustaining his art as a business. He designed his business after Walter Anderson's business model, maintaining a separate focus on drawing and painting in his own time and running his glass studio to earn a living. He is intensely interested in maintaining a balanced creative life while running a business.

"It's an odd thing to be an artist and a business person at the same time," he explains.

Considering the large size of his studio, Andy worries that there is a tendency to become very left-brain and analytical, which requires a lot of energy and can detract from the creative way of

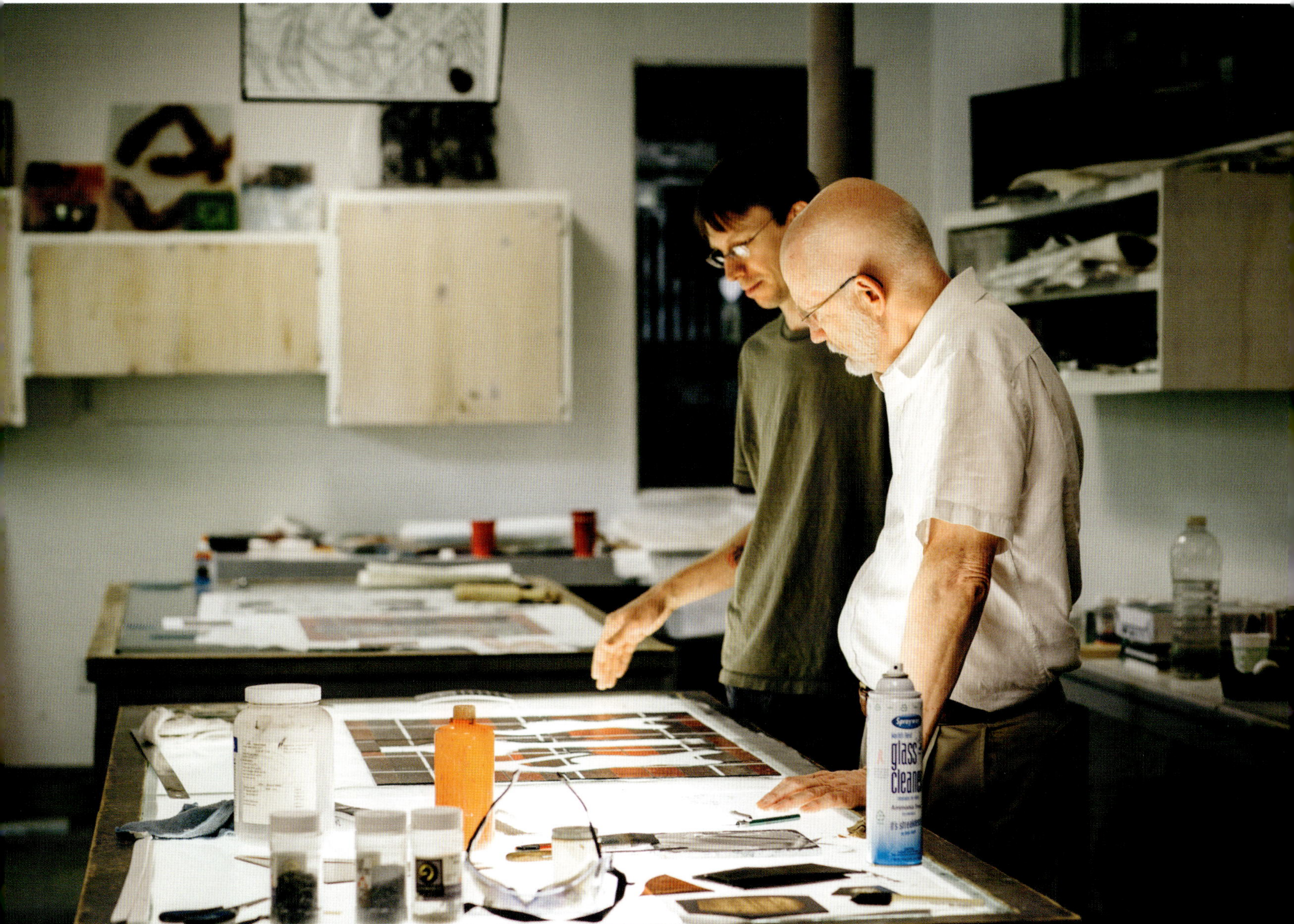

Andy and a member of the staff, Rob Cooper, consult over a project.

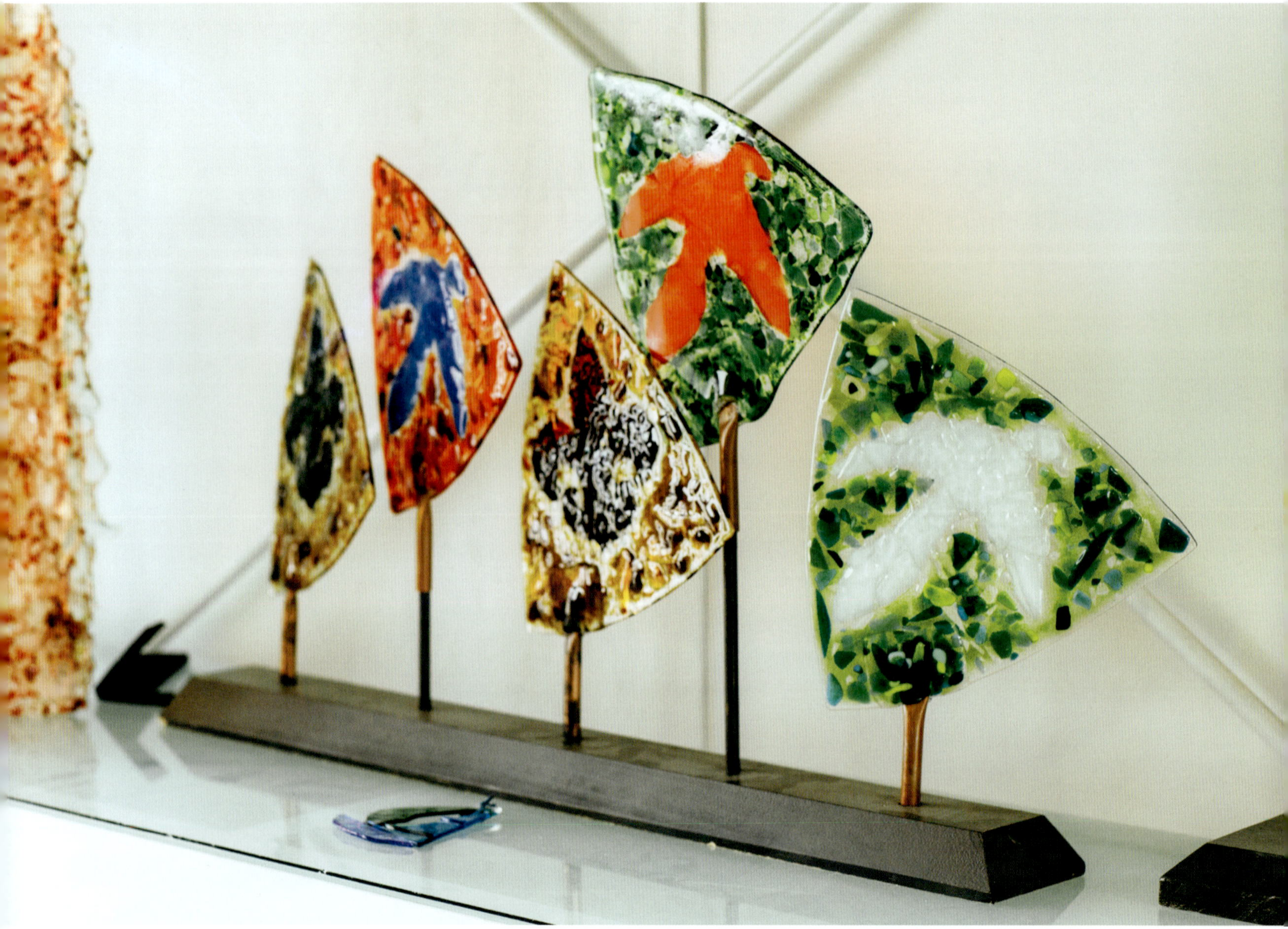

Creating art out of kiln-form glass is a contemporary part of the Pearl River Glass business.

looking at things. This can pose a problem for him, considering that he believes "you can solve most of your problems by thinking creatively."

Andy is a proponent of job creation in the creative class. His first employee was his college roommate, Reggie DeFreese, whom he hired in October 1975. Today, Andy employs more than fifteen people, all of whom, he says, are "artists in their own right." His current design master is Tom Crouch, and many local artists have done a stint at his studio before moving on to independent work, including Ginger Williams-Cook, Jerrod Partridge and Elizabeth Robinson.

"Stained glass propels itself into a business," he reasons. "Stained-glass studios naturally divide into a sense of operations, each one perfected by an individual."

To keep his studio profitable, Andy has begun working not only with stained glass and restorations but also with a unique method of craftsmanship known as "kiln-form glass," which he began experimenting with in 1980 and has spent years working to perfect.

"There was a limitation financially in terms of stained glass," he says.

In the last decade, Andy has become even more passionate about kiln-form glass, which he describes as the second leg of his company. Combining his knowledge of stained glass with the unique aesthetic of kiln-form glass, Andy feels that he has truly found the "dynamic simplicity" that he strives to produce.

"If you added one more thing, it would be too busy; if you had one less thing, it would not be enough."

He is famous for taking on projects with an enormous scale and has designed windows for prestigious organizations all over the country. He has a database of all of his drawings and designs, and most of the output of the Pearl River Glass studio is based on his personal sketches.

"I'm never satisfied with anything," he laments. "I'm always looking back at what I've done that I could change or improve. We're learning always."

Andy served as president of the Stained Glass Association of America from 2003 to 2004. With many irons in the fire, Andy finds focus to be a constant denominator.

"Creativity is as much a disability as an advantage," he explains. "Focus remains an issue. It's a challenge doing this for a living."

Andy is the recipient of many awards and accolades, including the Governor's Award for Excellence in the Arts in 2002 for Individual Artist Achievement. He was one of the earliest members of the Mississippi Craftsman's Guild and has continually pushed for economic growth in the arts community. His belief that any dedicated individual should be able to make a living from his or her art has propelled his creative visions for Jackson.

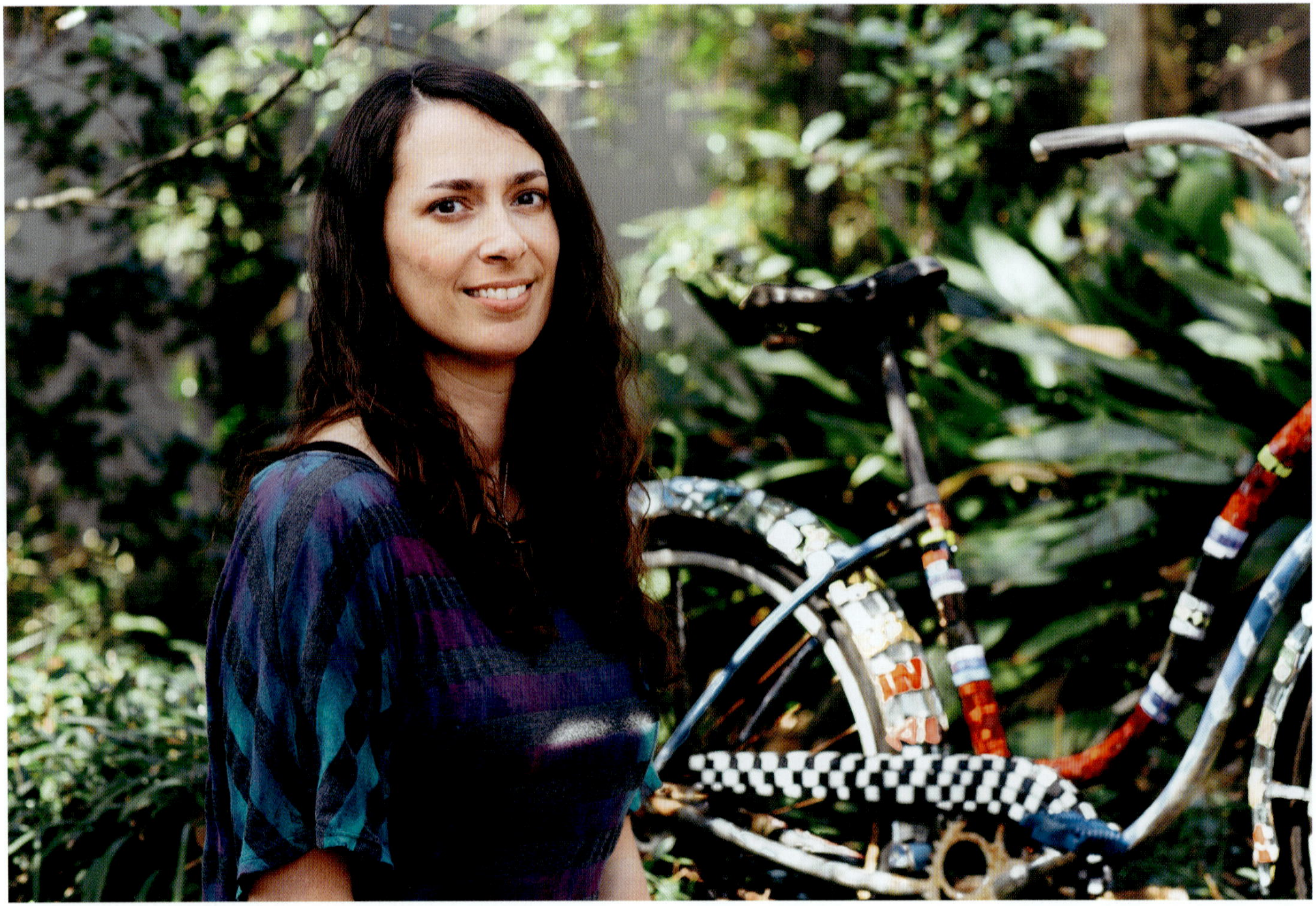

Teresa Haygood is a mosaic artist.

14

TERESA HAYGOOD

On any given day, Teresa Haygood may walk outside to find a cardboard box of dishes left in her driveway. Usually, it's broken china, remnants from an old set of dishes or even glass beads. Fans, friends and neighbors—anyone who knows Teresa—knows that she is usually scavenging for material, so they leave her these boxes. Such is the life of a mosaic artist.

Finding these boxes is a convenient surprise because Teresa runs Creative Minds Studio out of her cheerful, mosaic-saturated home in northeast Jackson, where she has lived and worked for twenty years. Her energetic approach to life is evident in her vibrant mosaic designs.

"My business plan is not to have a business plan," she explains.

Her dining room, which is converted to a sort of tiny gallery displaying her latest mosaic crafts, is open to the front yard, which is filled with all sorts of mosaic-encrusted delights: a bicycle, a birdbath or two, sundials, side tables, even bits of mirror strung up into the trees. She also does custom floors and countertop installations and pretty much anything else you can imagine. Teresa works for both private and corporate clients, including the Mississippi Bar Association and the River Hills Club. She is a member of the Mississippi Craftman's Guild and a frequent contributor to art shows and galleries, crediting a lot of her success to great connections in a supportive city.

"Jackson has been fantastic," she enthuses. "We have more talent coming out of this state than any other state in the nation. You kick up some dirt in the Delta, and it becomes a museum overnight. We have visual artists, craftsmen, writers, restaurants, theaters—why would you *not* be an artist if that is what you're put on this planet to do?"

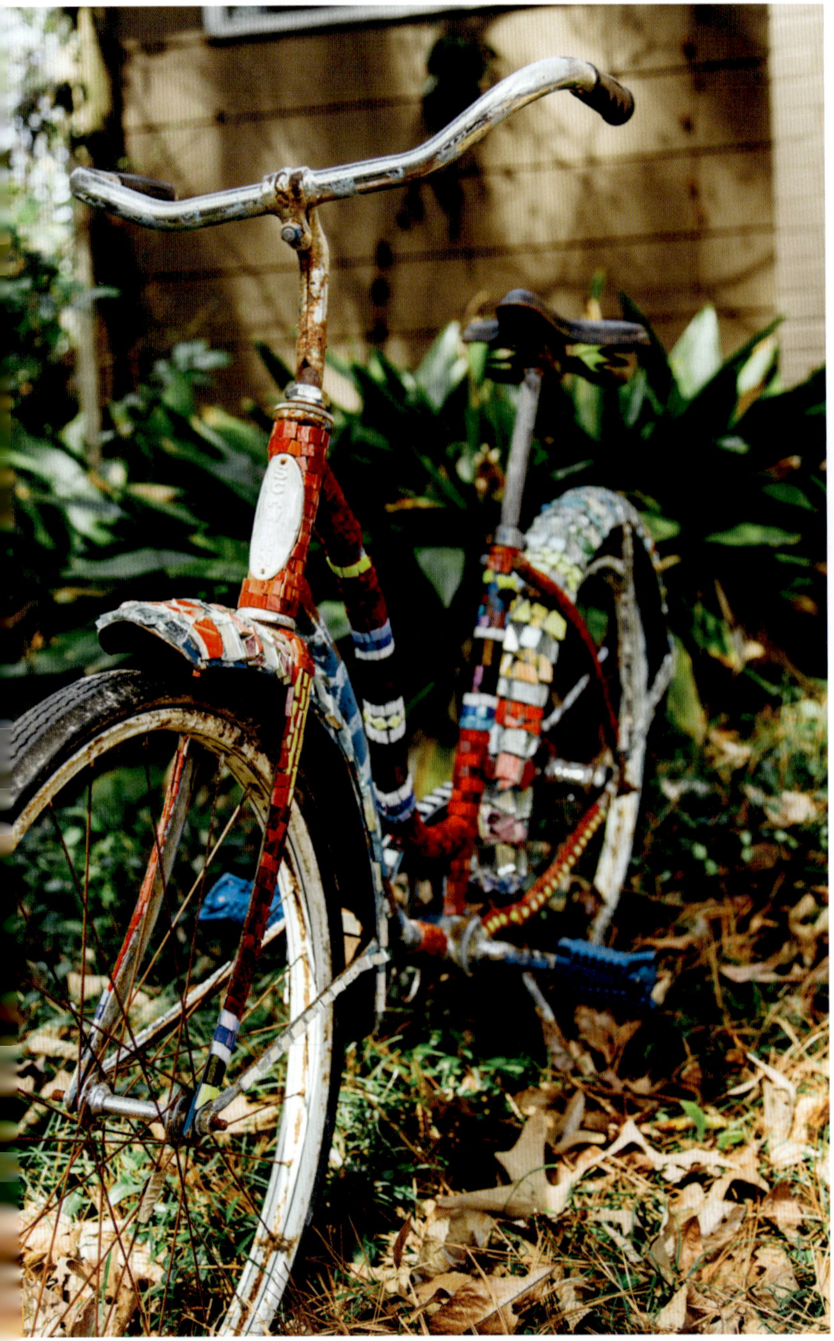

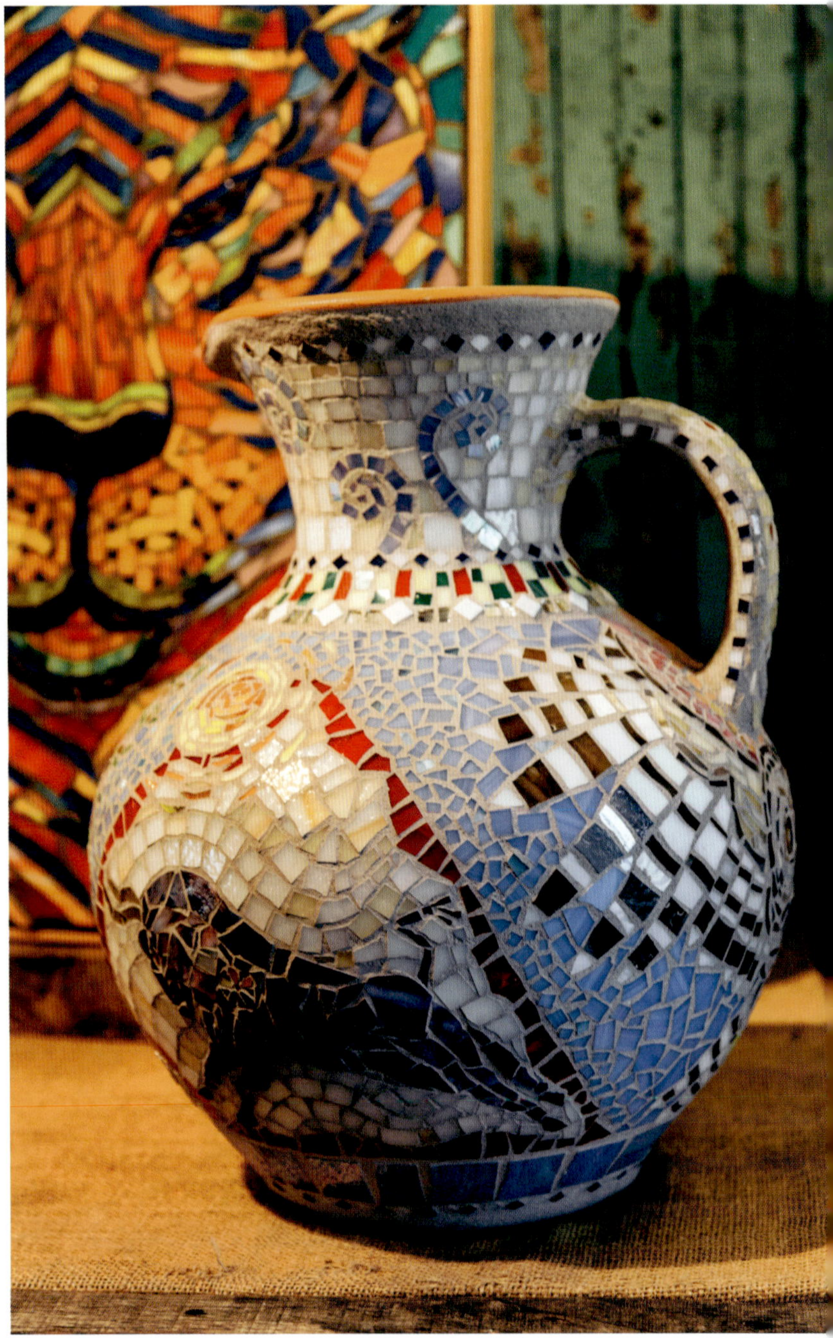

Teresa majored in geology at Millsaps College, where she worked part time in the geology lab. She sees this as a huge tie-in to the mosaic work she does today. In an attempt to switch gears from studying rocks and minerals to doing something creative with rocks and minerals, she took up stained glass, purchasing stained-glass materials and following instructions in a book. In 1996, in an effort to use up her extra glass scraps, she made the transition to mosaics.

"It was an epiphany," she gushes. "I loved the free form of mosaics."

By 2000, she was creating art in a hybrid of mosaics and stained glass. Teresa submitted some of her pieces for display at a local restaurant, Julep, and not long after, she received a life-changing phone call from glass-blowing artist Susan Ford, who wanted to buy one of Teresa's pieces. Ford not only bought Teresa's art, she took it to the Mississippi Crafts Center and showed it to members of the Craftsman's Guild of Mississippi.

"Susan gave me the encouragement to go for it," Teresa says. In 2004, Teresa was accepted into the Craftsman's Guild of Mississippi, and by 2006, she had embraced mosaics as her primary medium.

In 2006, Teresa also began teaching after Parents for Public Schools, a local activist group, contacted her about joining its arts development program. She also began teaching Introductory and Intermediate Mosaic classes as a part of the Community Enrichment Series for adults at Millsaps College, as well as a mosaic summer camp program for children at the Mississippi Crafts Center. Teresa's bright personality and enthusiasm bring delight to each classroom she enters, and she finds encouragement in turn as she experiences other people "getting the buzz," as she puts it.

Opposite, left: Teresa turned this bicycle into a mosaic yard sculpture.

Opposite, right: Teresa's mosaic jug is a modern interpretation of the ancient Grecian urn.

At Home and at Work

Teresa's home is a wealth of inspiration; it is a mosaic wonderland vaguely reminiscent of Cuban artist José Fuster's mosaic paradise. All of her bathrooms boast mosaic patterns, and her rooms contain her artwork and mosaic furniture. Her front yard is a garden layered with mosaics, from birdbaths to steppingstones, and she jokes that she had bottle trees before they became "cool." Her imaginative employment of her mosaics as yard art has made an impact already; she has been invited to address the Garden Club of Jackson, where she shared various ways to incorporate art into a garden. She has become so well known in the community that occasionally people will drop off boxes of mosaic supplies—tiles, broken ceramics, mismatched sets of dishes—in her driveway, a practice she adores because finding the right materials to break down into mosaic tiles is the basis of her entire craft.

"You have to be a scrapper to know how to direct your energies," Teresa explains of her creative process.

Scavenging, repurposing and "knowing how to ask for castoff items" are all part of Teresa's work; her studio contains dozens of coffee mugs, stacks of plates and saucers, broken pieces of fine china that others would have cast aside and boxes of broken glass.

Once Teresa selects a palette, she starts laying the pieces of tile and glass, which takes the most time.

"I don't even want to think about how many pieces of glass I've laid," she says. "Probably over a million."

Depending on the size and intricacy of a design, a creation can take up to two weeks to finish. Her studio is equipped with different work areas and task lighting, since tiling a birdbath, for example, requires a completely different space and process than laying tile for a piece of fine art. In her fine artwork—which she shows at Fischer Gallery in Jackson, Mississippi, and at the Attic Gallery in Vicksburg, Mississippi—Teresa is experimenting with using mosaic tile in the same way digital imagery uses pixilation. She completed a self-portrait in this style, and she hopes to do an entire series of subjects in this way to form a new body of work.

"If you step back, you see the image differently," she demonstrates, moving away from her self-portrait, which she keeps hanging in the "gallery" room at her home. Sure enough, from a distance the portrait smoothes out, but up close, it is composed of hundreds of tiny tiles.

Creative Economy

In 2010, a divorce pushed Teresa into a difficult decision: seek full-time employment or risk losing her house. Teresa took a job with the Mississippi Arts Commission (MAC), knowing that she would return to her artwork full time as soon as she was able. For the following three years, she worked as Malcom White's assistant, which gave her otherwise inaccessible insight into the backbone of Mississippi's creative economy. One of her first projects at the MAC was writing about the creative economy, and Teresa was obviously in a unique position.

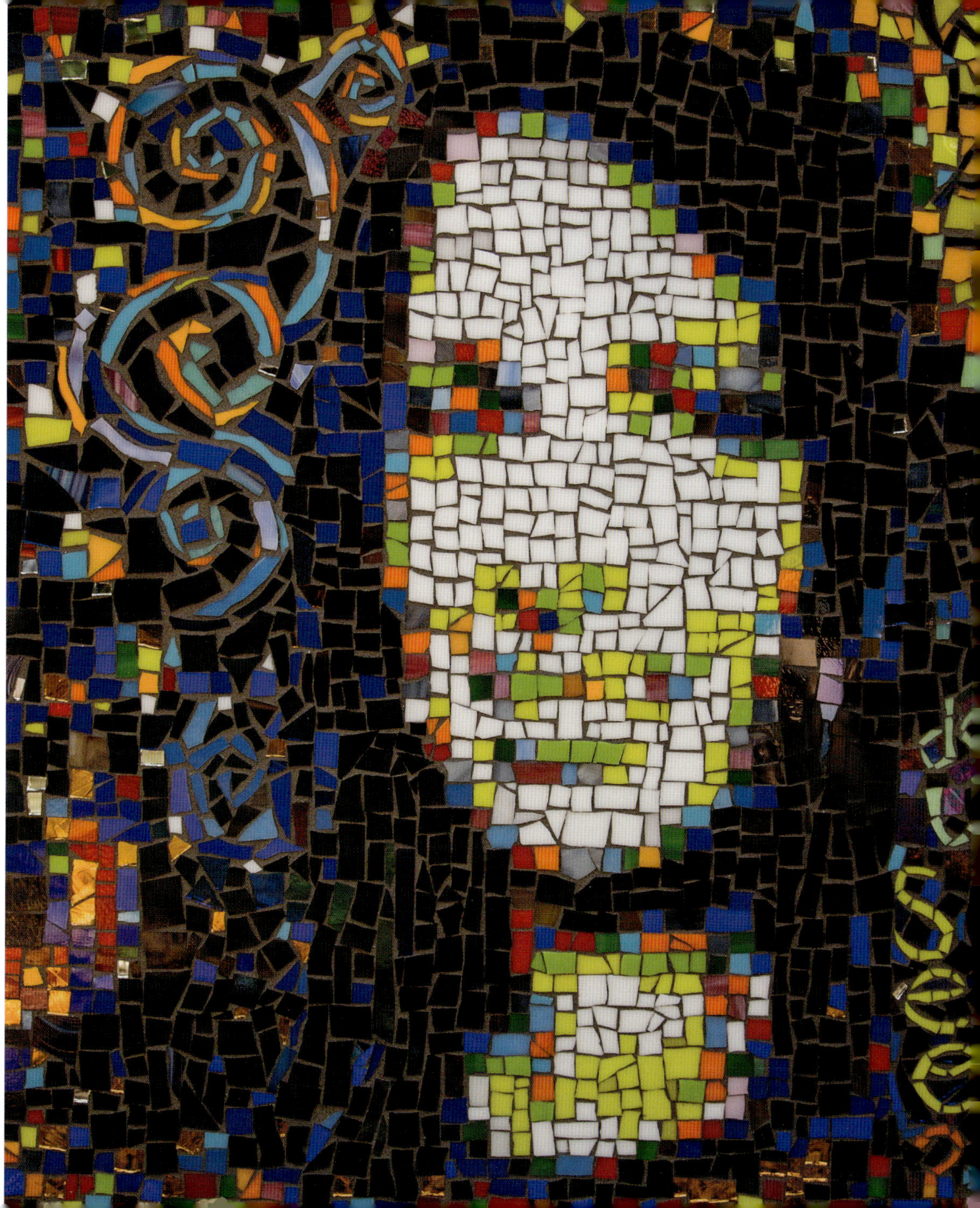

Teresa's mosaic self-portrait is designed the same way photographs use pixilation to create an image

"Members of the creative economy are the creative army," she says. "It's important that we see ourselves with value, and it's wonderful to know that people aren't saying, 'Oh, they are just an artist.'"

In 2010, Teresa witnessed the MAC form a partnership with the Mississippi Development Authority (MDA). Teresa knew that the announcement of 2014 as the Year of the Creative Economy in Mississippi might be received with mixed-reactions, even misunderstood. She maintains that although all sixty thousand members of the creative class may not feel the effects of this declaration immediately, by calling 2014 the Year of the Creative Economy, the governor is giving creatives "a lot of platform value."

"We are learning to see that creatives are an asset to our economy," she relates. "I see [all of us] in the future looking back on this year and saying, 'Wow.'"

In 2013, Teresa resumed her career as a full-time artist, knowing she was saying goodbye to a steady source of income.

"I would rather live ragtag not knowing what's in the future and figuring it out as I go along instead of the steady paychecks," she says.

Teresa has always felt that Jackson contained a community of artists. By appreciating and respecting all individuals in creative lines of work, Teresa believes that a collective self-esteem is established, allowing others to pursue their dreams. To an outsider, this may sound hokey, but Teresa's brief but poignant foray into government work allowed her the chance to see the picture from both sides of the frame. She honestly believes that by joining together, creatives gain respect.

"It is all about promoting one another," says Teresa of life among her fellow artists. "We all feel like we're on the same team. I love to collaborate with other artists on shows and projects. I love to be in a community of like-minded individuals, and I'm happy when another artist sells a piece because I catch their happiness," she smiles. "We share this common dirt. This is us."

15

WILLIAM GOODMAN

William Goodman is an abstract mixed-media painter. William is known for his large-scale murals, which are focal points of Mississippi institutions, including Viking Corporation and the Mississippi Museum of Art. His work has been featuring in *New American Paintings* and *Blue Canvas* magazine and is part of many corporate and museum collections throughout the United States. A Jackson native, William grew up in the Belhaven neighborhood, attended boarding school in Virginia and art school in North Carolina and returned to Jackson to live and work in his early twenties. For three years, William served as the creative director at the Mustard Seed, a home for mentally disabled adults. In 2004, he decided to

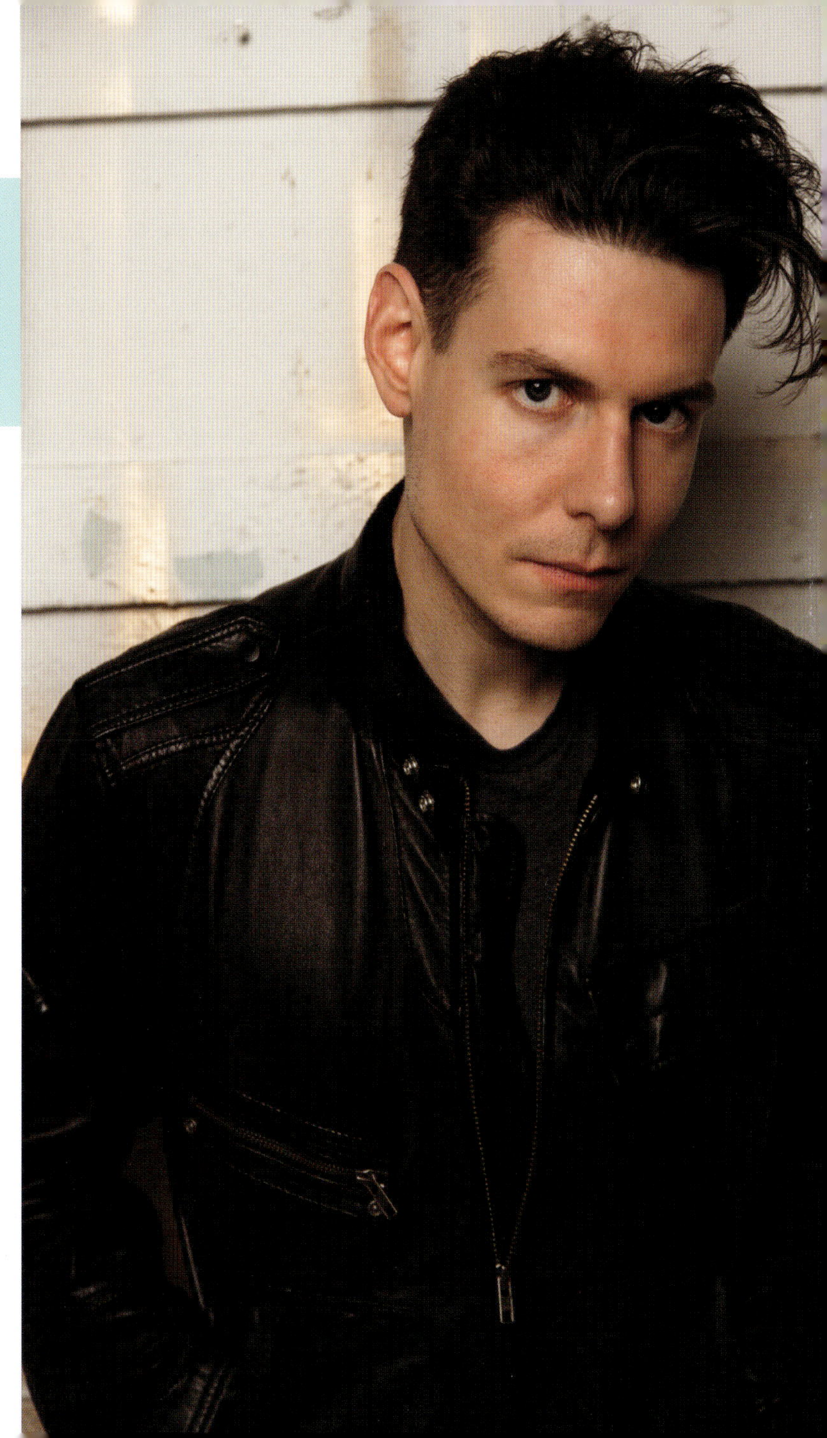

William Goodman shown in his Fondren studio.

try making art full time and see if he could live off his earnings. If he failed, he figured he could always find another job.

Colonizing Fondren

Early in his career, William was influential in establishing the arts culture in the Fondren neighborhood. William has worked in a studio at the Fondren Corner Building since Peters Real Estate renovated the building in 2003. He vividly recalls the renovation, which created what he describes as a multitude of "creative pockets" within the building, which eventually expanded into the Fondren neighborhood. His stepmother, Tommie Goodman, first told William about the renovation when she was contemplating moving her interior design business and furniture store onto the first floor.

"Tommie told me, 'Fondren is on a rise; lots of people are moving their businesses there,'" William remembers. "I went to looked at apartments, and when they finished, I was one of the first residents to move in."

William was quickly joined by a host of bright young residents who moved into apartments and studios in the building, including Ginger Williams-Cook, Josh Hailey and Jason Marlow.

"Fondren was such a fresh canvas," William recalls. "Looking back on it, I didn't notice it at the time, but other people realized that there was some new energy in Fondren. People were starting to take note."

In September 2003, William, Ginger and Twiggy collaborated on their first job together: creating art for Walker's Drive-In, Fondren's iconic fine dining location. Dubbing themselves the "Projectors," the team completed a mural together that launched them into years of creative collaborations. Over the next decade in Fondren, new businesses blossomed, and artists such as Chane, Elizabeth Robinson, Ron Blaylock and James Patterson eventually colonized the neighborhood.

"It quickly became all of us hanging out together all the time, bouncing ideas off one another," William remembers. "There was this energy that was definitely starting to take shape. At first, I don't know if people took us at all seriously—it was more experimental than anything."

Before long, the connection between local businesses and artists truly emerged in Fondren. It was a positive time in the arts world. William recalls that there was always something creative happening; "art parties," shows and businesses moving to Fondren and hiring local artists to design murals, signs and art—the more outrageous, the better. Hiring an artist was a point of pride for business owners, in part, William says, because "everyone wanted to be a part of the art community."

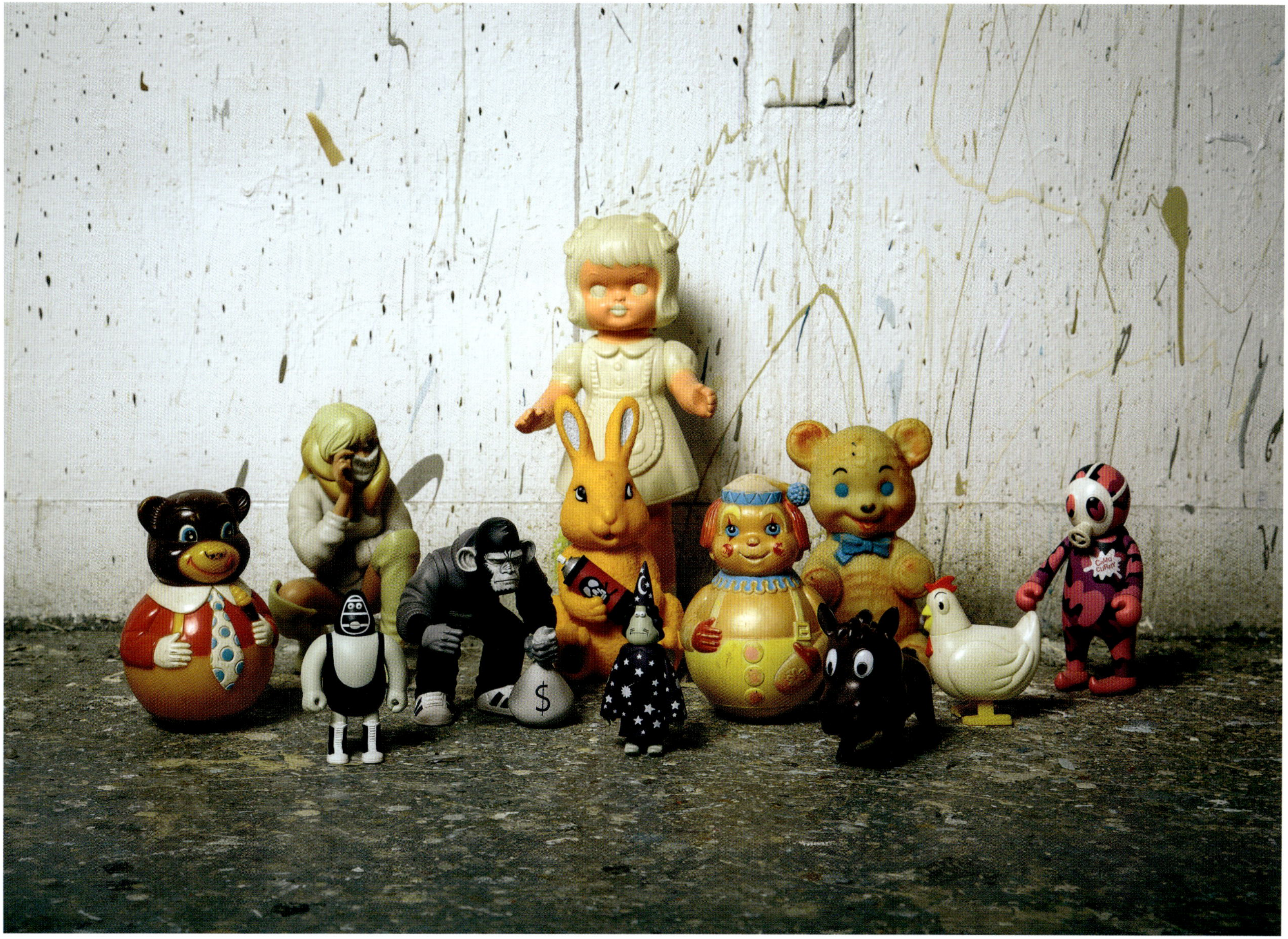

William's toy collection has grown substantially over the years and inspired an entire series of paintings.

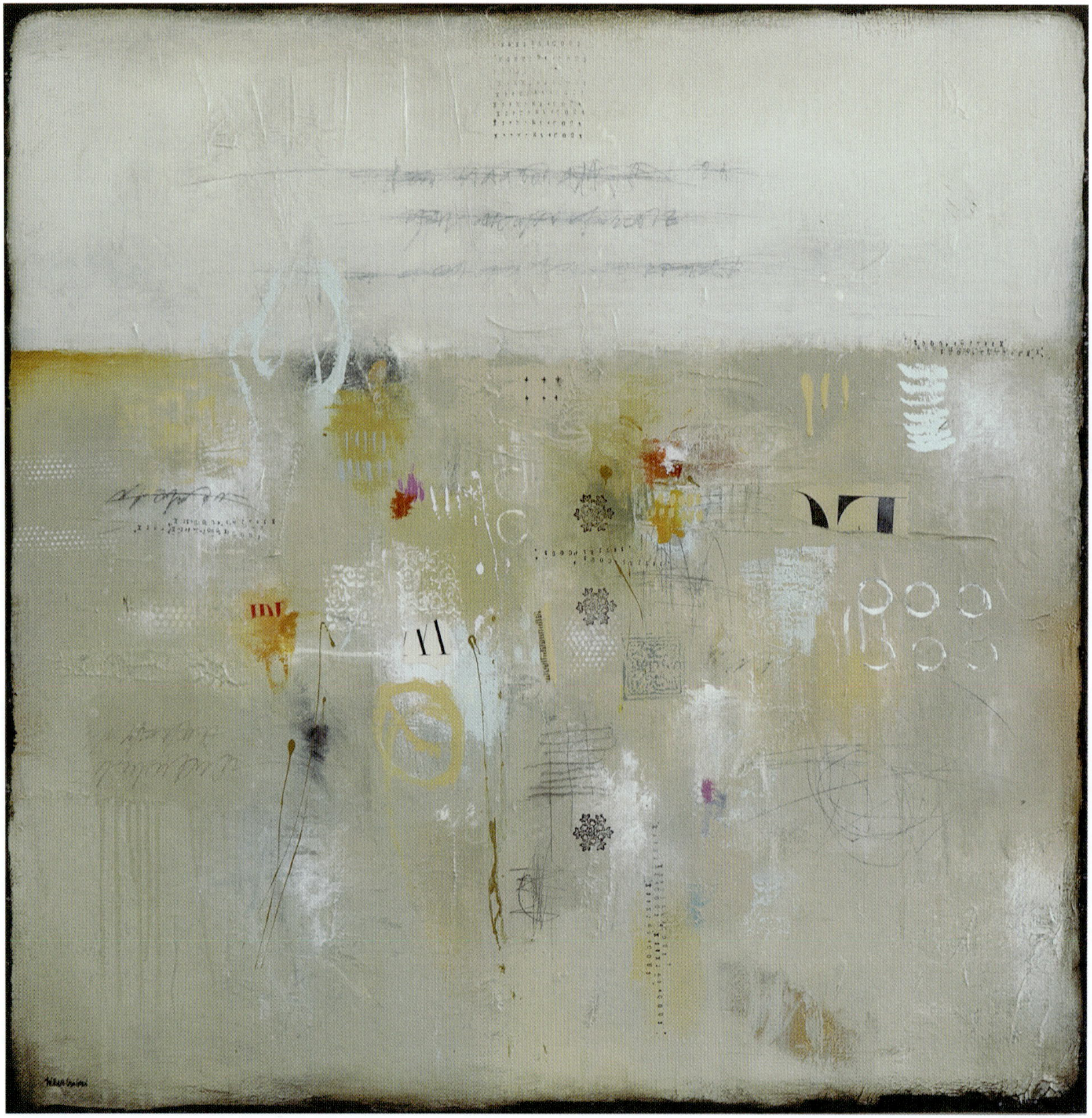

Quantum Relativity #1 by William Goodman.

In addition to his work in Fondren, William sent his fine art to galleries across the United States and began to show his work everywhere from Chicago to New York to Washington, D.C. He found that he could travel regularly while still living in Jackson, although he struggled when watching some of his friends move on to bigger cities to explore their art.

"There have been times when I have gotten fed up, wondering, 'How long can I keep doing what I am doing here?'" he admits. "But it is more economical for me to live somewhere that I can afford to do my work full time where rent is not sky high. A lot of people don't realize you take yourself wherever you go."

Instead of moving to a larger city, William joined Ginger Williams-Cook to live in Paris for a few months in 2007. They created a body of work together, and both of them returned to Jackson right before the beginning of the economic recession in 2008. The recession blindsided many Jackson businesses, ushering in a wave of closures and moves. Max Furniture was among many businesses to close completely, and others downsized or relocated out of Fondren. The Fondren art community, in turn, took a hit.

"I didn't necessarily feel the recession at first," William admits. "I had always had steady work, always had enough. Then sales slowed, then they didn't happen and, by 2009, galleries across the nation were closing and dropping me. Before the recession, I had done what I always wanted to do and didn't have to look at my art as running a business."

With seven years under his belt, William was forced to make adjustments. He found that making paintings with a "more versatile appeal" was preferable to making the type of work he describes as "more experimental." Abstract paintings were easier to sell than figurative mixed-media pieces, so in order to survive the recession, William turned his attention to creating very sellable work.

In 2009, William contacted his friend Marcy Fischer Nessel about opening an art gallery in Fondren that would feature modern art and sculpture. Marcy opened Fischer Gallery that year and began showing the work of Jackson artists, as well as the work of artists from other cities and states. William believes that Fischer Gallery connects clients on a local level, which is important for the city of Jackson.

"Art is all about attitude and perspective. Creative, deep and enriching things are here in Mississippi; you just have to look for it. Maybe Jackson is not inspiring, but something is keeping people here. The art community is very supportive. I am refreshed by a constant sense of support," he says.

"I think that it's wonderful that the creative economy is being celebrated and recognized.

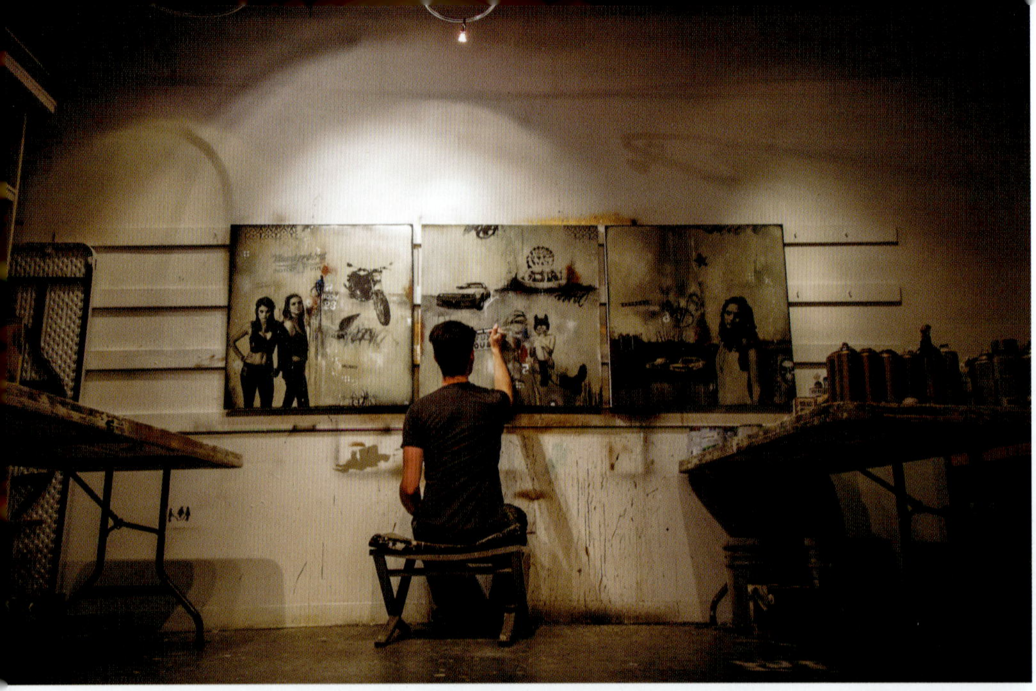

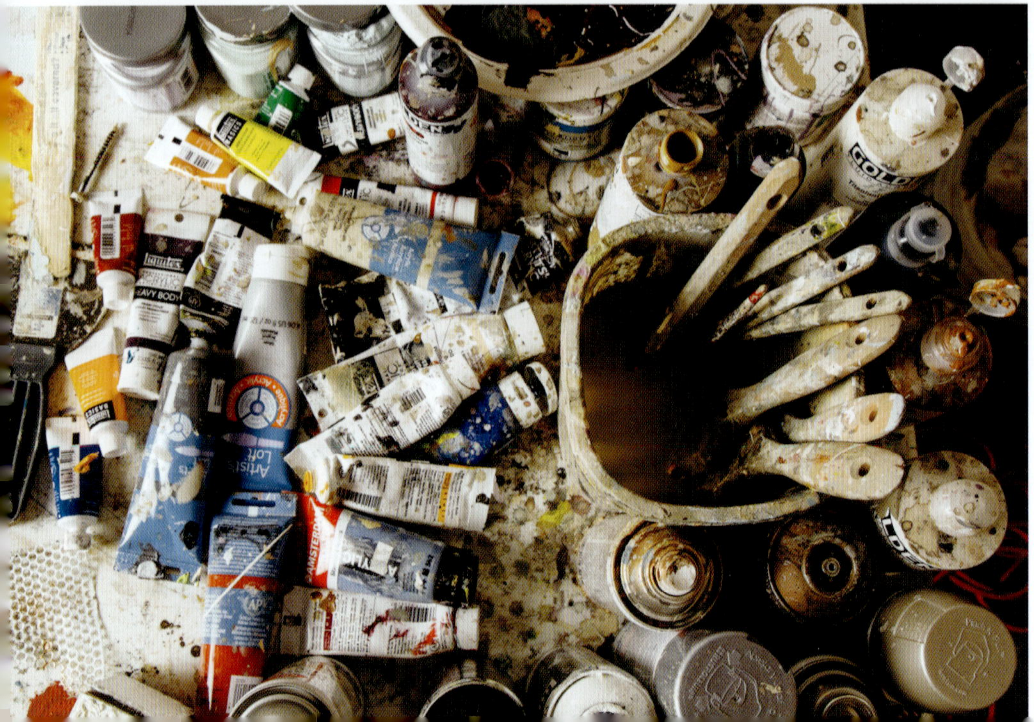

Artists in Mississippi don't get enough credit outside of our state, and when people find out about us, they are shocked. Really, it's not that shocking. We all feed off one another's creative energy, and it's a great thing to be part of."

In the Studio

William's studio space today is an evolution of the last decade of his work. In the beginning of his professional career, William painted in his Fondren apartment, eventually moving to a studio space on the fifth floor. He expanded his studio in 2008 to include more space for painting, track lighting and storage for his growing collection of retro toys.

Top: William's studio features track lighting and tables he can easily rearrange as he varies his styles of work.

Left: An array of paints and brushes form the chaotic base of what becomes a William Goodman mixed-media painting

"I don't see moving out of Fondren unless I were able to build a studio space with natural light that was even larger," William relates. "I enjoy being in this space. There's a lot of history here."

Although William no longer lives in the Fondren Corner Building, it serves as a reminder of all the creativity of early Fondren. He decorates the walls of his studio with pieces of art he collaborated on with local artists. Some of the walls of the studio feature small graffiti logos—"tags"—left by visitors and friends.

In addition to his collection of toys, William also collects vintage magazines, which he uses in his mixed-media paintings and collage work. He has hundreds of the old magazines on shelves in his studio.

"I started collecting magazines [when] one of my mother's cousins gave me her old collection of *Seventeen* magazines that she had saved from childhood," he explains.

William gradually expanded the collection of magazines, finding a lot of them on an abandoned property and on Craigslist.

"It's amazing how many magazines people save. I found one man with an old collection of *Playboys* from the 1960s and 1970s. I think he was sad to have to sell them, but his wife was pretty happy to see them go."

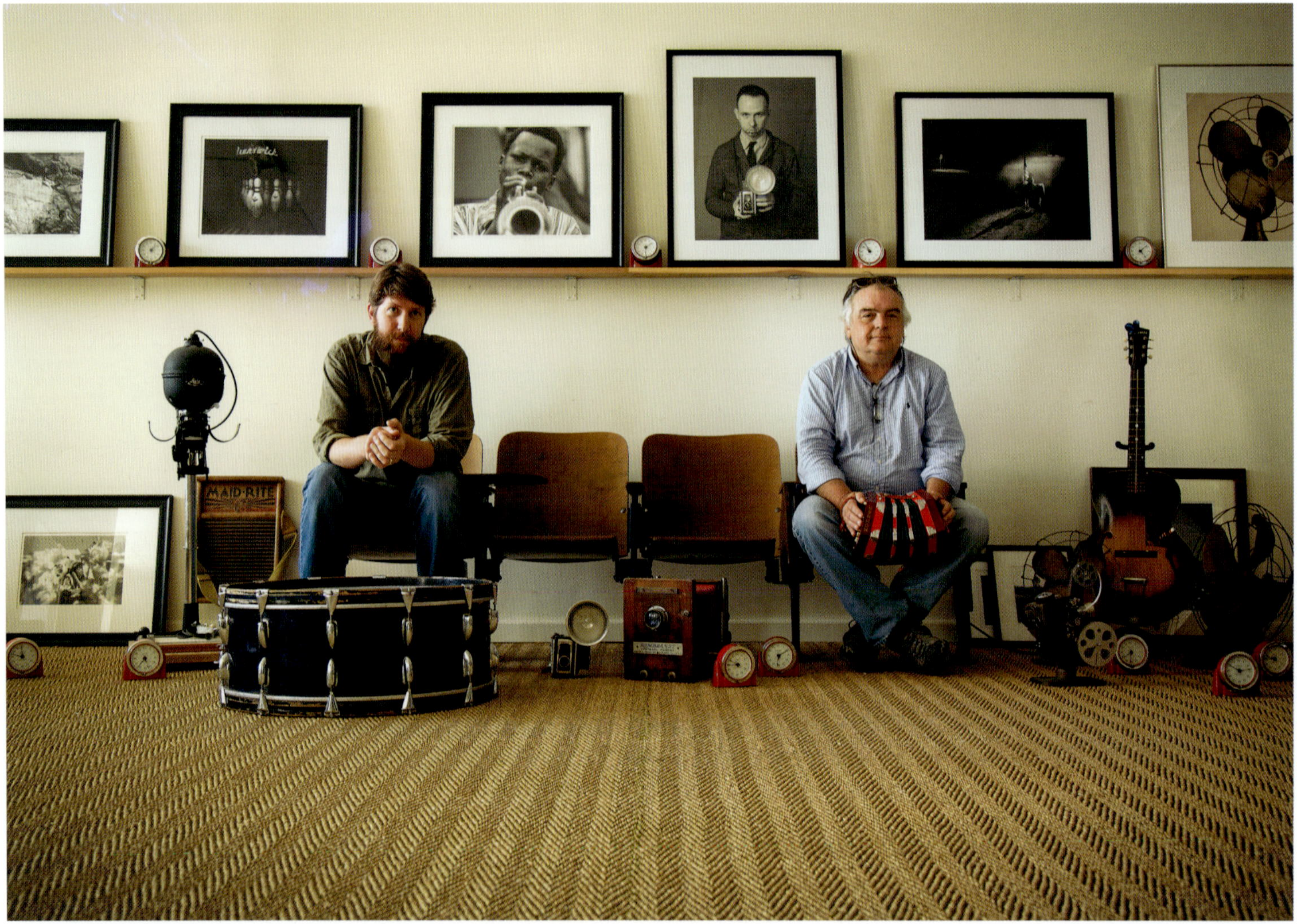

Ron Blaylock (left) and James Patterson (right) work in their Fondren studio.

16

JAMES PATTERSON AND RON BLAYLOCK

For the past decade, James Patterson's photography studio has occupied a prominent storefront on North State Street in Fondren, and for the last four years, he has shared the space with photographer Ron Blaylock, a Mississippi native who lived in New Orleans for years prior to Hurricane Katrina. In the decade prior to his move to Fondren, James owned and managed Gallery 119 in downtown Jackson, showing the work of many artists.

In the gallery space of their studio today, Ron and James show their fine art prints. James has spent twenty-five years photographing artists in Mississippi. He has also extensively documented the rodeo in Jackson and has worked on a series of photographs of an old beach motel.

Ron's photography engages the viewer in environmental landscapes. He is interested in the effect of "what humans have built and what humans have done," and he extensively photographed New Orleans in the year after Katrina.

Ron and James are the first to admit that selling fine art photography is a tricky business.

"I think one of the hard things about trying to sell art photography in Mississippi is there's little approval for photography as an art form," Ron observes.

James points out the irony, considering that one of the best-known artists from Mississippi is William Eggleston. Although James says there has been a handful of supportive collectors of fine art photography, Ron has noticed that most of his fine art prints sell out of state.

"A lot of support is the other artists," Ron adds. "I think a lot of people who really appreciate fine art photography can't afford it."

Instead of selling his work to other artists, Ron usually ends up trading or collaborating instead.

"That's the thing about the creative class. We give back all the time," he comments.

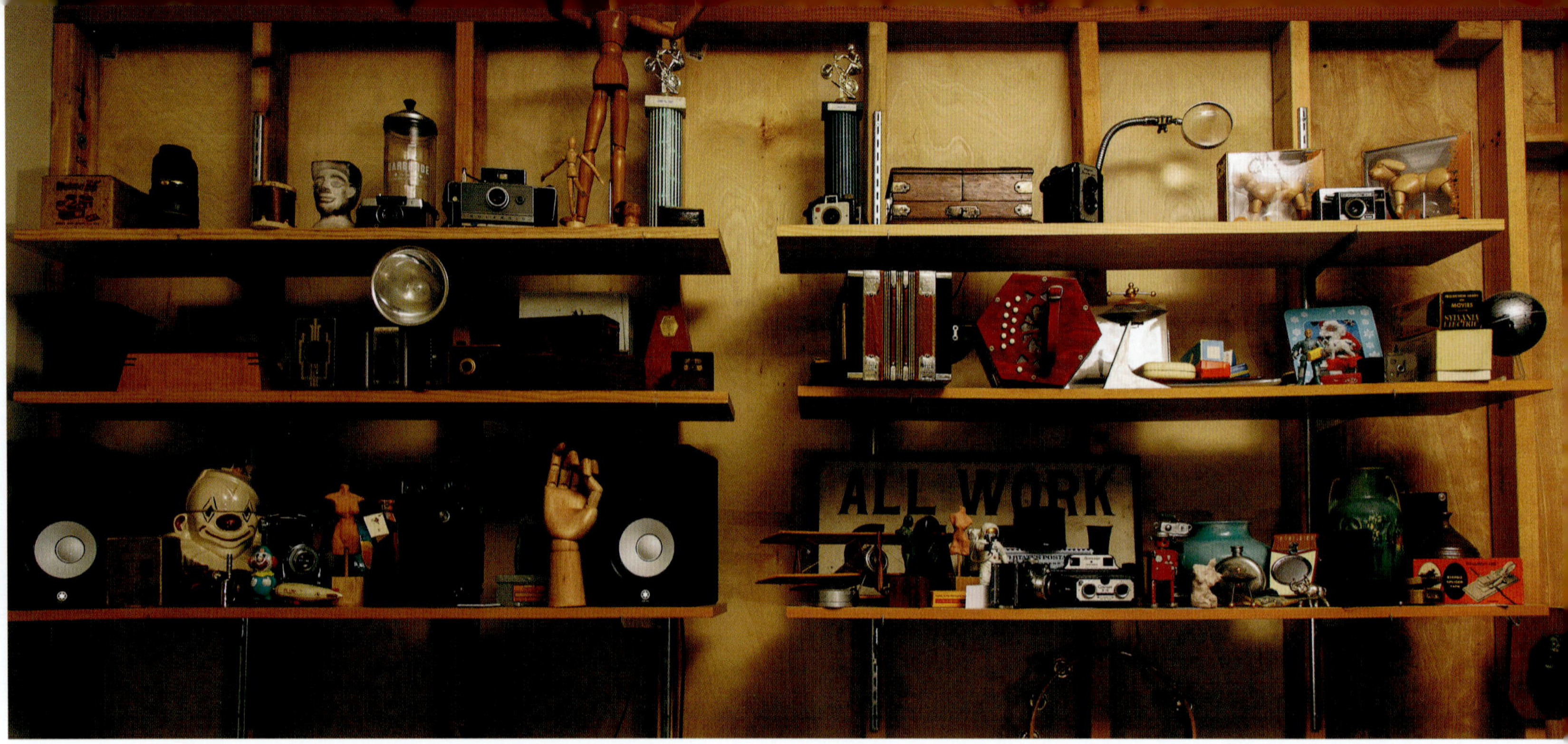

James's collection of vintage toys and Kodak timers add character to the space.

As artists, Ron and James remain interested to see the future of the creative economy in Jackson.

"If you are really going to have a campaign to push the creative economy, you need more than lip service," Ron puts forth.

James adds, "You can declare this the year of the creative economy, but I don't know that there's any grants or extra incentives."

James and Ron sustain their fine art photography by doing commercial shoots, portrait sessions and private commissions. James is a regular contributor to the *New York Times*, the *Wall Street Journal*, the *Boston Globe* and the *London Independent*, and Ron, who studied journalism and advertising at the University of Mississippi and the Rocky Mountain School of Photography, has worked for a range of corporate clients, including Viking and Entergy. They have both contributed to the *Washington Post*, as well as numerous local publications. When shooting for such clients, they have found that it is important to get into the right mindset.

"When you shoot for a magazine, you have to have a certain amount of negative space," Ron explains. "I think in a perfect world you'd approach everything like it's a piece of art."

"With photojournalism, you may have an assignment that is really vague and have to go and figure it out," Ron adds.

James chuckles, "I've been asked if I can 'run up to St. Louis' and shoot something."

With photography, James and Ron have found that the majority of people underestimate the levels of labor that go into capturing a single image.

"There's a lot of people who, from the outside, think that this is easy money," Ron points out. "It's actually a lot of work when you start putting hours to dollars."

To be a successful photographer in any capacity, James says it is crucial to think globally. He has observed how the world of photography has transformed in the digital age, and to keep up on a professional level in today's economy, photographers cannot limit themselves to film work. Mastering new technology is part of the business.

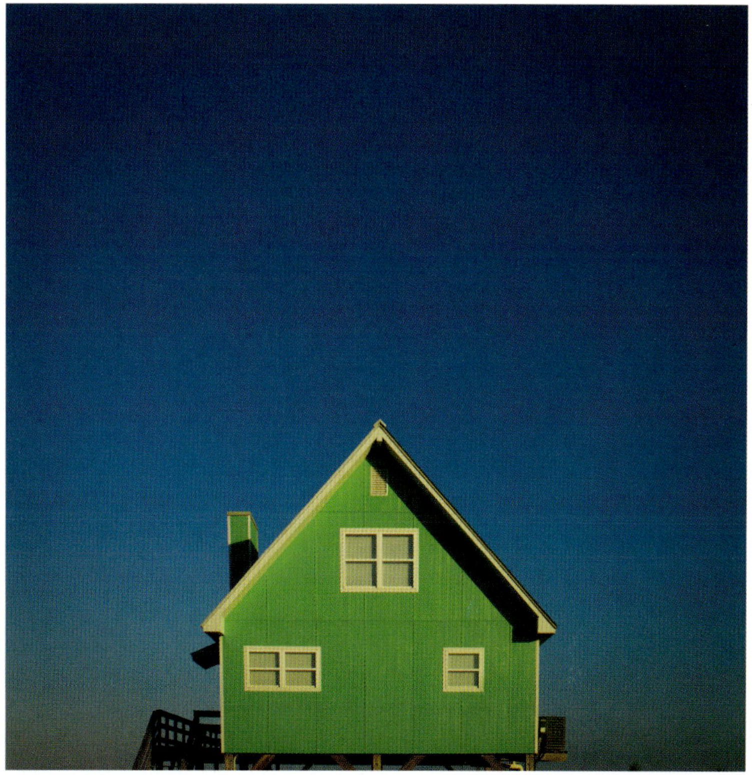

"Green and Blue." *Courtesy of James Patterson.*

"When I was growing up in photography, my best friends around the country were photographers and always supportive—it's not like that now," James says nostalgically. "If you want to get into photography, that's great, but everyone can't bring the tradition and craftsmanship to the table."

"Everybody wants it overnight," he adds with some cynicism creeping into his voice. "The film and paper I loved to use aren't even available anymore."

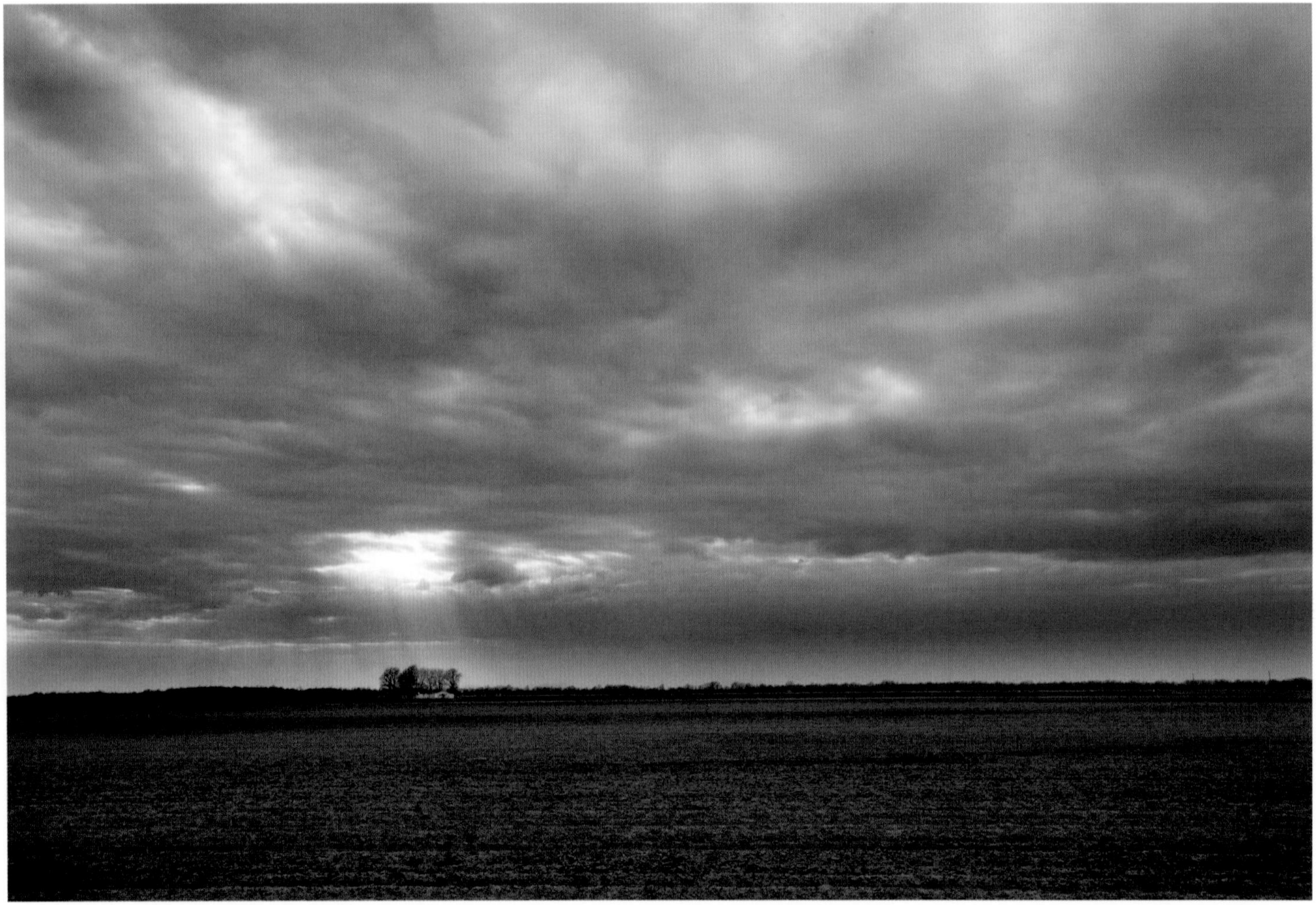

"Spotlight." *Courtesy of Ron Blaylock.*

Ron has noticed how technology has changed the precision of professional photography.

"When you learn shooting with film and printing in the darkroom, a mistake is very costly—you had to be a lot more careful and learn it like a craft," he explains.

"You covered your ass," James agrees. "And it's still a process on the computer. It takes as much time working digitally."

Ron agrees.

"We lament the end of film, but we're at an end where what some people are able to do with digital manipulation is an art unto itself," he clarifies.

Social media has also changed the way people view photography.

"I like Instagram," Ron admits. "But I am not trying to put anything serious on Instagram."

James remains cynical about many aspects of social media, although he uses Facebook.

"So much of social media is 'you are what you say you are,'" James posits. "The thing I always liked about art in general is that you put it in front of someone, instead of saying what you are, you actually are what you are."

Additionally, they have noticed how the trend of "street photography" has changed the way that people view having their picture taken.

People used to be open to being randomly photographed, they recall, whereas now, people are concerned that they might end up on the Internet, "the butt of some joke."

Even when Blaylock and Patterson are on an assignment from a major publication, they have run into trouble. They believe that the fear of terrorism may be part of the problem; they've been questioned before when photographing bridges or federal buildings.

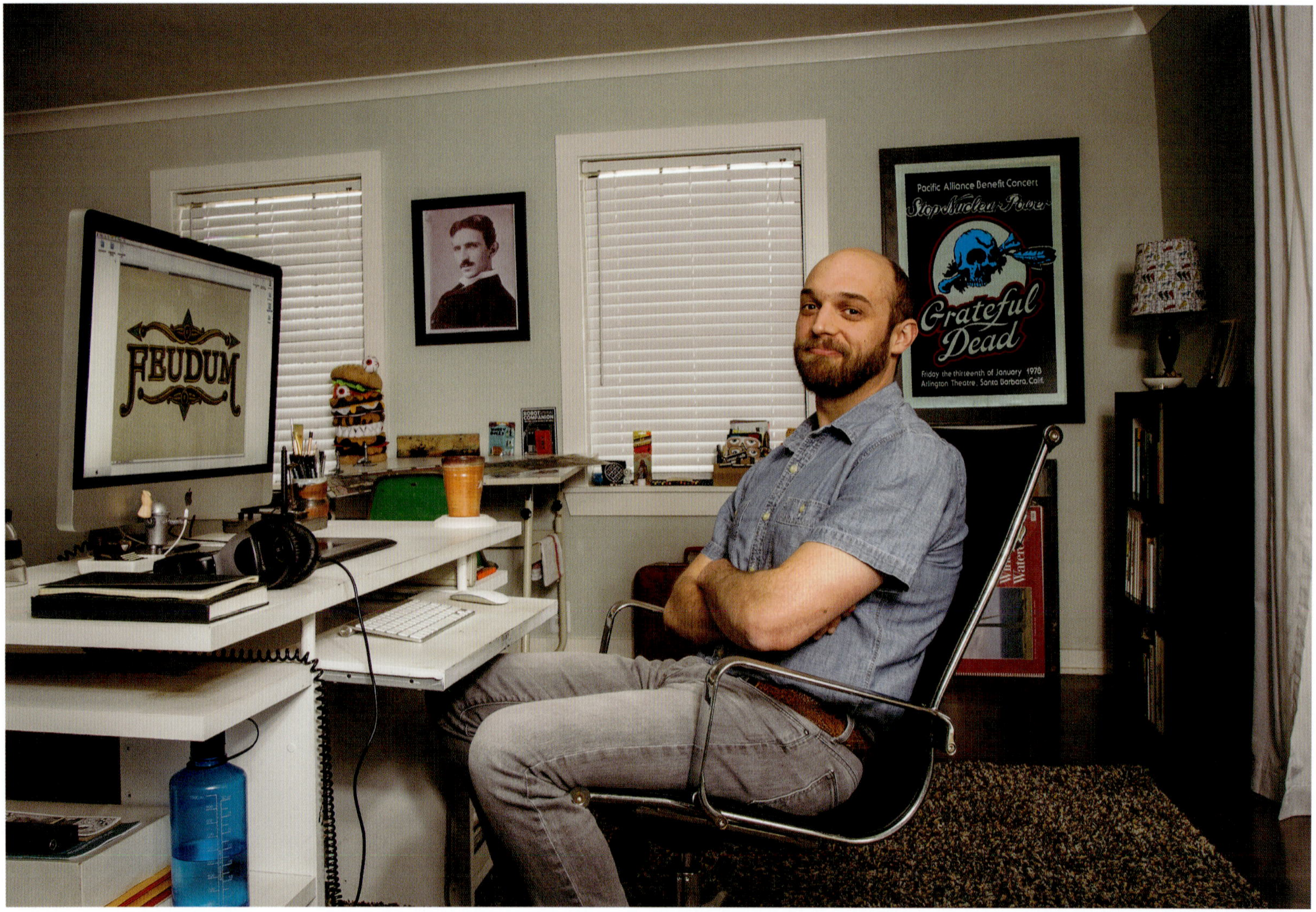

Justin Schultz is pictured in his studio.

17
JUSTIN SCHULTZ

Justin Schultz is working on a board game.

Schultz, a freelance graphic design artist and illustrator with a passion for working with small business owners, is known for his concert posters, which incorporate his signature imaginative illustrations and bright colors. One of his concert posters made its way from Schultz's home in Jackson, Mississippi, to Missouri, and Schultz found himself receiving an e-mail about a commission job designing imagery for a German-European-style board game called Feudum. The subject line of the e-mail was "a guy with a dream."

In the age of social media, the way that the board game creator discovered Schultz sounds old fashioned. Schultz describes himself as "cynical" about social media and calls his graphic design website the Flying Chair to avoid advertising his own name.

"The great thing about art is that it speaks for itself," Schultz observes. "You don't have to convince anybody. They can look at your portfolio, and it's very organic."

A graphic design major at Mississippi State University, Schultz cut his teeth in the design world working for notable Jackson businesses, including the Godwin Group, Cellular South (now C Spire) and Liquid Creative Marketing Agency. He enjoyed corporate work but also craved the freedom of self-employment. Schultz is attracted to projects that a corporate advertising agency might find a little odd and wanted time to pursue personal projects.

"I had this realization that I can help local small companies and friends," Schultz explains.

For the past five years, Schultz has been steadily self-employed, though he jokes—perhaps only halfway—that things can get scary when "you're surviving solely off your art."

Schultz has been fortunate to benefit from word-of-mouth marketing, or what he calls "the southern attitude and love of talking."

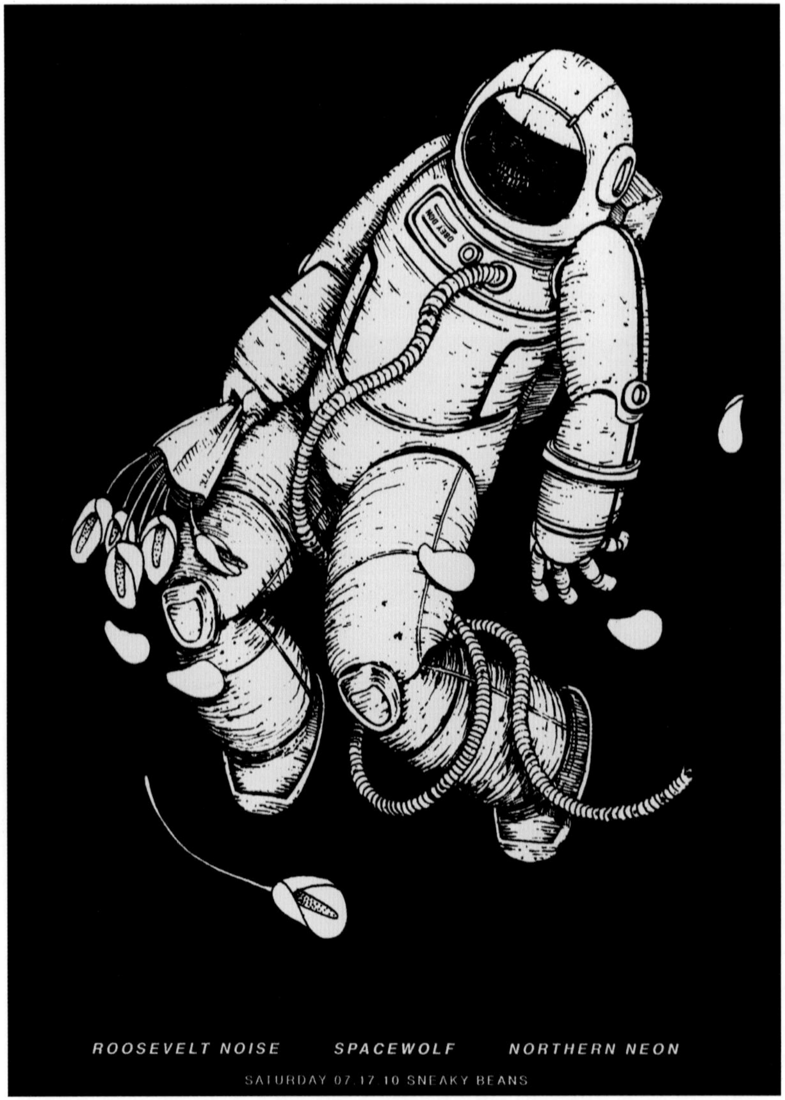

He has worked with a variety of small businesses, creating posters, designs, art and advertisements for clients such as Lemuria Bookstore, Bean Fruit Coffee, Cathead Vodka and *Mississippi Magazine*.

"I am really surprised by the support I get from the local community," says Schultz proudly. "In a bigger city, networking and connecting would be a challenge."

Schultz's work may originate in Jackson, but it is far reaching. For the past eight years, he has designed concert posters for bands across the nation, sometimes contacting bands as they tour through Mississippi and offering to create their unique concert posters for the Mississippi show.

When creating a concert poster, Schultz allows the music to speak to his illustrative style.

"I will literally take lyrics and create a scene from those lyrics, or it may be inspired [by] a random feeling evoked from the music," he says of the creative process.

Overall, Schultz says that about half his work is for corporate clients, bands and small businesses. The other half of his time is dedicated to his fine artwork.

A concert poster Justin designed in 2010 for a show featuring three Jackson bands.

In the Studio

Schultz's design process begins at home. He works out of his home studio in northeast Jackson, where he lives with his cat, Noren. The layout of his home and studio are very precise and organized; his walls are lined with books and posters, and old-school inspiration shines through his collection of midcentury furniture and objects of curiosity. His studio is flooded with natural light, with his computer desk in the very center of the room. Justin listens to music with large headphones while he works and prefers that the rest of the house remains quiet. He enjoys working in his home, though he knows that the home studio does not work for everyone.

"It would get out of control for me if I didn't focus," Schultz explains. "The whole reason that people have studios away from home is to step away and come back, feel movement and progression. It's cliché, but life is art. I like to be saturated in it. So the home office works for me."

Schultz is focused on finding his muse in everyday life—he looks to music and science to tap into a child-like creativity that is influenced by the work of Alphonse Mucha, Robert Crumb, Ralph Steadman, Jim Henson and Wayne White. Schultz describes his work as "cluttered," but it isn't, per se: it is busy and colorful, yes, but also very detailed and precise. Schultz acknowledges that he has tried to "stay child-like" in his creativity, sometimes surprising himself with his own creations.

"My [personal] style [of artwork] is not my favorite style, but it's what comes out [of me] so I don't fight it," he says, adding that while he often uses the colors sea-foam green, teal and hot pink, "I wouldn't even consider those my favorite colors."

Schultz thinks that color should be the "result of emotion trying to be evoked" rather than a direct representation of reality. He finds that music influences his color palate.

"Colors can control people's feelings," he asserts. "Think about a fast-food restaurant: the colors are red and yellow to get your heart rate up and get you in and out of there. A classroom or a hospital is a calming light blue."

Interestingly, Schultz's bedroom features blank walls and neutral colors, "a visual break of sorts," he explains.

"I don't think I could ever stop doing concert posters, and music is just this major quality of life to me," Schultz says. "It's amazing to me how much I'm pulled to music. Music is a very strong form of art. [It is a way] to be able to directly speak your feelings and evoke emotions through the actual work itself."

Schultz splits his time between doing corporate commissions and his fine artwork. He finds the two types of work to be very different, though his method of creating is the same:

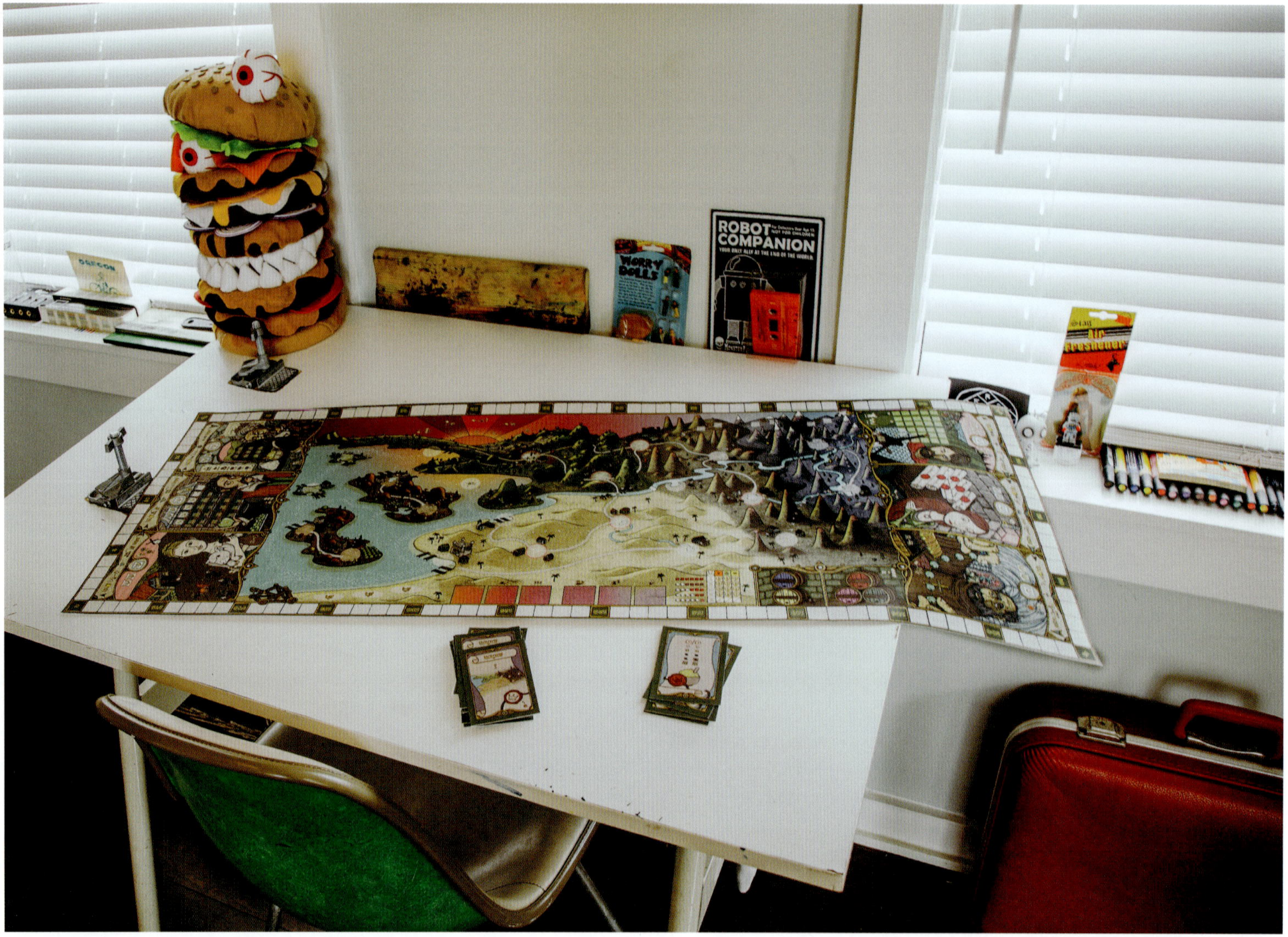

Justin's studio is filled with objects he has collected and created, including the plush hamburger puppet and his current project, the board game Fuedum.

almost all his work is done on the computer using the Wacom graphic tablet, a perk of the digital age.

"I've learned to accept that the computer is a tool just like any other tool—paint, chalk, pencils. All [the computer] will do is open up more doors," he says. "Fine art is more difficult because of the openness," he explains. "Fine art is very intentional. My [corporate work] isn't abstract. The message has to be there."

Living in Jackson

Schultz's commitment to the Jackson community extends far beyond his business connections.

"The music scene is a unifier for the artistic community," he says.

Schultz lived in Jackson's Fondren neighborhood for a while but says he never really identified with one particular Jackson neighborhood, preferring instead to be a social "floater." He believes that a creative economy can originate in a creative community, citing Nashville and Austin as examples.

"[Nashville or Austin] show that a creative community can create a creative economy. If people support the arts, it becomes a more interesting city," Schultz says. He goes on:

> *Mississippi is a unique place for positive and negative reasons. Creativity is parallel with uniqueness. Jackson goes in waves. It's a neat time to be here because we are on an upward push. Many people* [in the arts] *want to be saturated with music and culture so they move to a big city. I don't blame people who have negative statements about Jackson. Maybe one day we will be one of those creative cities that people seek to move to, but then we will probably just complain about how we miss the way it used to be. The grass is always greener.*

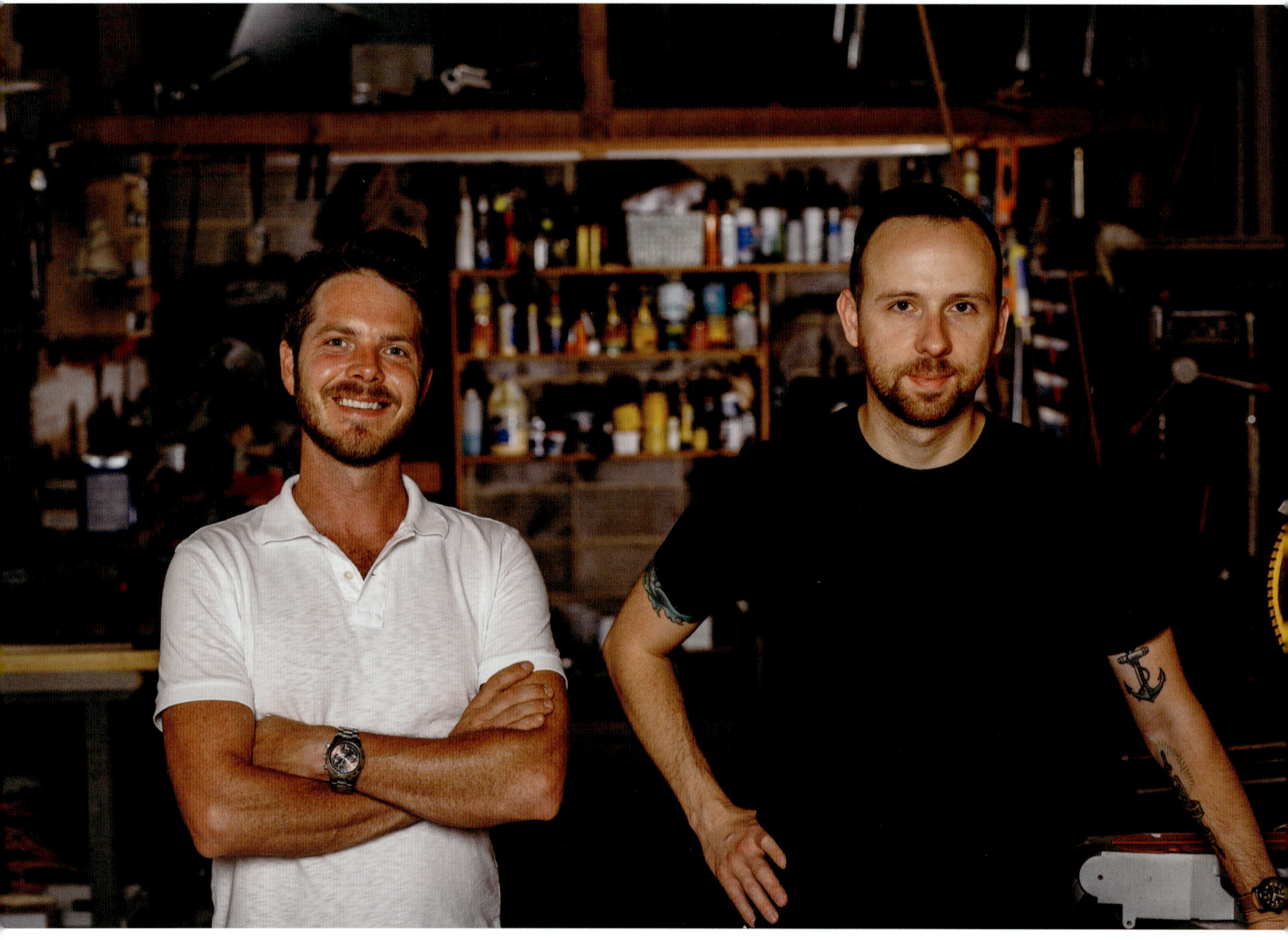

Josh Bishop (left) and Jason "Twiggy" Lott (right) work in their downtown woodshop.

18

555 CUSTOM SALVAGE DESIGNS

JASON "TWIGGY" LOTT AND JOSH BISHOP

Josh Bishop and Jason "Twiggy" Lott co-own 555 Custom Salvage Designs, a specialty furniture business focused on using salvaged items to create industrial-inspired, midcentury modern designs. Josh, who has been a builder for over fifteen years, began his career in the floral design industry, and Twiggy has a long background in fine art. With their unique blend of talent, the two have created a harmonious workshop in downtown Jackson.

Custom Salvage Business

Josh and Twiggy began building furniture together in 2013, although Josh has been a woodworker for as long as he can remember. The challenge of building furniture, however, was not something Josh wanted to do alone.

"I needed a partner with creativity, and someone to hold me accountable," Josh recalls.

Josh worked with a few other artists, including their mutual friend artist William Goodman, before he partnered with Twiggy. When Goodman's schedule pulled him away, Josh began working with Twiggy, and the two clicked immediately, relocating from Josh's garage to a warehouse space in downtown Jackson near Twiggy's Belhaven apartment. There they could focus on what they call their "individual and collective vision." Twiggy brings an artistic vision to their designs while Josh's experience in the construction industry offers technical knowledge, specifically when it comes to power tools.

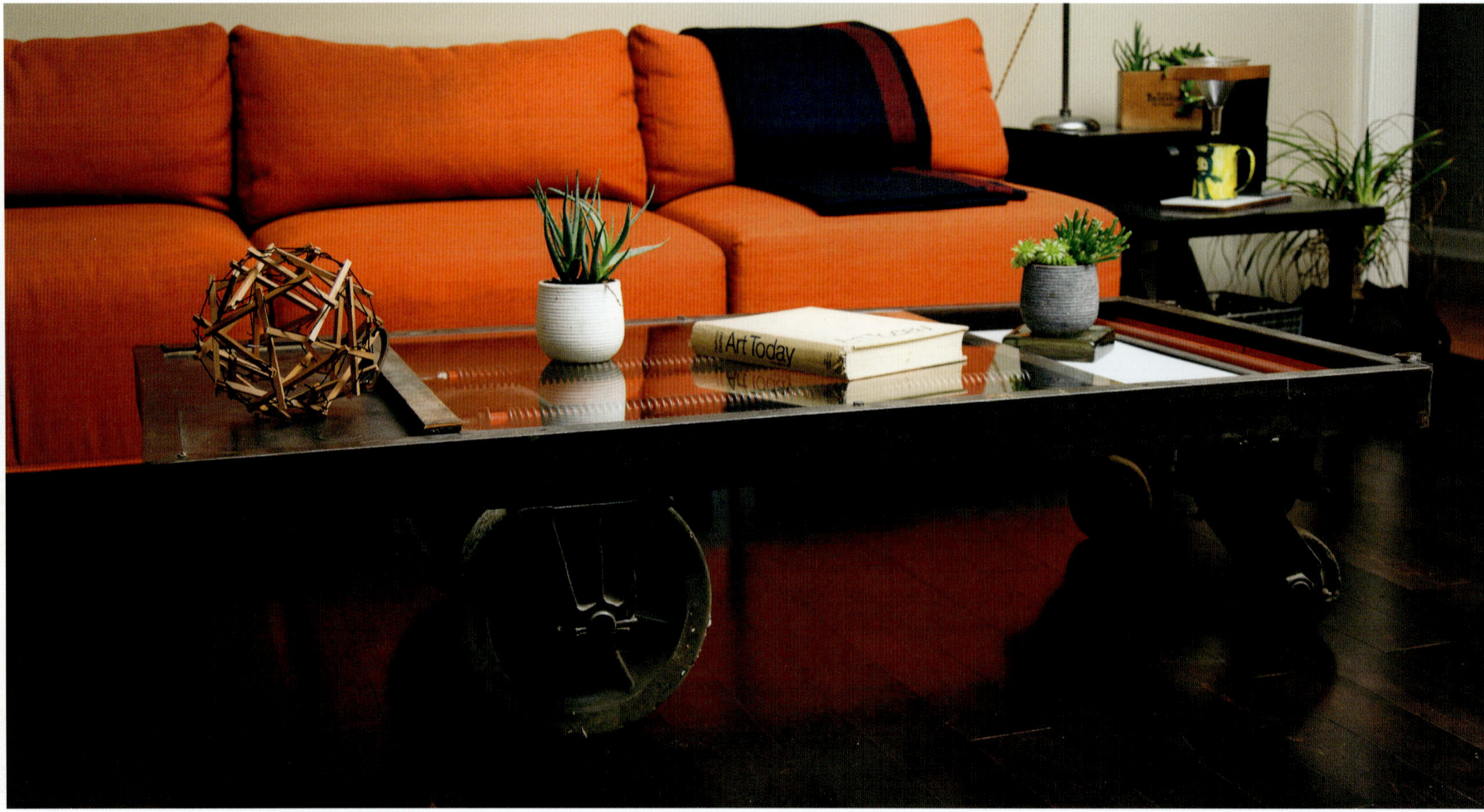

So far, Twiggy and Josh have found that Jackson is supportive of their work. They show their pieces through various interior design connections, and their biggest client to date is Fondren Church, for which they have created several pieces furniture and where Josh is an active member.

"I feel like I'm doing what God wants to do when I'm building something," Josh explains. "I feel like everything in my head slows down. Creating something is God-like, because God gives us the same satisfaction that he had when he created."

One cannot help but remember that Jesus himself was a carpenter, but Josh only smiles widely when this similarity is pointed out.

"I just like designing stuff," he says humbly.

Twiggy also embraces the spiritual side of woodworking and says spirituality plays an enormous role in his personal art, as well, agreeing that whenever he creates he feels a sense of peace.

"We wouldn't be doing this if we didn't like it," Twiggy says. "We feel like we are contributing something to the world instead of following a big corporate machine."

Both Twiggy and Josh recognize the value of owning custom furniture, and they feel that Jacksonians do as well.

"The industrial and midcentury furniture look is a national fad right now," says Twiggy.

Opposite: A 555 Custom Salvage Design coffee table is a sturdy, artistic piece.

Right: This coffee maker is intended to resemble a vintage, midcentury model.

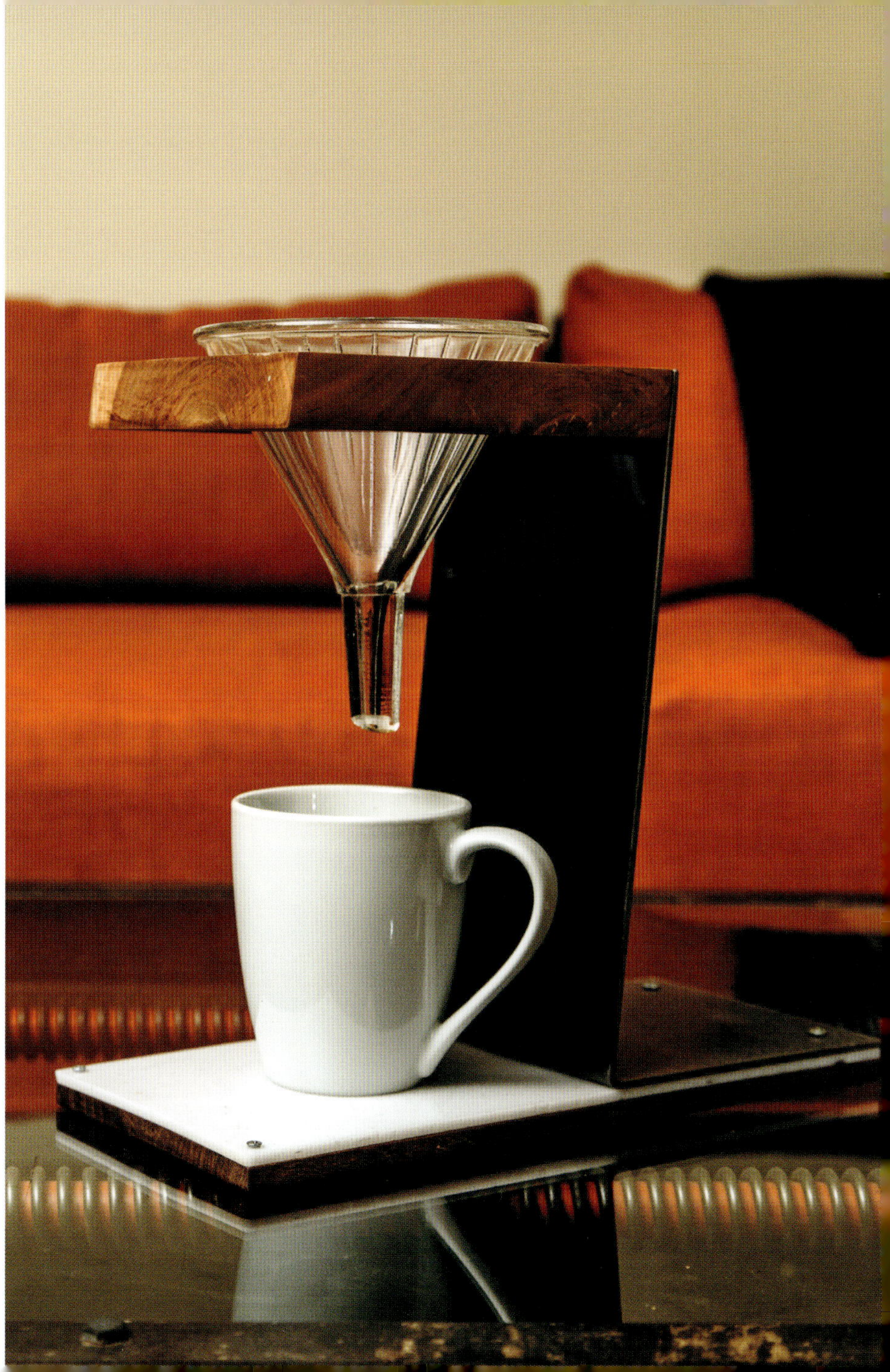

Josh agrees that the type of furniture they are building may be popular at the moment but that the sentimental element of owning a custom, repurposed design is what attracts their buyers.

"If you go out and buy a Herman Miller chair, that's not sentimental," Josh argues. "I always appreciate something more if I have a personal attachment to it."

Josh's home is full of authentic midcentury pieces that he inherited from his grandmother, whose style he always admired. With 555 Custom Salvage Designs, Josh and Twiggy draw from their mutual love of midcentury pieces while combining more rustic, industrial elements. Whenever possible, they source their materials locally, maintaining that it is important to use "found" items but acknowledging they purchase a fair amount of new material as well. "Salvaged" is a confusing term, but to the two of them, it means that their ideas themselves are what are salvaged in their designs.

"When I think of creativity, I think nothing is really new. You're taking other people's ideas and adding to them to make them your own," Josh explains.

"If I see something that really inspires me, I take that idea, and in the process, I'm doing my own thing, making something I think is really cool," Twiggy adds.

Walking around their studio, you can see many pieces that blend the old and new, including rewired long-neck desk lamps from an old drafting table that Twiggy and Josh have attached to wood blocks, creating one-of-a-kind sconce lights. There is an intentionally sturdy quality to their work because, as Twiggy tells me, these are designs built to last one hundred years. My eye settles on an old midcentury side table that I learn they found at a flea market and restored, adding an oblong set of filing cabinet drawers to the top. I express admiration for the piece, and Twiggy makes a scoffing sound.

"That piece," Josh groans. "We can't get that right."

"We've reworked it about six times," says Twiggy, rolling his eyes.

Creating "Twiggy"

Twiggy describes his personal artwork as "a blend of beauty and decay." He likes to make a mess when he creates, but his resulting inventions are orderly and precise. Known for his mixed-media assemblages and detailed oil paintings, Twiggy says he cannot remember a point in his life when he did not identify as an artist. When people nicknamed him Twiggy, he adopted the name as part of his artistic persona.

Growing up an only child, Twiggy took private art lessons to supplement the classes and training he received in school. He matriculated at Mississippi State University to study graphic design but

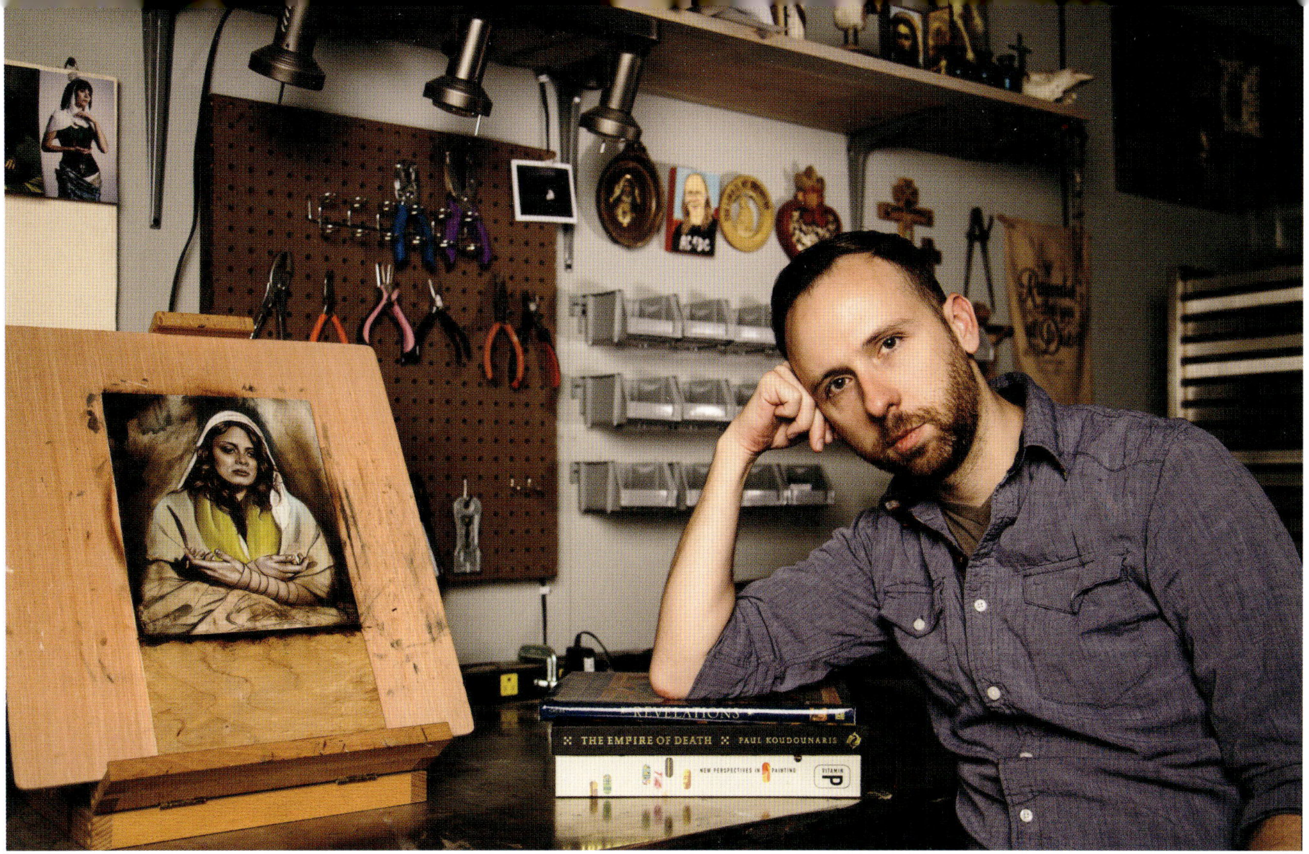

Jason "Twiggy" Lott is pictured with one of his oil paintings, which will form the basis for an assemblage piece.

dropped out after a few semesters, a decision that he sarcastically describes as "really responsible."

In the summer of 1999, he took an internship with a small advertising agency, where his co-workers took him under their wings and encouraged his inclination toward graphic design. After the internship ended, the company gave him a full-time position.

By 2003, Twiggy was deep into the corporate design world when he met William Goodman, who was living in Jackson's Fondren community and creating art full time. Twiggy was fascinated.

"William rekindled my desire to make art for art's sake," Twiggy recollects.

Twiggy vividly remembers the night that he and William met; they hung out with artists Ginger Williams-Cook, whom Twiggy knew from high

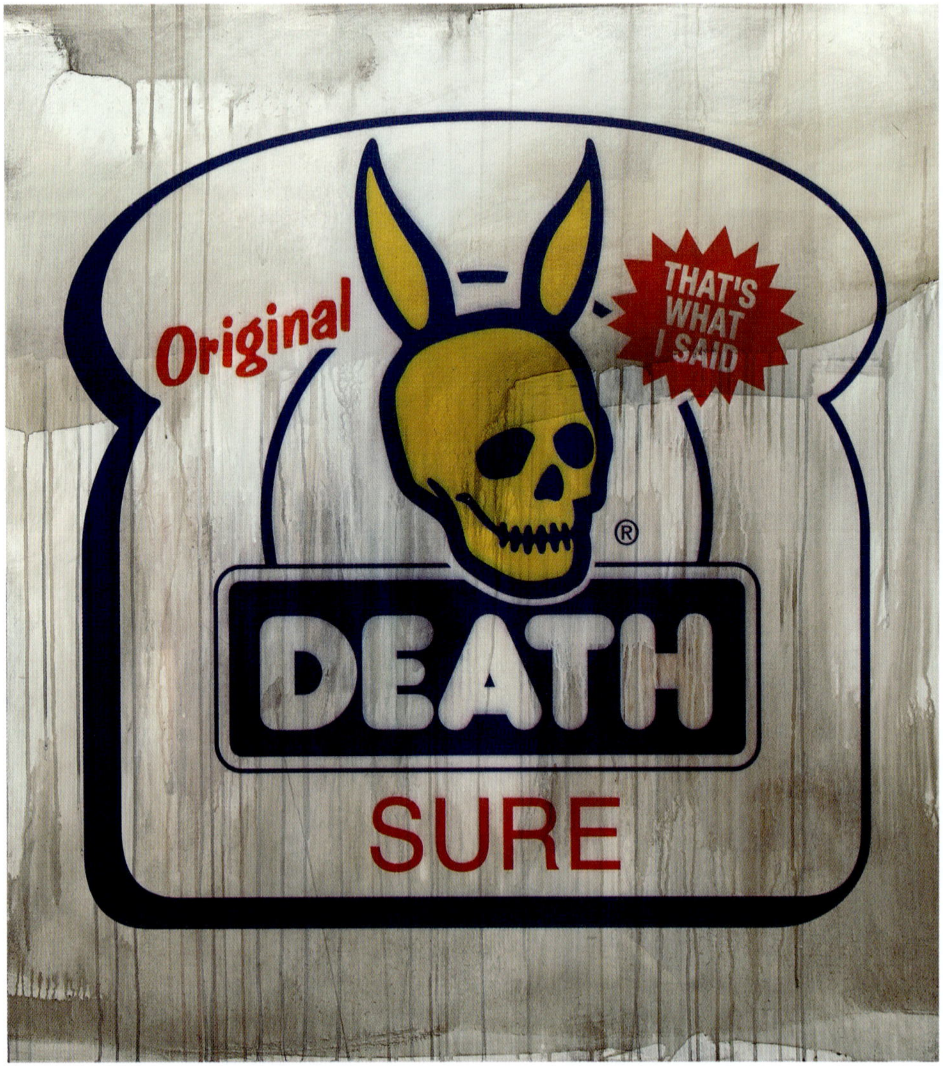

school, and photographer Josh Hailey. The four artists began to spend time together in the Fondren community, establishing relationships with other creatives, including Ron Chane and Jason Marlow. William and Twiggy collaborated on multiple bodies of work, which supplemented Twiggy's income from his career in advertising. Then in 2009, Twiggy lost his job. He began making art full time as a necessity.

"In 2009, I began a really creative experimental time," Twiggy explains. He took a trip to Switzerland, which, he says in retrospect, "deeply inspired" him.

"Every time I travel out of Mississippi I am getting inspiration, even if I don't realize it yet," he declares. "I am becoming more interested in telling a story or making a very specifics statement with a piece of art. My biggest thing in the past several years is the examination of the ideas of death and rebirth."

Opposite: *Rest Assured* by Jason "Twiggy" Lott.

Right: *St. Rita of Cascia* by Jason "Twiggy" Lott.

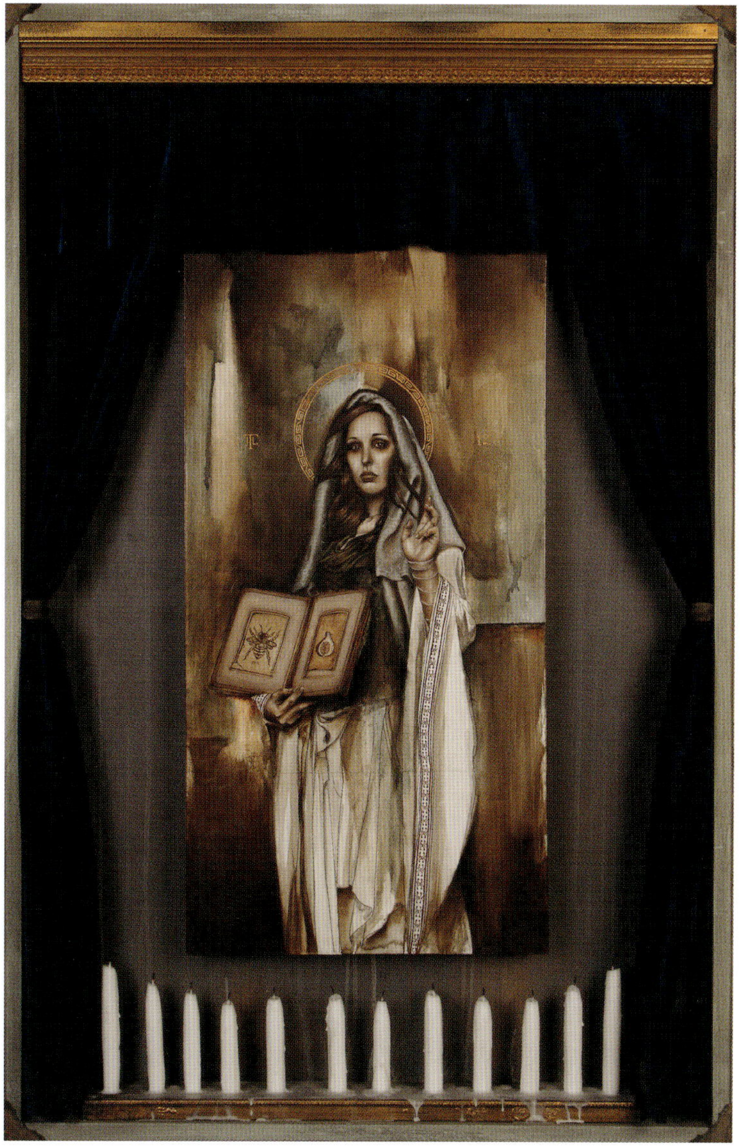

For a long period, Twiggy was transfixed with creating assemblages, pieces of art that used many different elements to tell a story. He built the assemblages inside old desk drawers or mounted on pieces of wood. Oftentimes, a tiny oil painting formed the focal point of the piece, resembling a sort of miniature shrine. Twiggy's latest abstract paintings, meanwhile, combine acrylic and oil paint. Lately, he's begun blending flora into the abstracts, choosing dried plants that he finds around town. Despite the variety of his creative output, the Jackson market has never proven financially supportive of his artwork. Twiggy shows his work at Fischer Gallery from time to time, but he relies mostly on out-of-state sales. He currently shows at the Rymer Gallery in Nashville, Tennessee; Søren Christensen Gallery in New Orleans; and M2 Gallery in Little Rock, Arkansas.

"I can do anything I want to do from Jackson because the Internet market will get it out there," Twiggy explains. "There's just not a lot of market here for the art that I make."

The 555 Revolution

Both Twiggy and Josh believe that Jackson is the right market for their custom furniture.

"Jackson is the place for this to blow up," Josh says emphatically. "The way I look at it is: build some cool stuff and give people a place to buy it."

Although Josh and Twiggy are not planning to open a storefront, they are interested in furthering the idea of an art collective in the downtown community. Josh in particular seems fascinated with the idea of a place where artists and craftsmen can work together; his long-term goal is to open a center for the arts. Josh's vision includes a large community space such as a warehouse, where people who are making art but need a place to study and learn could take advantage of low rent and learn the business tools to get on their feet.

"Our business is contingent on collaborations," Josh explains. "My main motivation in having an art collective in one building will be to have a showroom where we can showcase what everyone who is involved is doing."

"When I can bounce ideas off someone else, it helps me stay focused," Twiggy admits, adding that he likes the idea of giving other people a space to "do what they do."

"When you see somebody create something, you grow yourself. I believe God wants us to be a community," Josh elaborates.

Josh sees basing this art community center in downtown Jackson, which Twiggy jokes is a location that is "dead after dark." Twiggy is not alone in this line of thought; other artists, including Andy Young and Kristen Ley, have commented that weekends in downtown Jackson are notably quiet. But Josh believes that this art collective could dramatically rewrite the story of downtown Jackson, bringing a new life to the area.

Twiggy remains skeptical.

"We aren't trying to start the revolution," Twiggy mollifies, but Josh interjects.

"Actually, I *am* trying to start the revolution," he smiles. "The groundwork for a revolution was started by William [Goodman], Twiggy and their friends a decade ago. The reason it had so much potential to take off is there's a blank slate here [in Jackson]. You make more of an impact when more than one person is involved. No one person is going to change the face of Jackson, but [the city] will appreciate what you are doing to support it."

Josh pauses to give Twiggy a pointed look, to which Twiggy responds by laughing and shaking his head.

"It'll happen," Josh tells him. Twiggy nods but keeps laughing.

"It's a vision and dream," he says, addressing me confidently, "but it'll happen."

19

ELIZABETH ROBINSON

Elizabeth Robinson's journey into glass began after college, when she took a job at Pearl River Glass studio in Jackson in the late 1970s. Studio owner Andy Young hired her for a position that she describes as a "sort of secretary," but it was not long before Elizabeth began learning the craft of glass working from the ground up.

"Back then, there was a big division between whether you were an artist or a craftsman," she recalls. Craftwork, she remembers, was seen as more folk art than fine art.

"Fletcher Cox, Susan Ford and Andy Young began to show what could happen to crafting as fine art," she says. Before the founding of the Craftsman's Guild, Elizabeth felt that Mississippians were isolated from the rest of the craft world, and

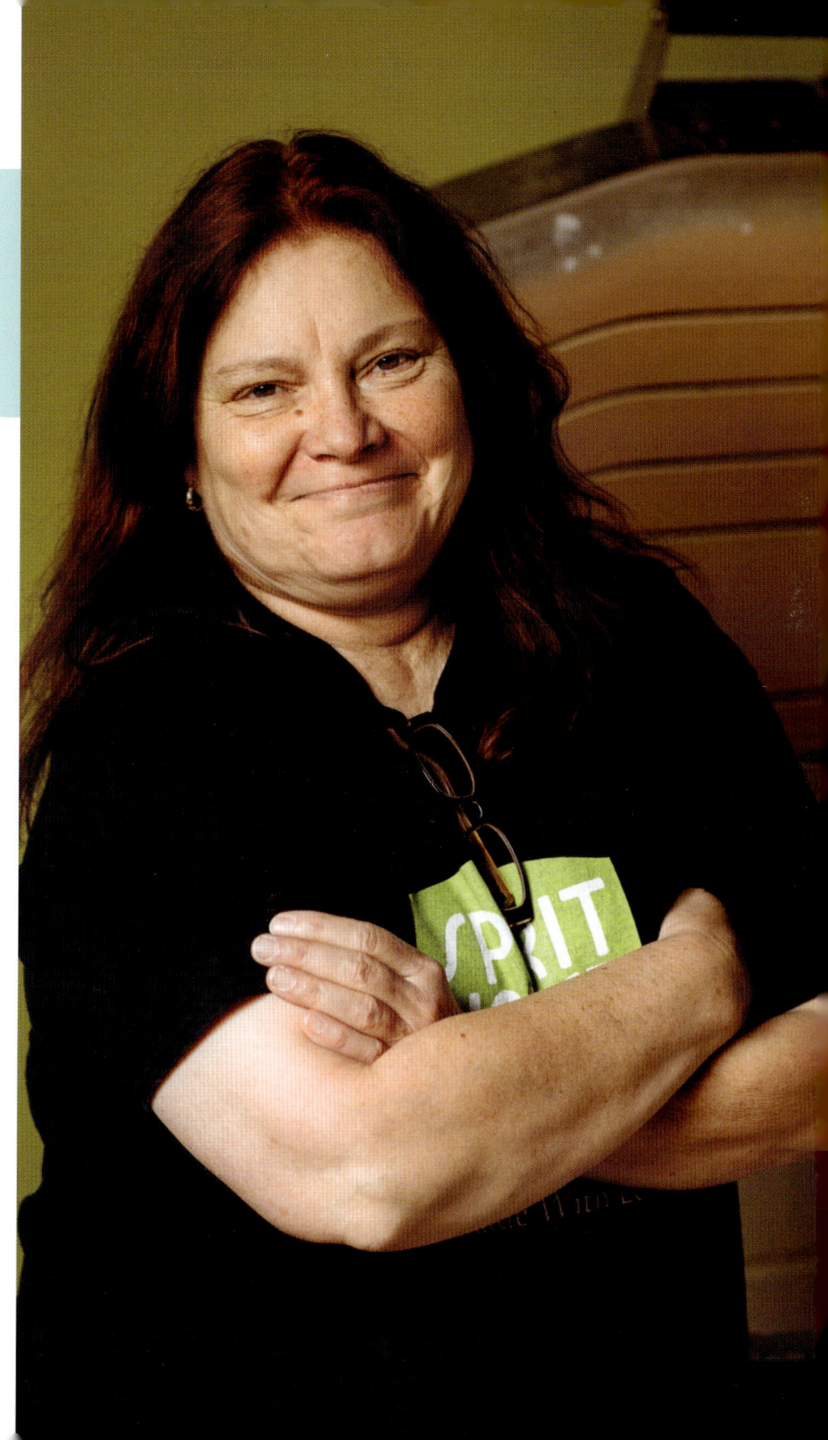

Elizabeth Robinson runs her studio in the basement of the Fondren Corner Building.

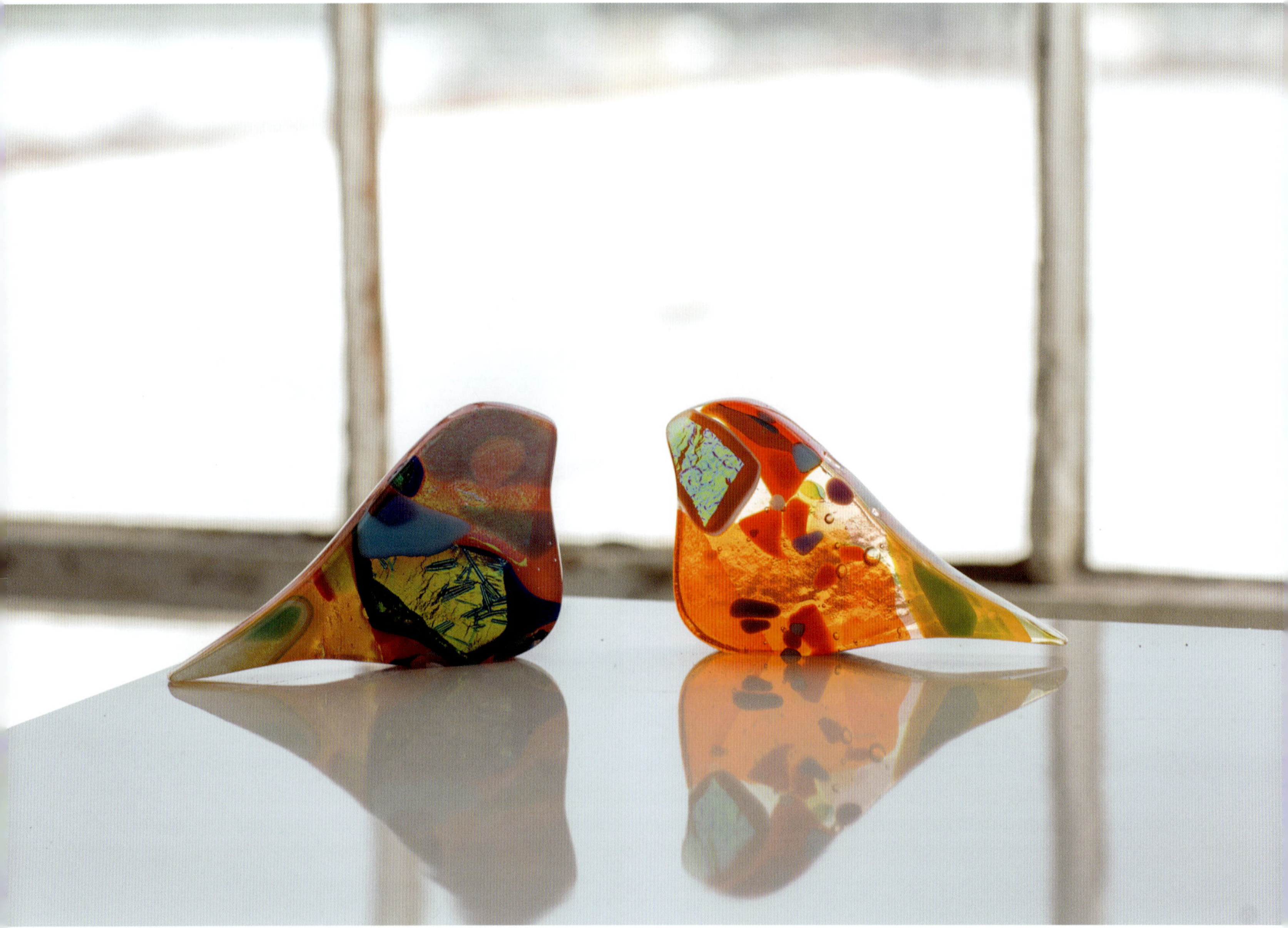

Glass birds remain among the most popular of Elizabeth's creations. She encourages collectors to send her pictures of the birds in natural settings.

the Jackson art community was small. In the early 1980s, she started making glass in her own studio in Midtown, which she shared with her friend Kay Holloway. In 1985, she joined the Craftsman's Guild, and she fondly recalls the new support she found in the fledgling group as the lines between fine art and crafts began to fully dissipate.

Still, in those early days Elizabeth worried about making enough money to maintain her craft, and to compensate, she ran side businesses for years. Instead of attempting to design items that made lots of money, she focused on perfecting the things she loved to make. It came as somewhat of a shock, therefore, when her small glass birds suddenly became wildly popular.

"I made six glass birds for the Chimneyville Craft Festival, and they all sold in the first thirty minutes," she recalls. "The kicker is that every one of them is different."

Elizabeth's birds have a pleasing, elegant and simple design inspired by the tranquility she finds in nature.

"The best part of your day is when you are somewhere quiet and hear the birds peeping," she says.

Her birds are beloved by collectors, and the price point makes them an ideal gift. Mother's Day and Easter are top sales periods. Elizabeth sells them out of her studio, and she also sells them "by the flock" through the website Artful Homes. A flock of five birds will feature completely different individual birds, since no two birds are alike.

"You get whatever is hatching at the time," Elizabeth laughs.

Additionally, she's created different species of birds. One of her personal favorites is the "Southern Carnival" breed.

Since her glass business has picked up, Elizabeth has been able to let go of her side business ventures and focus her creative energy on Spirit House Glass Studio. To keep Spirit House Glass economically stable, Elizabeth is careful to match her prices to the cost of the labor and the glass itself. Only a limited number of companies produce glass specifically designed for use in the kiln. Beautiful, multifaceted dichroic glass, which Elizabeth loves to use, is the most expensive.

Elizabeth has also expanded her studio space and hired a like-minded team.

"I bring in artists who have a voice of their own and can express that in glass. You need experience to be able to make this product," she explains.

Currently, Elizabeth has three employees: Kay Holloway, Kelley Williams and Rebecca Wilkinson. All of her employees are part time, and each one brings her own personal talents and designs to her work. Kelley, for example, is experimenting with glass jewelry. In addition, Elizabeth enjoys collaborating with other artists, including William Goodman and Ginger Williams-Cook. Almost three

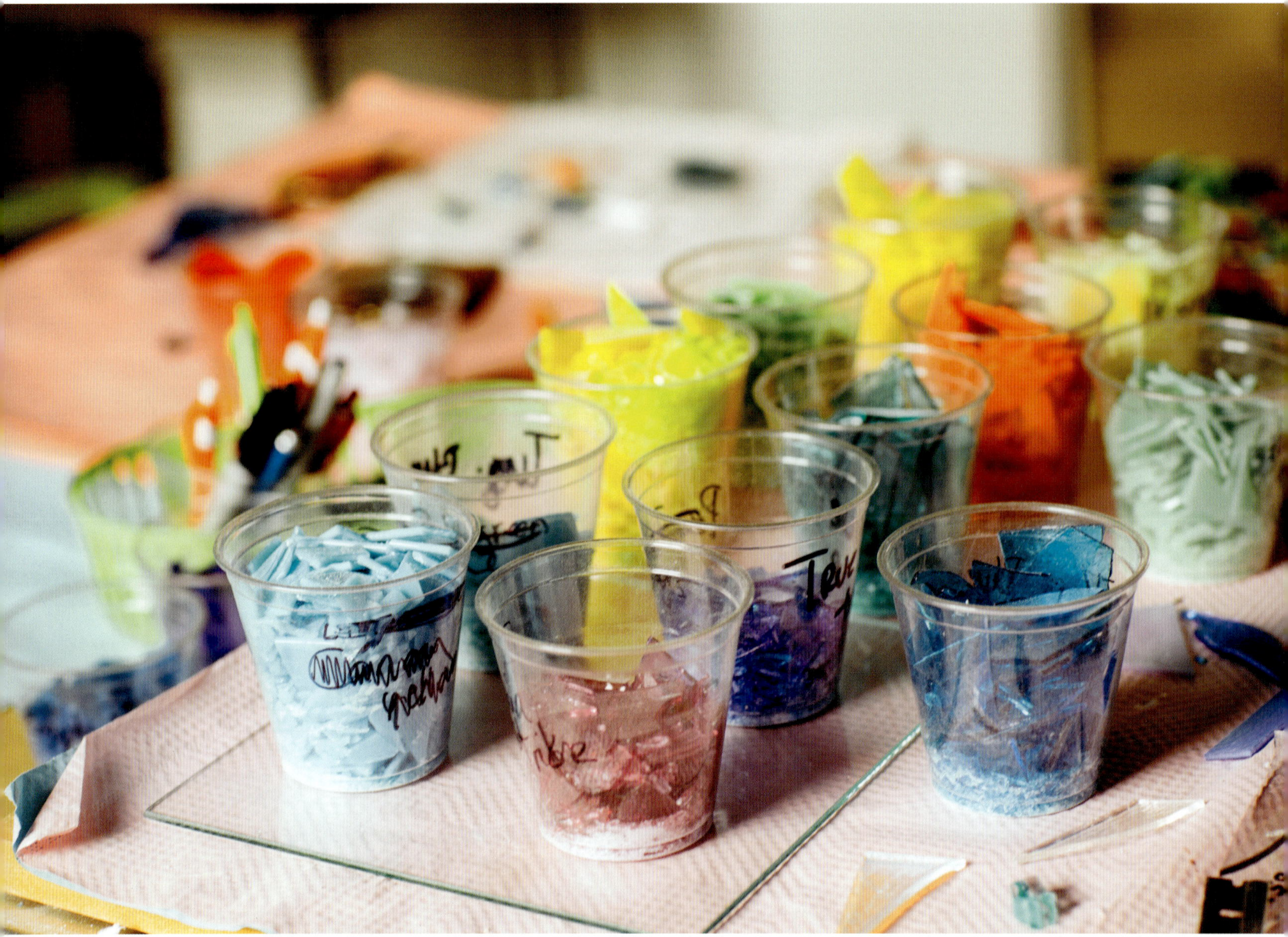

Shards of glass are organized by color and opacity level.

decades since joining the Craftsman's Guild, she marvels at the transition she has witnessed in the Jackson art world.

"There are fewer divisions in the creative community," she explains. "Now you can be an artist *and* a musician."

The city of Jackson has also changed dramatically over the years, she says, and it has finally become a place that sustains creative minds.

"Jackson is coming around and seeing that if you allow art to grow and flourish in the city, then businesses will have success and residential areas will get safer," she says.

She admires the concept of the Year of the Creative Economy, which she sees as a "start."

"I see more respect now for creatives than ever before," she observes.

Elizabeth's successful Fondren studio is proof that a creative business can form and thrive, but it has taken time. To grow, an art community requires money and dedication, she says, but first, "squatters" have to come put their creative touch on a neighborhood. Only later do commercial real estate investors notice the area and come in to build it out.

"Creatives move into an area that may be blighted, and they cultivate a creative fire. Chefs then come to cook over the fire. Musicians then come to warm their hands over it."

Thus, a creative community is born.

Fine glass is expensive, so broken shards are salvaged and transformed into new creations. A single bird can features dozens of pieces of glass.

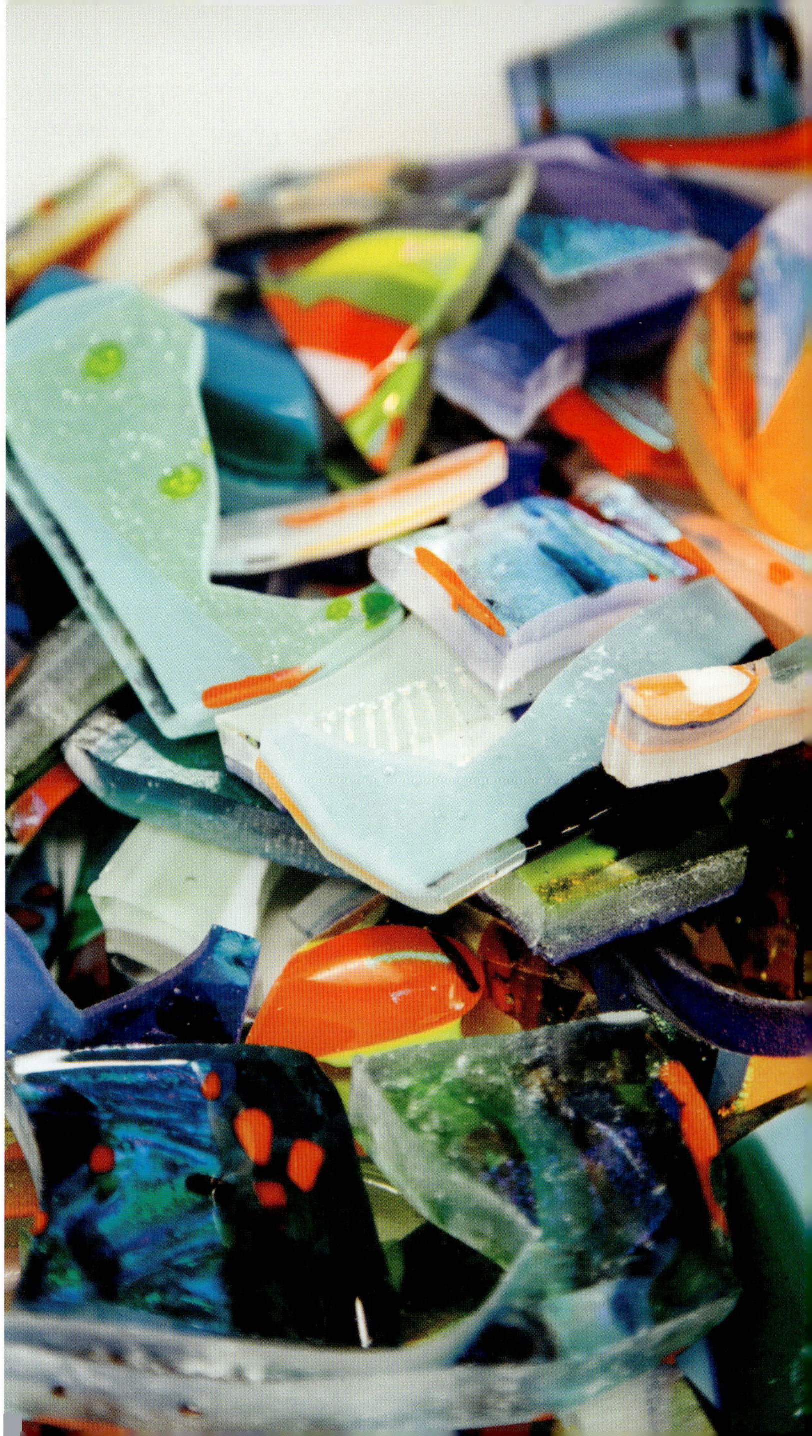

20

CHANE

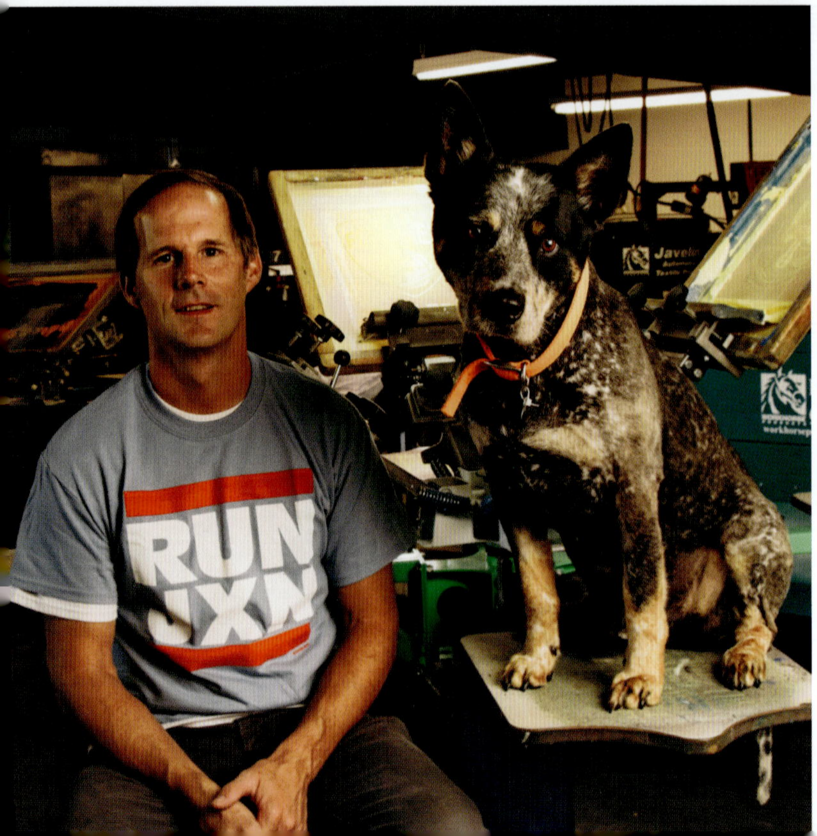

Chane and his dog, Zero, hang out in Chane's print shop, located in the basement of the Fondren Corner Building.

The rebel spirit of Fondren is the mononymous Chane, who has dedicated his life to the Jackson community by fighting against corporate takeover, filling in potholes and making really cool T-shirts. Call him what you will—a graphic designer, a screen printer, a vigilante, a visionary—Chane is a man who has taken the law into his own hands more than once in the name of art, community and development. When he is not sweeping the streets for criminals and potholes, Chane is running multiple businesses in the Fondren community (he has signed eleven leases in the past sixteen years), each one grounded in his personal belief that only through art will a community grow. Chane is the founder of

Agents for Change, an endowment that issues grants to emerging artists, and he is fiercely dedicated to convincing Jacksonians to support the arts and push—sometimes even demand—Jackson to move forward.

Background

Born in south Jackson, Chane attended Forest Hill High School and studied at Hinds Community College, Mississippi State University and the University of Southern Mississippi, finishing at the latter with a degree in marketing and advertising. By his last semester of school, Chane had lined up employment in his field. Then, the night before graduation, one of his close friends and roommates was killed, tragically and suddenly. The subsequent feelings that Chane experienced were life changing, and pondering the ephemeral nature of human existence rendered him unable to justify a life of corporate servitude. Instead of heading to his desk job, Chane headed to New York City, where he rented a couch in a hallway that he had to share with a three-legged dog named Goliath. He sold his screen-printed T-shirts on the streets of New York until his life philosophy of "live fast, dream forever" led him to Florida, where he lived for a time in Pensacola Beach, working at a surfboard camp.

"I hustled T-shirts out of my backpack," he recalls of his time in Florida. "I had no real plan, no business mindset."

He toured the country for three years, living out of his car and selling T-shirts. In 1994, Chane came through Jackson, stopping at Cups in Fondren for a coffee. For the first time, Chane felt what he describes as an "indie, hipster hope" for Jackson, specifically the Fondren community. The space next door to Cups was up for rent, and within thirty days Chane had signed a lease and opened his first business, a "hodgepodge" shop where BMX enthusiasts and skateboarders came for T-shirts and supplies. Still, Chane was dissatisfied with the city of Jackson overall.

"I hated Jackson," Chane admits. "I thought I would go back to New York. I thought Jackson was the dumbest place ever—and then the artist revolution hit Fondren."

Art Revolution

"The words 'artist' and 'revolution' weren't on my radar until 2004," Chane explains. "Then a new group of people who I didn't know came in and were doing something I didn't understand."

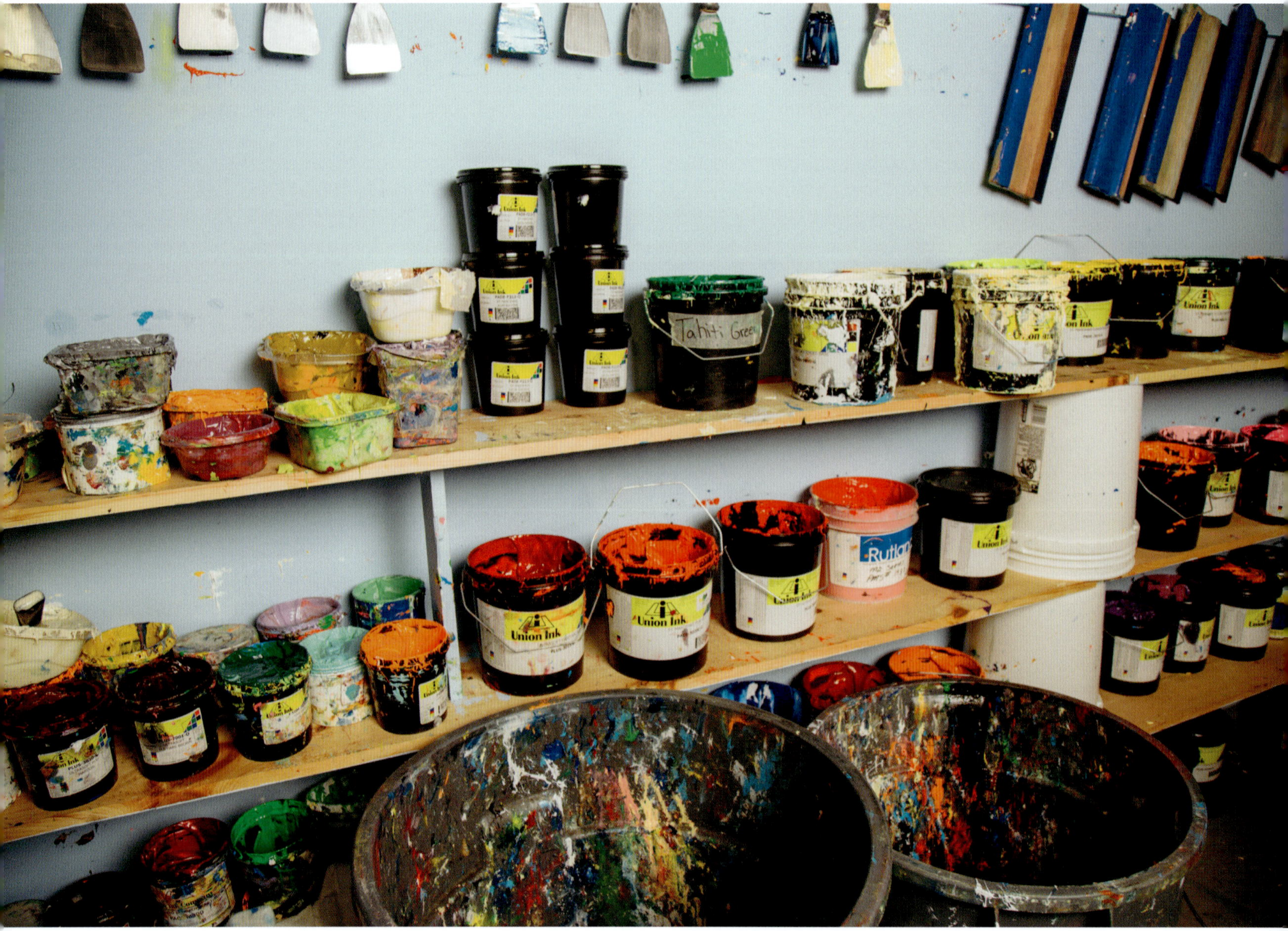

Ink is applied to a screen and printed onto T-shirts by machines, which are operated by members of Chane's print shop staff.

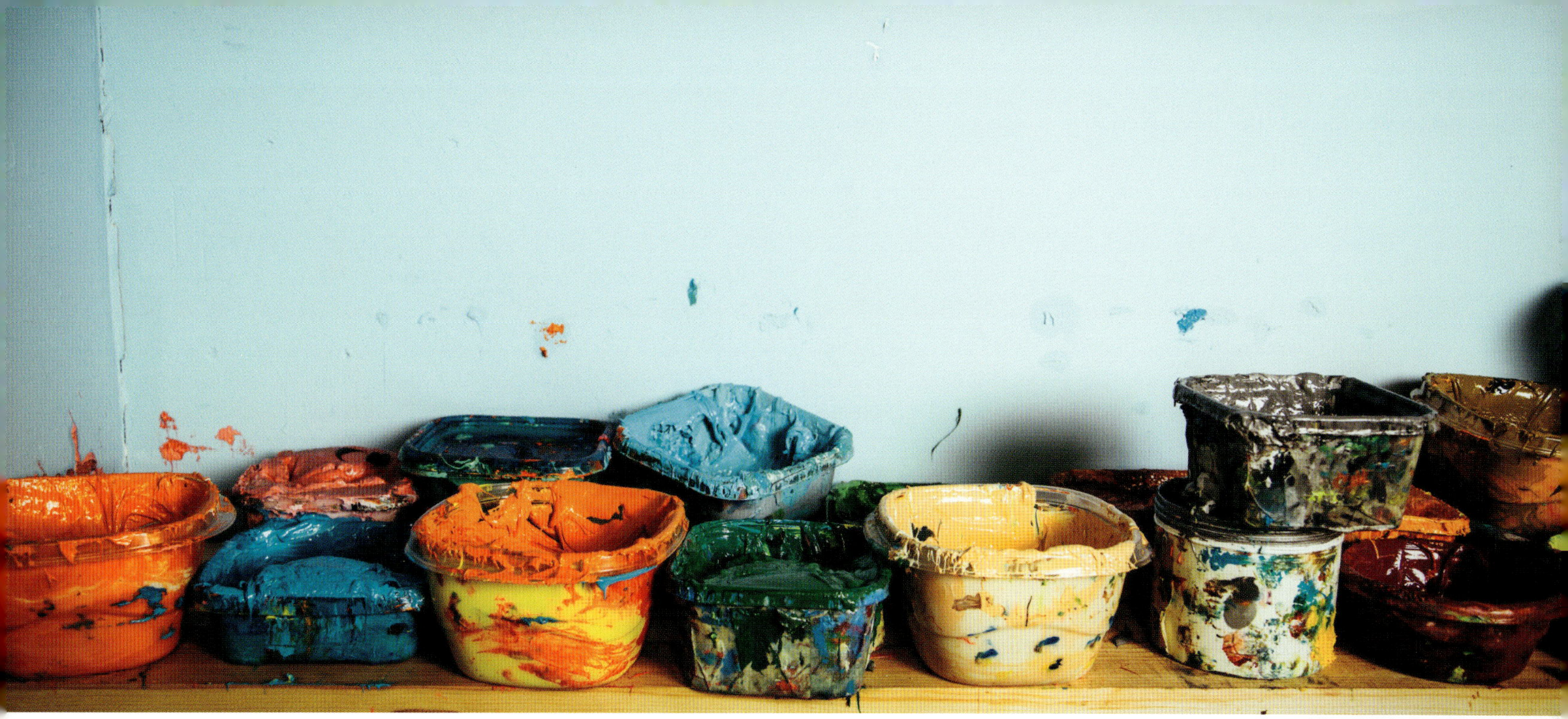

Containers of ink wait to go onto a screen-print machine.

Chane had never seen a group of artists in Jackson come into a neighborhood and create their own society.

"Maybe in New York City," Chane remembers thinking, "But not Jackson. The art scene was born. That is what changed Fondren—the art scene went from nothing to all encompassing. Fondren became something. Jacksonians began to notice the neighborhood."

The artists who were moving into Fondren and setting up shop included a young group of friends: William Goodman, Ginger Williams-Cook, Jason "Twiggy" Lott, Josh Hailey and Jason Marlow, among others. All of these Jackson natives had decided to call Jackson home, forming an art district by living and making art in the Fondren neighborhood.

"I was inspired to dip back into canvas art," says Chane, who had long given up on his own fine art pursuits.

Chane was thrilled to see young artists who were determined to make a living from their artwork, and he was happy to share with them the business skills that he had learned the hard way.

"I understood synergy. There was a network," Chane recalls. "My visionary is William Goodman, the first artist I knew in the Fondren Corner Building. I saw people like him come in as a bulb and bloom into a flower. I pushed William to do his art full time."

All the while, Chane pursued his own passion: designing and screen printing the most outrageous, limit-pushing T-shirts that he could imagine.

Pushing Limits

The name Studio Chane, which Chane has always used, refers today to the screen-printing factory that Chane runs out of the basement of the Fondren Corner Building. Chane has more than four hundred T-shirts that he has designed by hand, beginning with sketches on paper featuring his observations of the city of Jackson. His sketches are inspired by the classic "I Heart NYC" designs. Some of his Jackson designs highlight negative aspects of the city, including shirts that read "North Jackson Swingers Club" and "Government's Bitch." He has a shirt poking fun at the frequent "boil water" alerts that plague Jackson; he has a shirt that makes fun of the mostly abandoned Metrocenter Mall.

"It's the Southpark of T-shirts," Chane jokes, basically implying that he will make fun of everything and everyone. "I'm not trying to start the revolution, just be funny, fresh and raw. All the reality is already out there—you can take the crap of life and make art out of it."

Although he takes on corporate printing jobs, even making T-shirts for clients like C-Spire, he sells a T-shirt that reads "Corpophobic." He uses money made off corporate jobs to fund his grants for artists through his Agents for Change Endowment Program.

"I think [what] people have learned about our store [is] that we have enough balls to stand up for what we believe," Chane says.

Screen printing is only one component of his business; his retail shops, including Slavebird for men and Wilai for women, sell products that Jacksonians cannot find anywhere else. His approach to retail mirrors his approach to life—lots of attitude and aggressive marketing. Chane is adamantly "anti-mall," but he maintains a good relationship with other Fondren retailers while openly acknowledging that he is taking a completely different retail approach. The Wilai storefront is a few doors down from an upscale Fondren boutique that sells items such as designer jeans and Chanel handbags. Chane quit selling jeans at Wilai after other local boutiques started carrying the same brands.

"Wilai is the bitch of the local fashion industry," says Chane, his voice welling with pride. "We're

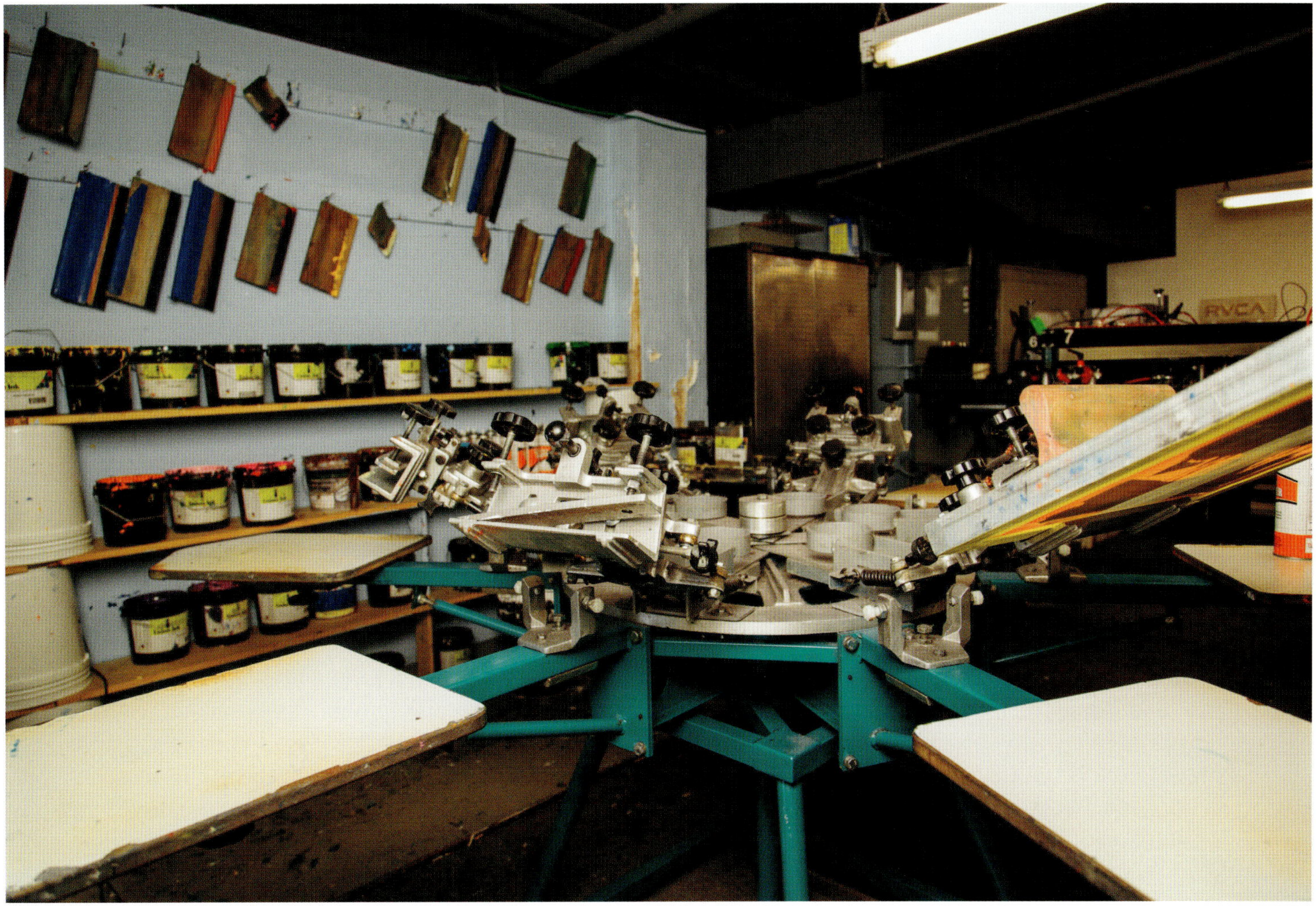

A screen-printing machine in Chane's studio is operated by just one employee at a time.

against the grain. We may make less money, but we're strong in our non-sellout plan. There is no intellect behind Wilai: I'm not rich. I'm not a girl. I'm not a fashionista. Ignorance is our genius."

Chane also runs what he calls the "mothership" of his businesses, Swell-O-Phonic, a retail shop that offers T-shirts and specifically caters to skateboarders. In addition to all his Jackson business ventures, Chane remains devoted to New York City, maintaining an apartment in Brooklyn and commuting to New York on a regular basis to sell his T-shirts at pop-up shops

"A lot of people gave me crap about New York City, but all of that New York income I am bringing back here and investing in Jackson," he explains. He is an advocate of creatives who leave Jackson and come back, asking rhetorically, "How much further can you make it if you leave and bring some culture back?"

As the Fondren neighborhood continues to gentrify, Chane has become even more grounded in his belief that "too much nationwide business" can "take away the luster" of a neighborhood.

"We aren't gritty or grainy anymore," Chane says of Fondren today. Still, the grittier art district of Jackson, Midtown, has caught Chane's eye.

"I feel a responsibility to give back to Fondren and also to extend love to Midtown," he says. "These are the last meccas for independent creatives who aren't sellouts."

Chane is dedicated to finding angles for artistry that other people will not notice. For example, Chane saw that a series of potholes was disrupting the stretch of North State Street that he refers to as the "Fondren-Midtown corridor," so he decided to get asphalt from the city's supply and fix it.

"We stole it," he says of the asphalt. "That's the art behind the whole deal. My thought was that after we did the first few, the city would keep coming behind us to cover them up. But then they stopped."

A big fan of the street artist Banksy, Chane spray painted the words "Citizen Fixed" on the street by the potholes he repaired in creative attempt to draw attention to the problem of the city's poor roadways. Then CNN showed up at Chane's Brooklyn doorstep, demanding to know if he was the "Pothole Robin Hood" of Jackson. In the end, it was CNN who protected Chane from prosecution by the City of Jackson, which dropped charges against Chane when threatened with negative national media attention.

"I'm not a big media whore," Chane declares. "I've suffered for my art in New York, and I can suffer in Jackson. If you want to be an artist in any form you have got to suffer. Whatever is considered artistry or not with me, I've always had the understanding that it's OK to ride the short bus and swim in the shallow end of the pool."

21

LIGHT AND GLASS STUDIO

JERRI SHEARER AND ROY ADKINS

Roy Adkins and Jerri Shearer are a husband-and-wife team who together formed Light and Glass Studio in downtown Jackson. Roy is a photographer, and part of their studio functions as his photography space. Jerri works with glass to create sculptures and dishes, which she shows in a gallery at their studio. They also show the work of other artists, including some of their friends and colleagues, and they frequently use their space to host events and art shows.

Roy and Jerri have occupied their current studio for about seven years. Jerri, a native of Clinton, Mississippi, calls Jackson her "adopted" home city.

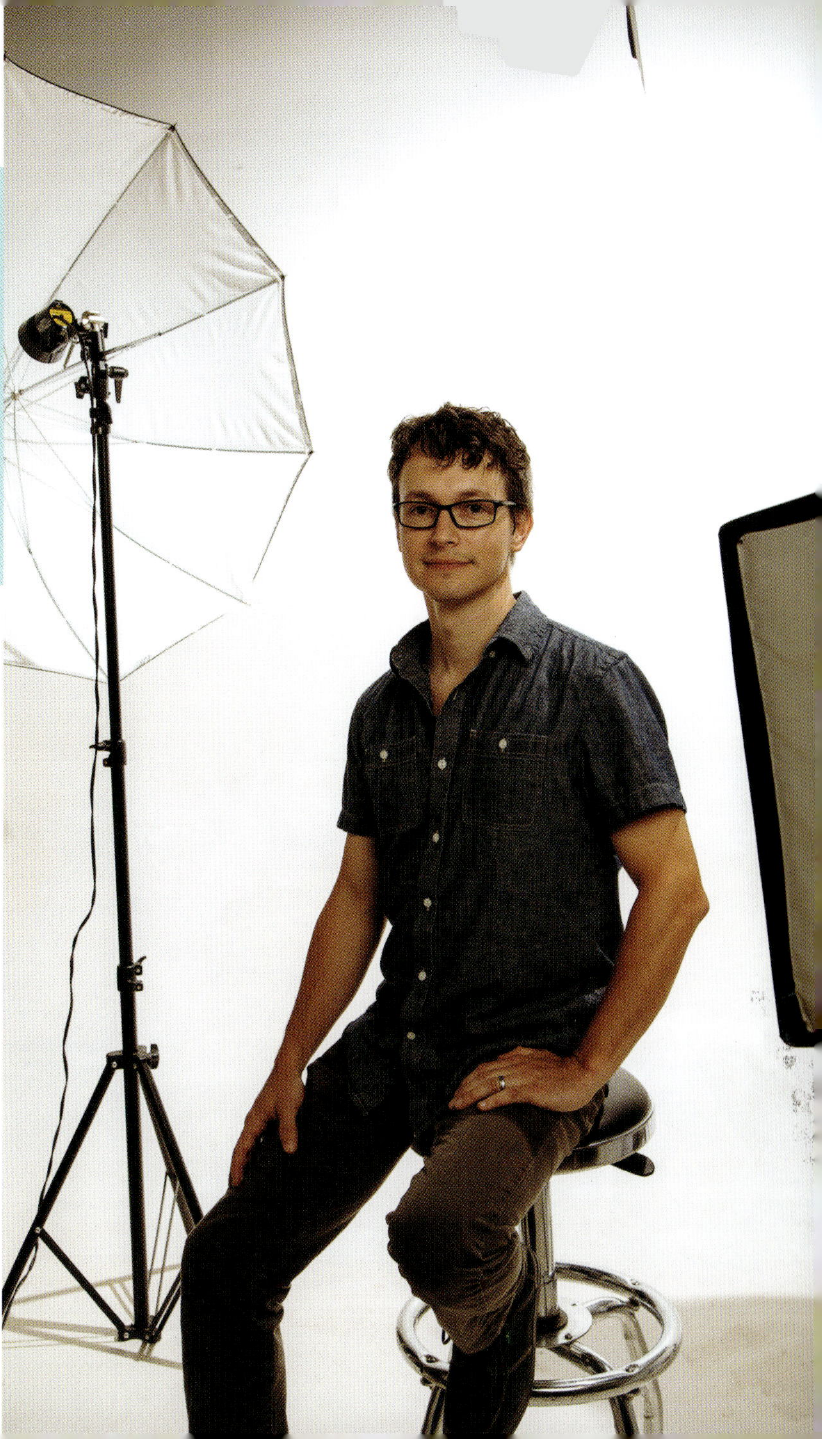

Roy Adkins works in his downtown Jackson studio.

The two met as students at Mississippi State University, where Roy studied psychology and fine art photography. Roy's interest in photography began as a high school student, and he took a specialty class offered by Birmingham-Southern where he could experience working in a darkroom. Photography is, he believes, his true calling. Jerri's interest in crafting began at a young age. She remembers seeing mosaics at a craft fair in Memphis and immediately wanting to learn how to make them herself.

After graduating from Mississippi State, the couple moved to Savannah, Georgia, to "get the hell out of town." In Savannah, Jerri worked for a woman who made stained glass that she showed at Renaissance festivals.

"The woman's husband made Renaissance leather boots," Roy remembers.

Jerri was paid for each piece of glass she made, and the Renaissance-enthusiasts introduced her to the basic principles of blown glass. Later, she

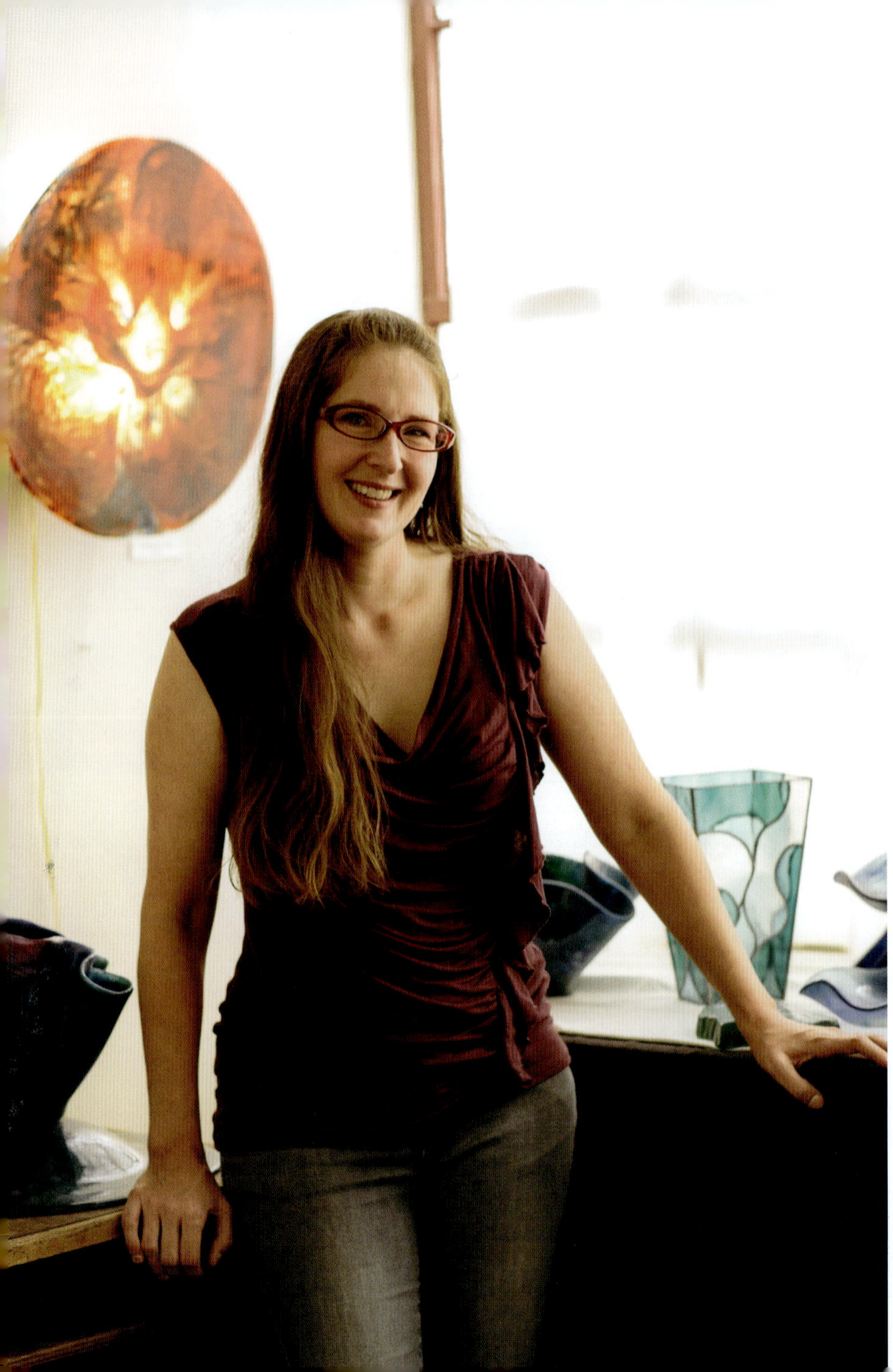

Jerri Shearer, Roy's wife, keeps her kilns at their house in Belhaven and shows her work at their studio.

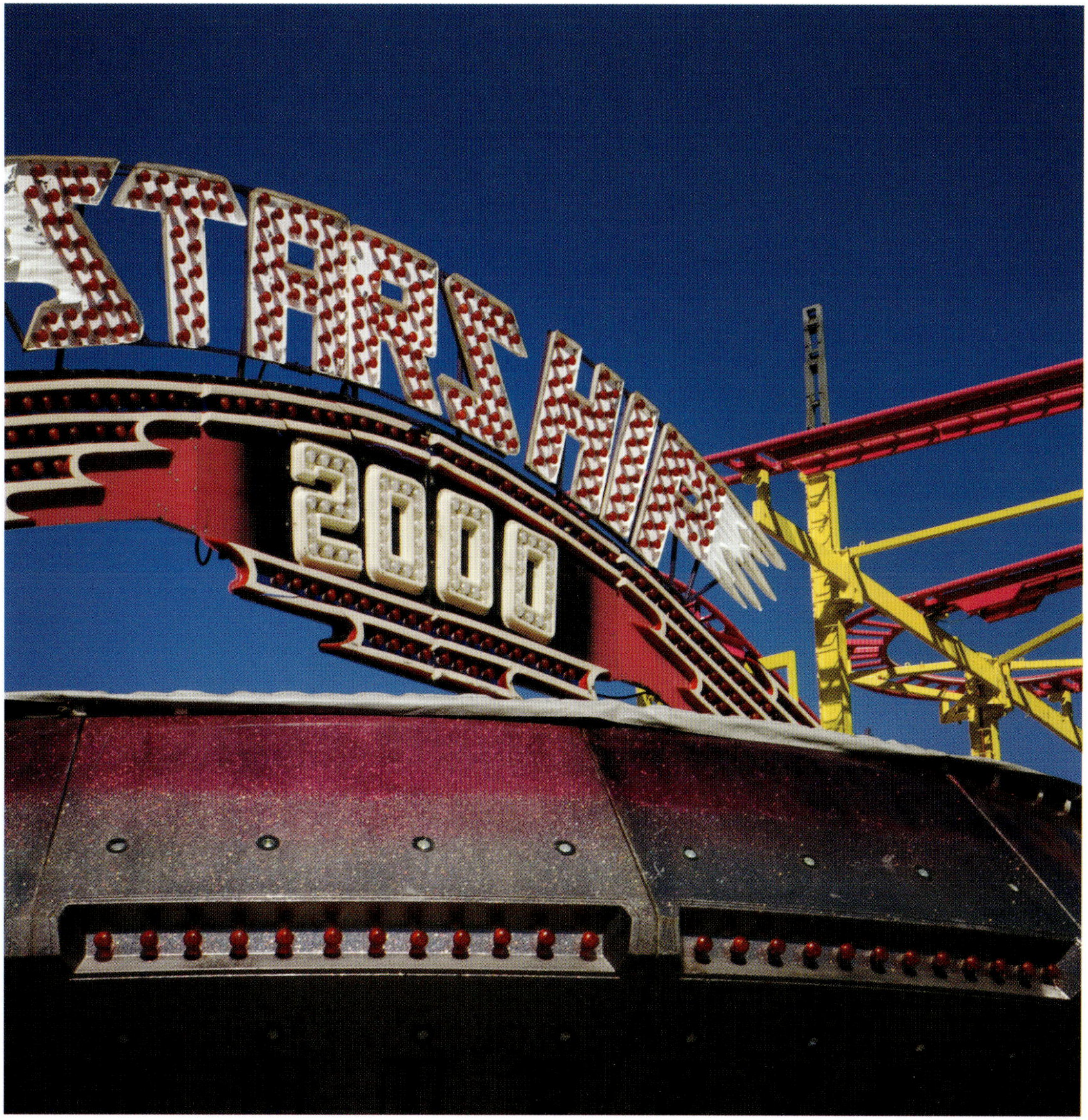

"Starship 2000."
Courtesy of Roy Adkins.

received a kiln as a Christmas present and began studying blown glass on her own.

When the couple returned to Jackson, Jerri began selling her crafts. For a fee of only twenty-five dollars, the couple could set up a booth all day at Belhaven Market, selling jewelry, little vases, bowls and pendants that Jerri made by hand.

"Belhaven Market was a great small business incubator," Jerri recalls.

Meanwhile, Roy had begun exhibiting his photography in juried shows and art exhibits.

"It was skin thickening in a way," he recalls. "We began doing outdoor craft festivals, traveling in bigger cities—at those shows, you get a better response to fine art photography."

Like many photographers, Roy has noticed that fine art photography can be a difficult sell.

"Nobody wants to think of their art needing to match someone's décor, but that's reality," he admits.

Roy expanded his work to include mixed-media photography pieces, which he found made popular commissions. The couple continued to travel to multiple craft shows a year, but in 2008, the economic recession put the brakes on Roy and Jerri's ability to travel, so they began to focus on their work in the local market.

"Jackson is a small community with a lower cost of living; it's easier for people to know you and easier for you to get involved," Roy notes.

Both Roy and Jerri have found a support network through the Mississippi Craftsman's Guild, where Jerri serves on the standards committee and Roy is on the board. The couple also has a great working relationship with glassmaker Elizabeth Robinson, who helped them curate a show at Light and Glass Studio in February 2014. Roy and Jerri try to host a few art shows each year, where they display their work alongside the work of peers whom they invite to participate. They joke that they "aren't great self-promoters," but their business would suggest otherwise. Although they have both shown their work at other galleries, they find that the majority of their sales happen at their own studio by appointment. Although Jerri keeps her kilns at a studio in the backyard of their Belhaven home, Roy does the majority of his business at their downtown studio.

"We always end up doing well enough, and we've stayed out ahead of this as much as we can," Roy says. Jerri insists that the key to sustaining their business is planning ahead.

"There's spillover between our work," she explains. "We segment things, like when we put frames together. I coat them and make all the kiln molds—it's a practical division of labor," she smiles.

"Jerri is really good at being the other person in the room during a photo shoot and giving positive feedback," Roy adds.

Currently, Roy does commercial photography for *Southern Living* magazine and *Garden and Gun* magazine, as well as many local publications and clients. Until 2007, he worked with a photography group. He is now mostly self-employed, which he said was frightening for a while but liberating overall, especially as it allows him time to work on his mixed-media art. He is a "stay at home dad," and his two-year-old daughter, Georgia, accompanies him to the studio and on many of his commercial shoots. Additionally, Roy received fellowships from the Mississippi Arts Commission in 2010 and 2012. Meanwhile, Jerri has taken on part-time work in the sales industry while she plans the work she wants to explore next. "I gave myself permission to enjoy this downtime to recharge and have creative thoughts and not worry about the details—[I'll] flush out the details of what I want to do when I get back into it again," Jerri explains.

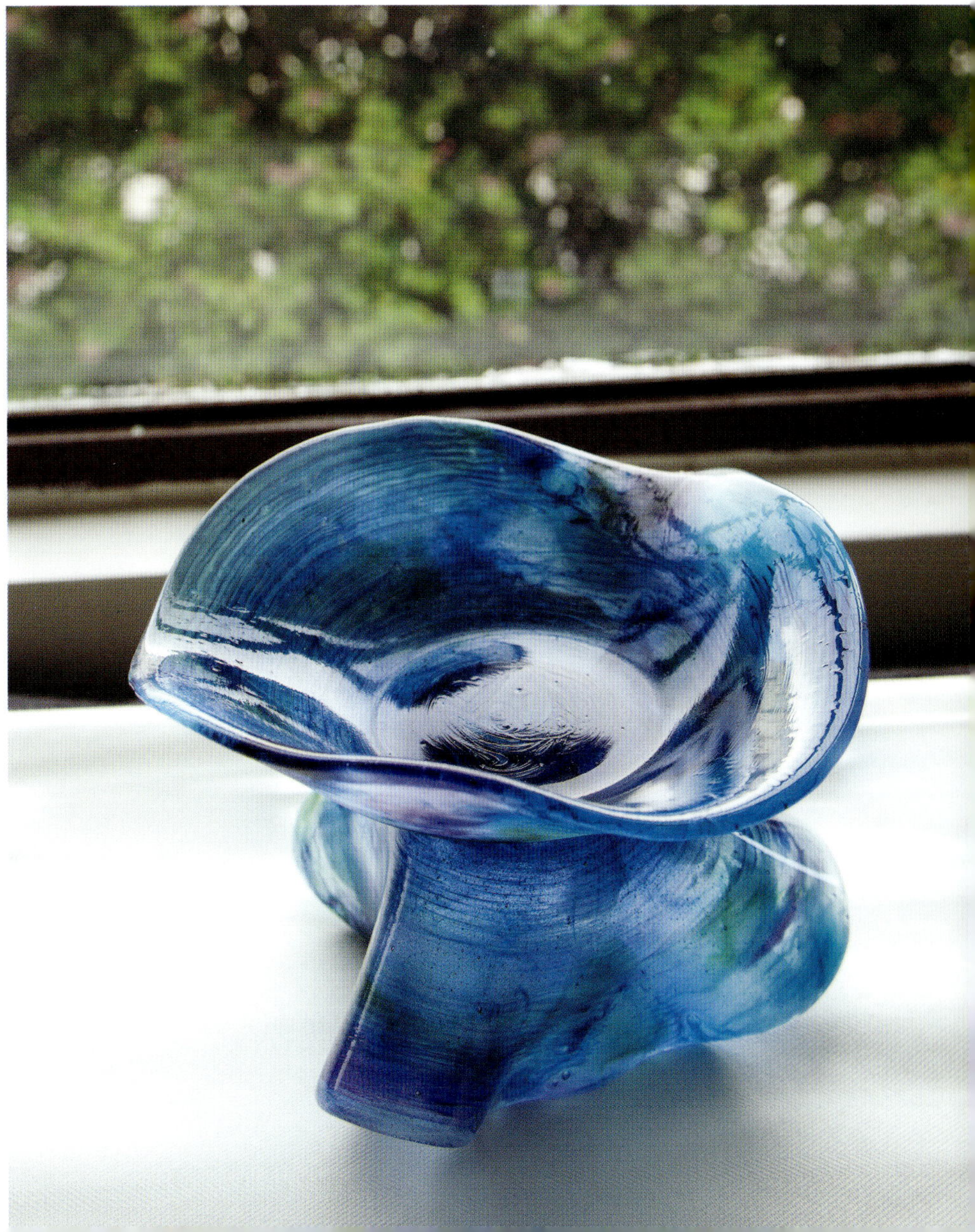

A Jerri Shearer blown-glass creation. Jerri's work is on display at Light and Glass Studio.

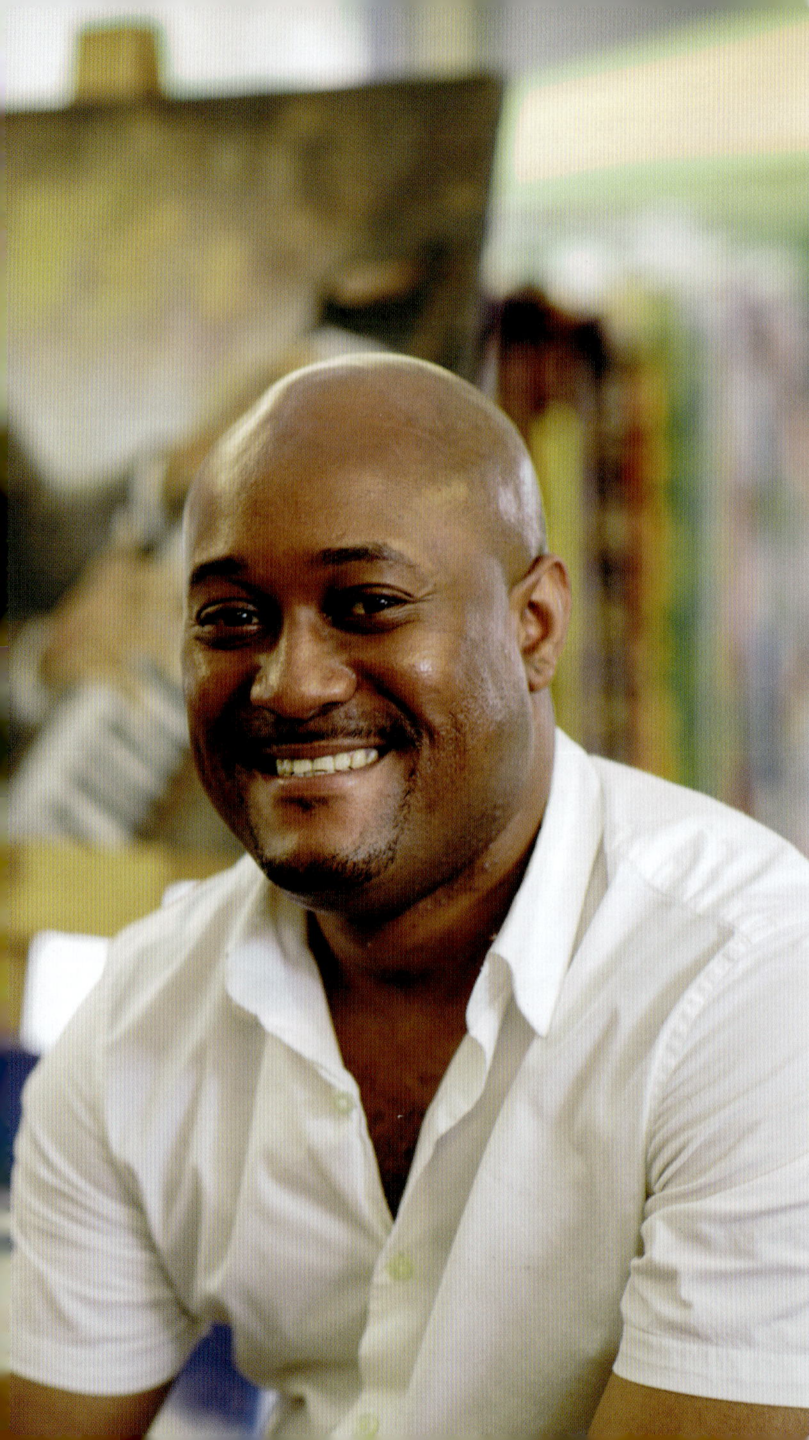

22

TONY DAVENPORT

For painter Tony Davenport, the city of Jackson is his studio. On Saturday mornings, he can be found in his booth at the farmers' market in downtown Jackson, working on one his paintings while chatting with friends and visitors.

"I have a show every week," he jokes, gesturing around his booth. "I'm immersed in the arts every day," Tony says. "I am a full-time artist; I create art, and I teach art."

Tony grew up in Vicksburg, drawing cartoons and exploring art on his own.

"Other people said I was good at drawing and creating," he remembers. "I thought, let me see what this 'creativity' is all about."

Tony attended Jackson State University, where he majored in fine art despite regular reminders that in the art world, it can be hard to survive.

Tony Davenport strives to make a difference in the respect given to future generations of Jackson artists.

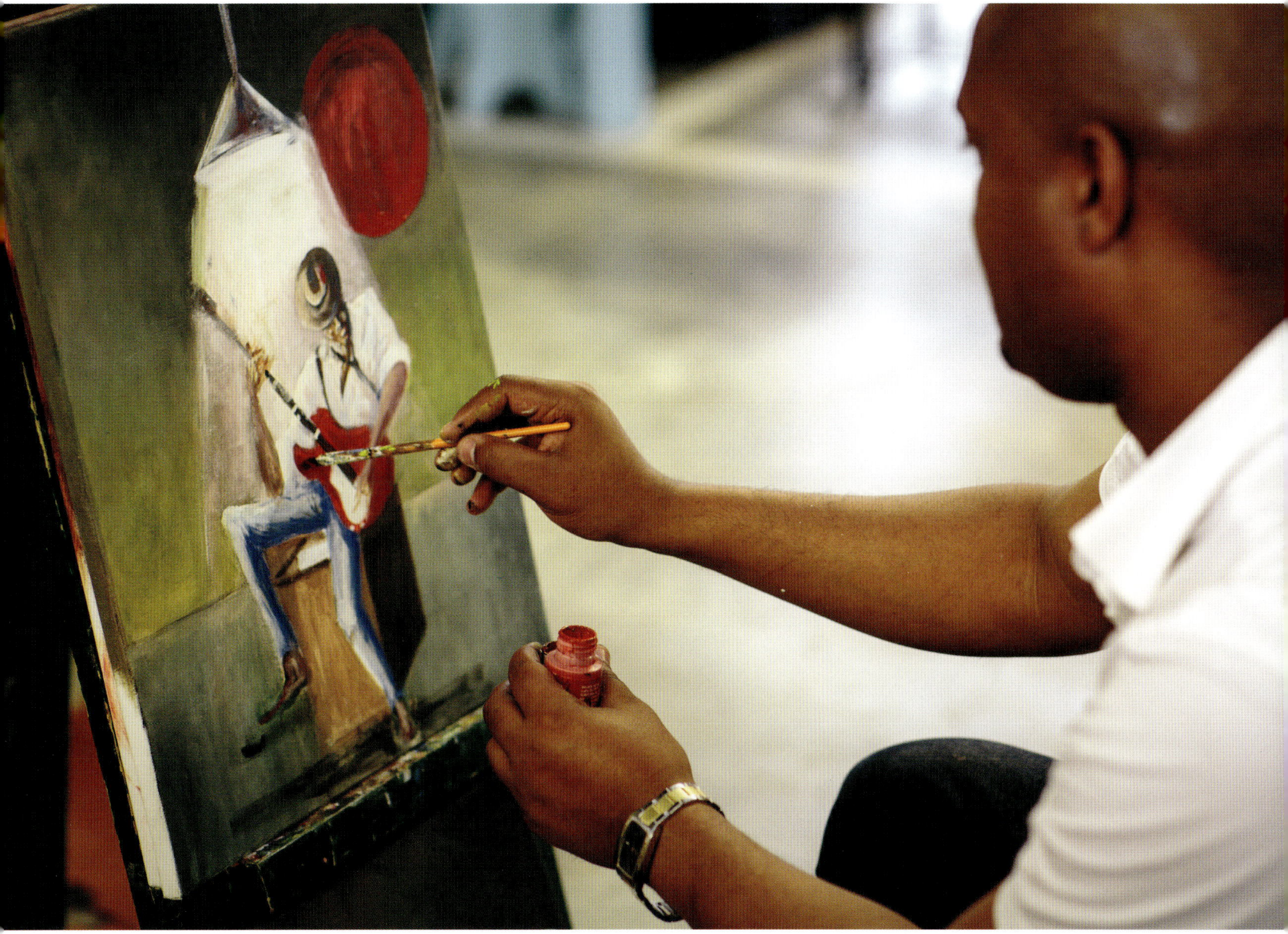

Tony paints at the farmers' market in Jackson on Saturdays.

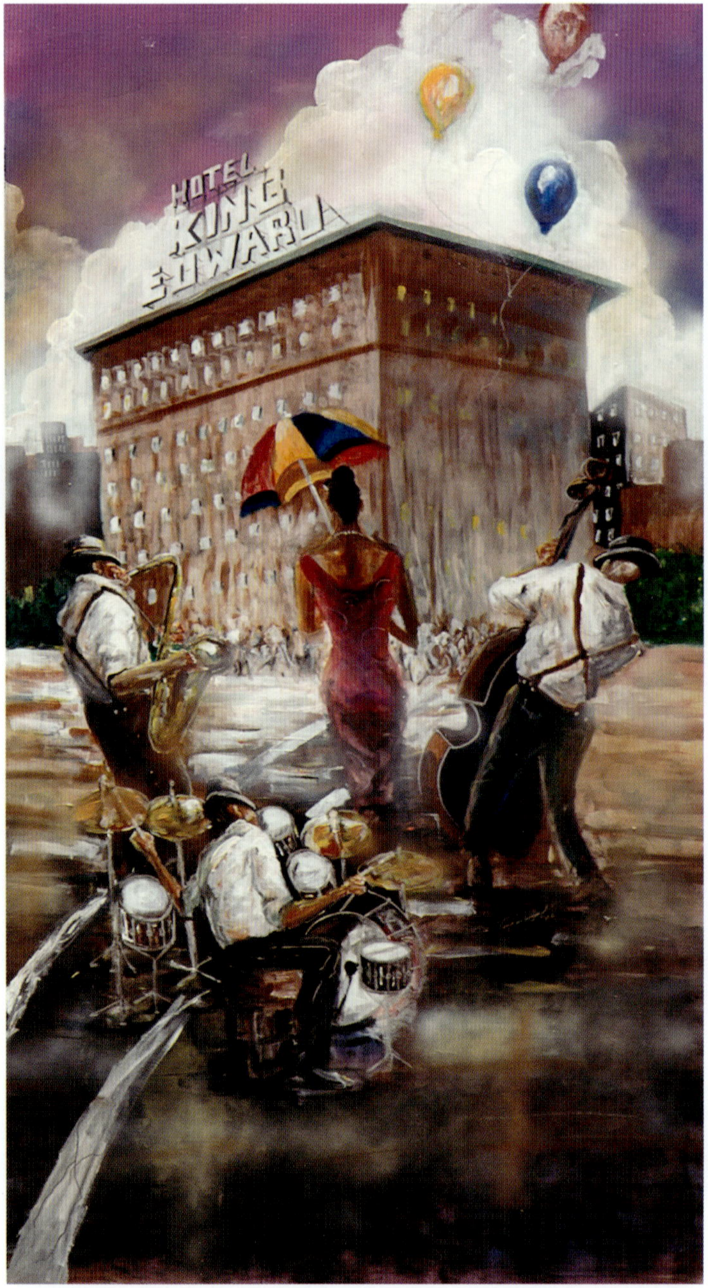

"How are you gonna make money? You know you're going to have to have a part-time job, right? Some of that may be true, but right now, I get to get up in the morning and do something I love to do, using my degree—I don't consider that a bad thing," Tony says. The real difficulty as an artist, he says, is finding your own voice and identity.

"I used to be scared of painting," he says. "How do you put colors down and blend and make things realistic? I've learned from watching other successful artists."

Tony has found his own realism, through bright, energetic paintings that feature bold colors and radiate timeless images of people from all walks of life.

"I want to create art that transcends time," he reasons. "We've always had music, we've always had buildings—it's about getting the viewer to slow down, pay attention. I want to cause the viewer to slow down and ask questions."

In 2007 and 2008, Tony was part of the Jackson Arts Collective and worked in Midtown with fellow artists, including his friends Chad Mars and Ellen Langford. He found it important as an artist to be surrounded by other people's creative energy. When the Jackson Arts Collective dissolved, he

Tony's artwork is reminiscent of the jazz age but incorporates iconic buildings for a timeless feel.

began painting at his apartment before going out into the city to create his work.

"The group is still alive on social media, where I can post what I am doing in the community," he says.

Tony is a proponent of introducing art and art education to parts of the Jackson community that do not have easy access to the arts. For Jackson to excel as an artistic community, Tony believes that the key is instilling the value of creativity in all areas of the city, especially with the next generation. Many young Jacksonians, he worries, have a warped view of the art world. He worries that they see artists as leading reality show lives when the actual reality is that making a living as an artist can be challenging.

"It is not always about the artists right now," he expounds. "It's about the artists coming behind us."

As the artist-in-residence at the Mississippi Children's Museum, Tony admired the natural creativity that many children inherently possess and the next generation's willingness to explore its own creativity.

"Sometimes, with age, we think we can't do something," he notices. "Kids are always ready to learn. It's all about presentation. You can't teach talent, but you can inspire."

As a substitute teacher and a teacher of "elective" art classes in the Jackson Public School System, Tony has witnessed young Jackson artists developing their talent, though he finds it frustrating that many students do not receive the opportunity to take art classes until as late as middle school.

"As an 'elective' teacher, I really think I'm not given the same value as other classes," he admits. "But the electives are what hold everything together—music, arts, theater—the kids who excel at those things have higher test scores. If arts are integrated across the curriculum, then all students can achieve."

The best example that Tony sets is living the life of a true artist every day.

"All the artists that I've seen succeed *worked*," he relates. "They painted and painted, not worrying about what to do next. The just painted—no guarantees, no promises. I'm doing what I love to do. If you're an artist, every year is the creative economy."

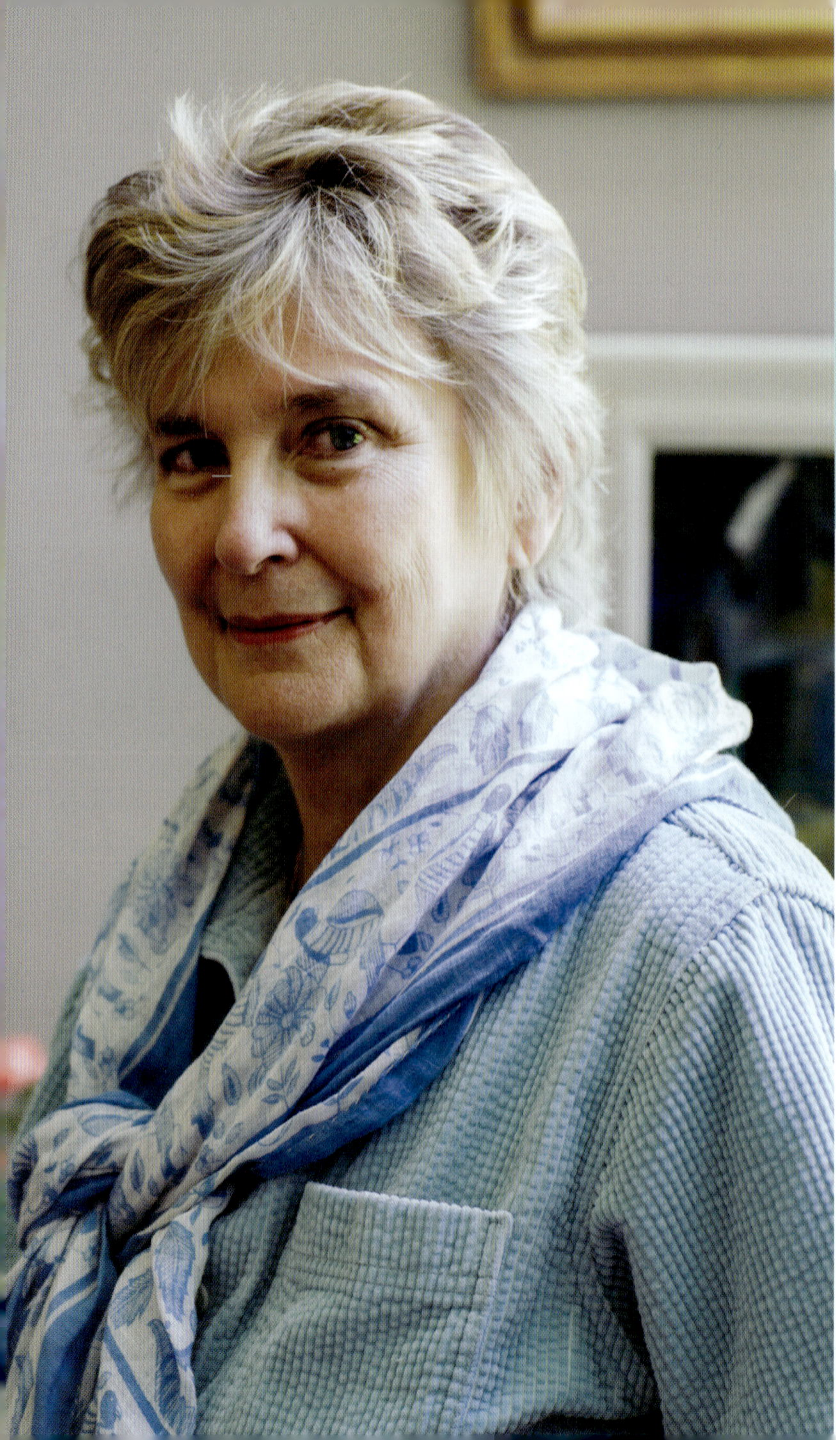

23

WOLFE STUDIO

BEBE WOLFE

Wolfe Studio is one of Jackson's oldest studios. Founded by Karl and Mildred Nungester Wolfe in the 1940s, today the studio is run by their daughter, Bebe Wolfe. The studio is still in its original location, tucked between office complexes and Interstate 55 off Old Canton Road in northeast Jackson. Hidden from the street by trees and flowering shrubs, the architectural buildings and the sunlit gallery of Wolfe Studio are filled with the ceramics, including the famed Wolfe Birds.

Left: Bebe Wolfe is the second generation of the Wolfe family to own the iconic studio.

Opposite: Each Wolfe Bird is a remarkable work of craftsmanship.

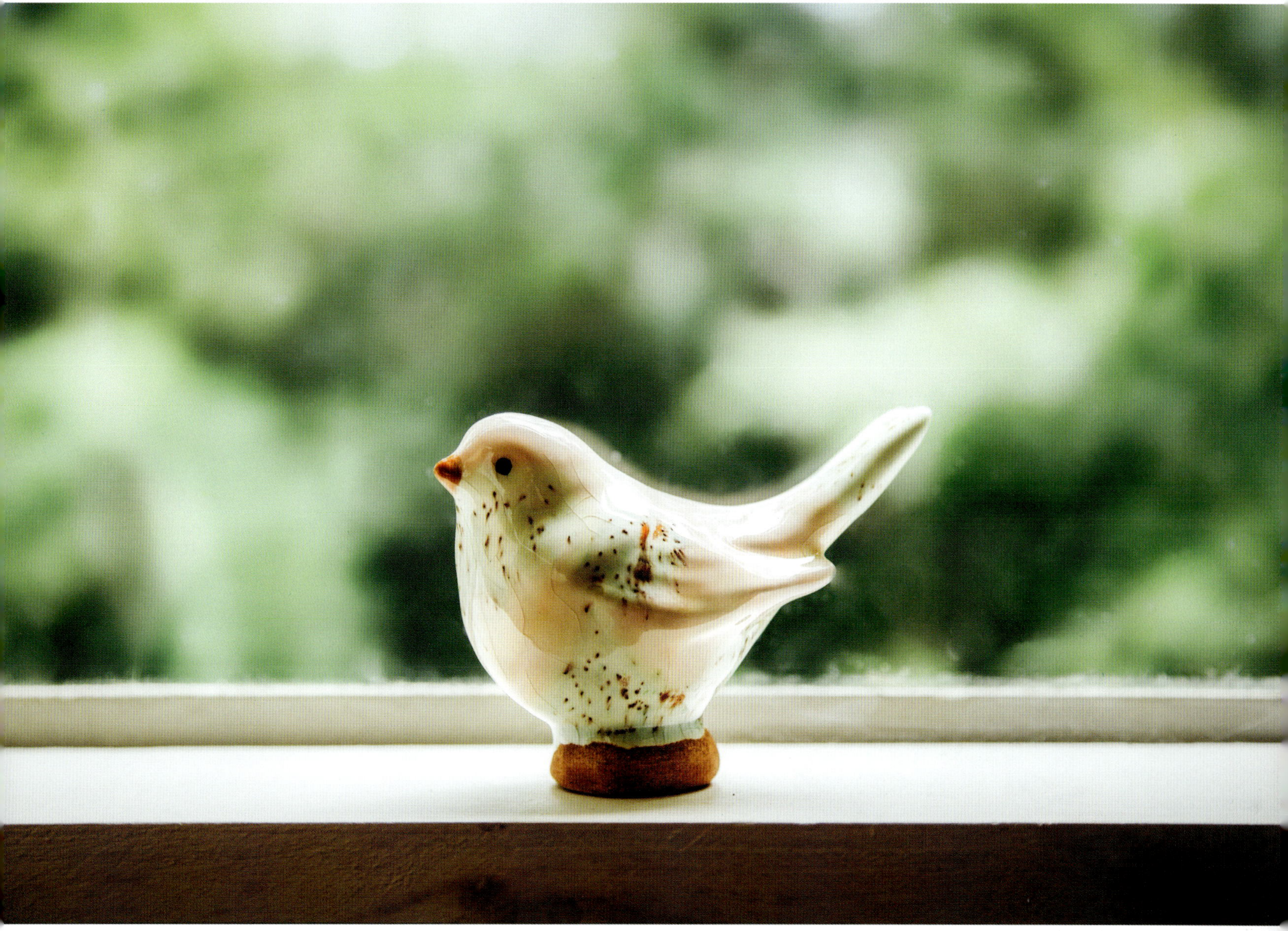

Wolfe Studio History

Bebe Wolfe has lived on the studio property since the 1940s, when her parents founded Wolfe Studio. Her father, Karl Wolfe, originally purchased the land in the 1930s. He and his wife, Mildred Nungester Wolfe, were painters, and they built a studio and eventually their family home on the property, where Bebe was raised along with her older brother. Bebe's parents were both respected artists at a time when a career as a professional artist was not common in Jackson. Their contemporaries included William Hollingsworth and Marie Hull.

"I think my parents helped inspire generations of artists in Jackson," Bebe shares. "They were determined to have a studio where people would come to them."

Bebe's parents eventually began creating pottery together after they were given a kiln. They did a show at the Municipal Art Gallery in Jackson every Christmas season for many years. At one of these shows in the early 1950s, Karl and Mildred debuted a new creation: a unique jar with a bird perched on the lid.

"Everybody was nuts about that jar," Bebe recalls. The Wolfe Birds were born. Her parents converted part of their home to a gallery, and it was not uncommon for people to come in to buy a bird and decide to commission a portrait as well.

Bebe recalls making her first bird when she was less

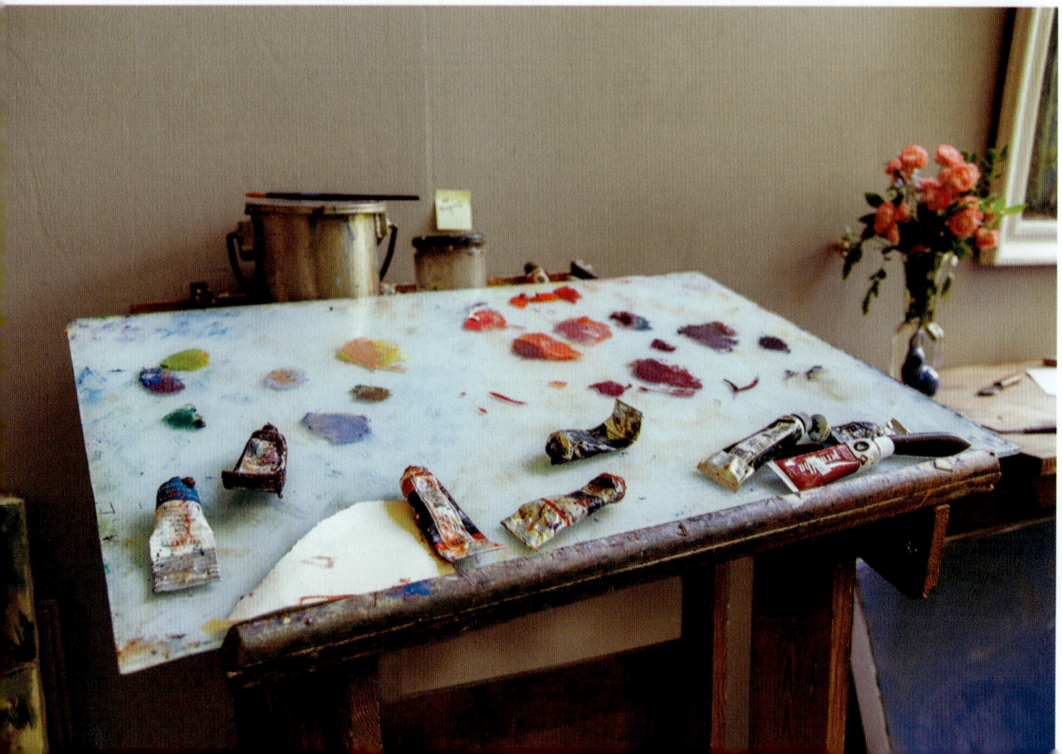

Left: Bebe's father, Karl Wolfe, built this worktable, which Bebe uses as a paint palette.

Opposite: Bebe Wolfe's oil paintings are inspired by nature, much like her birds.

than ten years old. Her parents made molds of the birds that she created, but sadly, they were lost in a studio fire in the 1960s, along with the other original molds. Her parents built a new studio with a gallery space and continued to create new designs. After leaving Mississippi for art school in the 1980s, Bebe returned to Jackson to help her mother continue running the business after her father's death.

"I was not an employee, I was an indentured servant," Bebe jokes.

One of the first employees at Wolfe Studio was Bebe's mother's good friend Linda Bartling, who works there to this day.

"Linda is an untold help in all kinds of ways—she has good

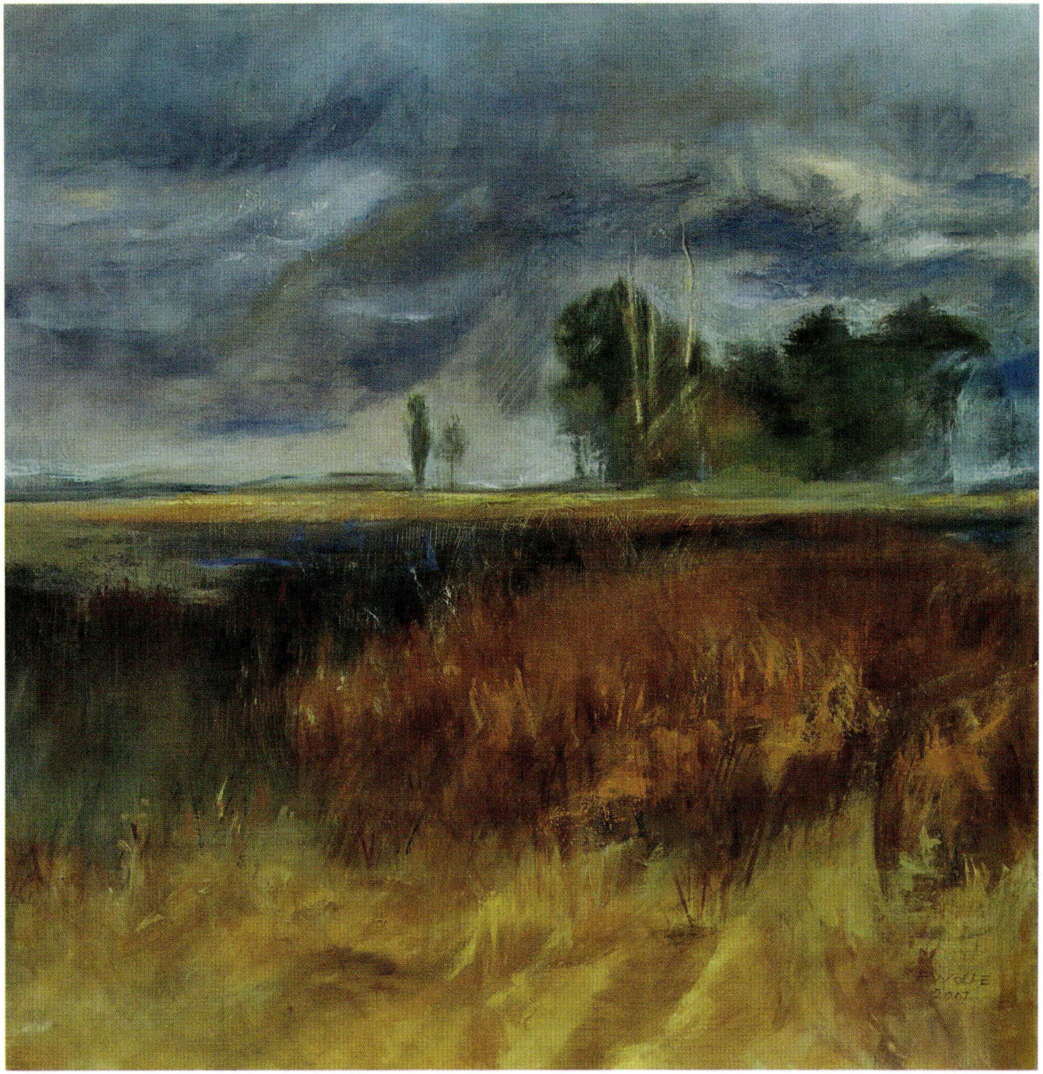

instincts on what people will buy," Bebe comments.

Each year until Mildred's death, the three women would prepare for a holiday showcase, filling a large table with their collected work.

"My mother's idea of 'sprucing things up' was to lay an old shower curtain over the table," Bebe remembers with a smile.

The holiday open house showcases were the only time that the public got a chance to get a first look at new designs. The studio was only open for the few weeks leading up to Christmas each year, and the rest of the year was dedicated to creating new designs. Bebe soon hired Wendy Eddleman to join the team.

"When you have an employee, you've got to generate some year-round income," Bebe notes. "I was a very inexperienced business person. It's tough. I'm still learning how to do it."

The Wolfe Studio Model

In the last decade, Bebe and her husband, David Weidemann, have continued to expand the studio space off Old Canton Road. She and David have their own house there, and she has a personal studio for painting. There are also studios for developing new mold designs, housing the kilns and glazing the ceramics.

"The business has always evolved, but it's always been that way. It was evolving when they did it," Bebe ruminates.

Bebe has resurrected from memory many of the original designs that burned in the 1960s, as well as created hundreds of new designs. She has added employees over the years, too, creating part-time jobs for young artists and employing up to eleven people at a time. Although Bebe designs the majority of the products for sale in the gallery at Wolfe Studio, she encourages her employees to utilize their own craftsmanship.

"I look at it as the art of the tribe," she says. "I don't look at the Wolfe Bird as being all of my doing—I look at it as a collective effort. They always evolve. To me, that's what makes it so interesting and vibrant and keeps everything from getting stale."

Bebe's employees go through an extensive training period to master the craft. The process of making a new design takes time—sometimes Bebe will redo a design hundreds of time to get it right. Bebe designs the majority of the ceramics coming out of Wolfe Studio, though it is a point of pride for Bebe that her employees create designs also. Once Bebe approves a design, a wax model is sent away to a mold maker to create a master model. For a long time, Bebe created the master molds herself,

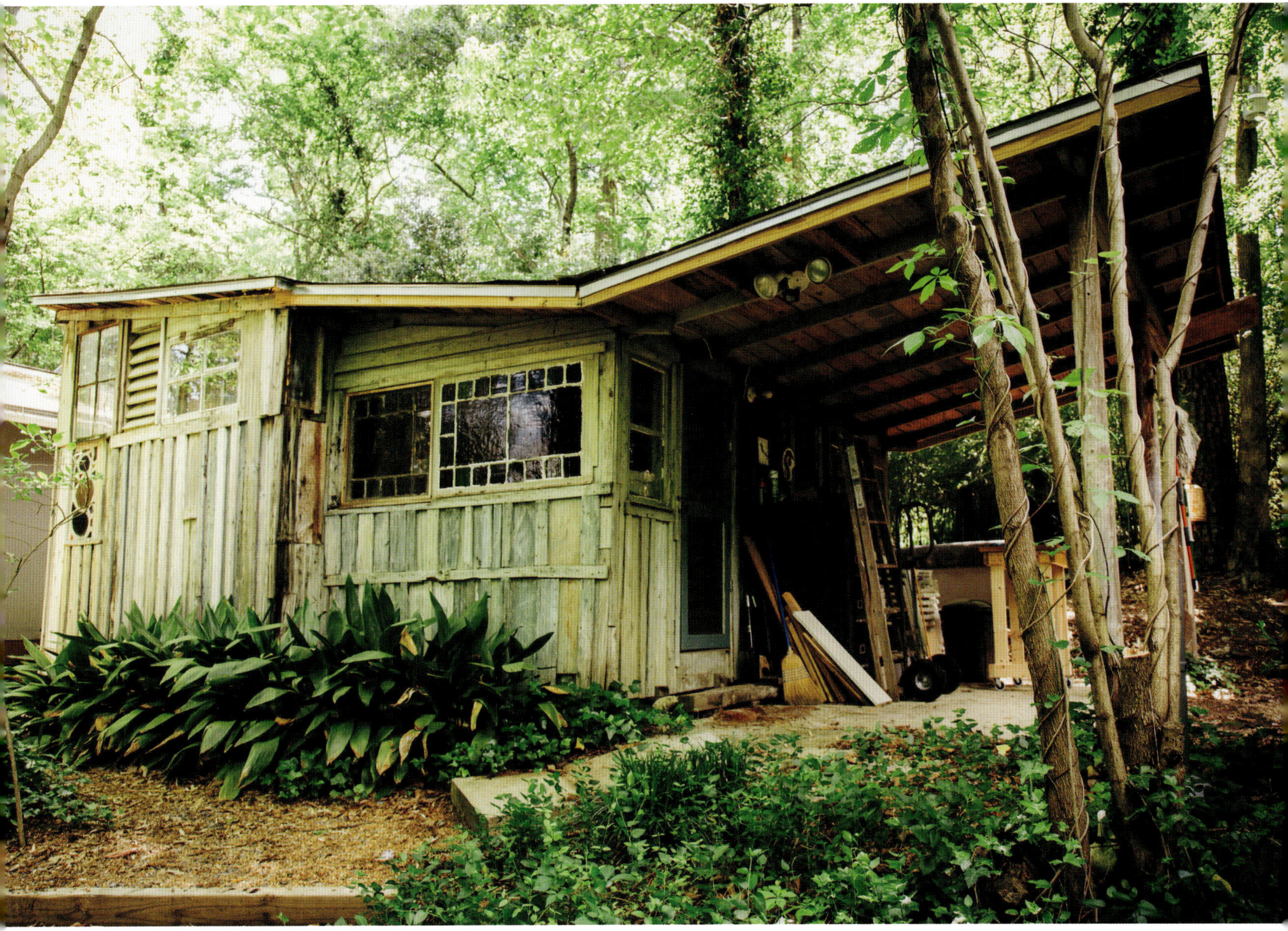

Pictured is one of the many unique buildings that make up Wolfe Studio.

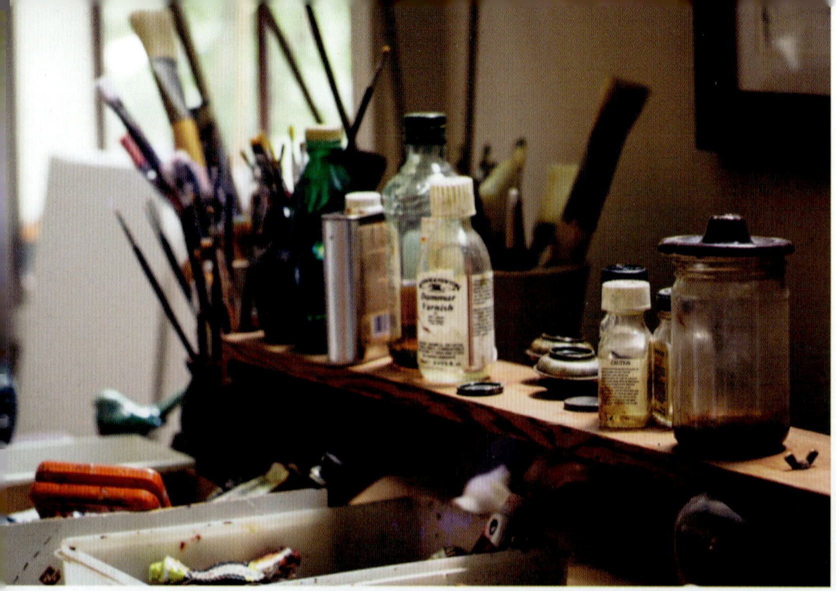

Painting supplies are ready to go in Bebe Wolfe's studio.

but she could not continue to create and meet production demands. As fate would have it, she found a master mold maker in Bovina, Mississippi.

"It was just a fluke that he was located so close to us," Bebe remarks. "He makes molds for people all over the United States. I don't know what I would have done if this hadn't been the case."

Once the master mold returns to Wolfe Studio, it is stored in a studio room that contains hundreds of master molds. They are poured and set, fine tuned, fired and then glazed in another studio space. When it comes to glazing, she says it takes new employees months to get a handle on the different color palettes. Adding to the complications is the fact that the glazes that Wolfe Studio employs are commercial grade, and therefore, the availability of certain colors fluctuates.

"There's a huge amount of stuff you have to learn," she explains. "I rely on everybody's interest in learning about the colors. They have an opportunity to invent new ways and colors. The production in the studio is an ever-changing, organic thing," she says. "My job is to appreciate it and learn slowly how to steer it a little bit...I have never run into any other outfit that approaches it this way."

In keeping with a tradition begun by her mother, each year Bebe sends out a postcard featuring the latest designs.

"Mailing is expensive but effective," she says. "I have people tell me they have every postcard from the past twenty years. The hook of being made in Mississippi and having the history is a big selling point."

The majority of Bebe's sales are generated from ceramics sold out of the gallery at her Jackson studio. She also sells some giclées of her work and some block prints of her mother's work, but she has not found the need to do much wholesale or online business. Her observation that Wolfe Studio is doing things differently is correct. Wolfe Studio is a model business that has created jobs and demonstrated to Jacksonians that fine craftsmanship is something to admire and cherish within the community. Wolfe Studio remains a treasured part of Jackson's creative culture.

ABOUT THE CONTRIBUTORS

The Author

Nell Linton Knox studied English and classical studies at Millsaps College and holds a master's degree in southern studies from the University of Mississippi. A Jackson, Mississippi native, Nell is a contributor to publications and organizations including *Portico Magazine*, Mississippi Encyclopedia, the Southern Foodways Alliance and the Mississippi Department of Archives and History. This is her first book.

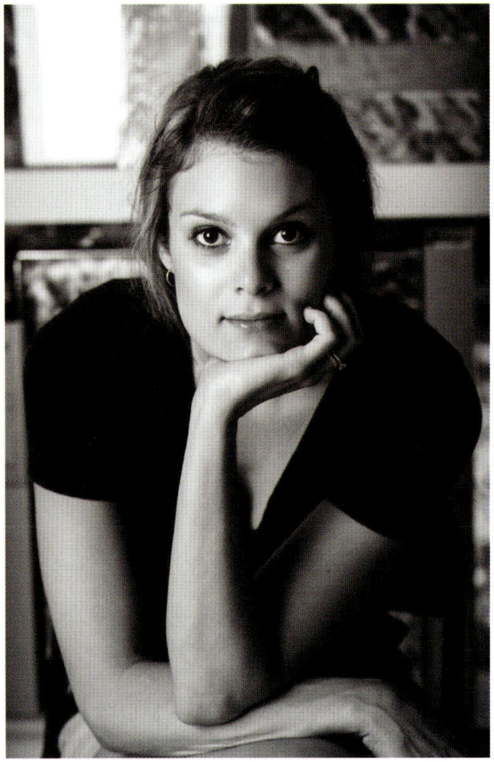

The Photographer

Ellen Rodgers received her first camera, a hot-pink-and-lime-green Polaroid "Cool Cam," at age seven. She recalls using the camera to photograph her toys; she was reprimanded for trying to sell the photos to friends at school. She majored in fine arts at Belhaven University in

Jackson, Mississippi, with a concentration in photography. A Rolling Fork, Mississippi native, Ellen is currently based in Jackson, where she does commercial photography for a number of freelance clients, as well as portraiture. Ellen shows her fine art photography at Fischer Gallery in Jackson and M2 Gallery in Little Rock, Arkansas. This is her first book.

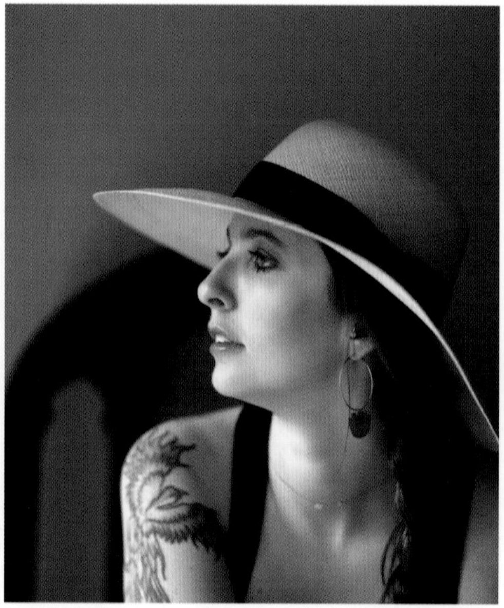

The Foreword Author

Malcolm White is the director of Visit Mississippi, the tourism office of the Mississippi Development Authority (MDA). In this role, he is responsible for the overall management, development and implementation of Mississippi's story, along with the creation of economic growth and opportunities for Mississippi through tourism.

Malcolm joined MDA in 2013 after serving as the executive director of the Mississippi Arts Commission (MAC) for seven years. In that position, he was responsible for overseeing the agency's staff and operations while driving its mission of supporting and celebrating the arts in Mississippi and the state's creative culture.

From rural Stone County, Mississippi, Malcolm was raised in the hamlet of Perkinston. He graduated from Booneville High School in 1969 and studied at various Mississippi institutions of higher learning before ultimately graduating from the University of Southern Mississippi. He is chairman of the Mississippi Blues Commission and Mississippi's Bicentennial Organizing Committee.